Learn iOS Application Distribution

Successfully Distribute Apps

Hagop Panosian

Apress®

Learn iOS Application Distribution: Successfully Distribute Apps

Hagop Panosian
Yerevan, Armenia

ISBN-13 (pbk): 978-1-4842-2682-7   ISBN-13 (electronic): 978-1-4842-2683-4
DOI 10.1007/978-1-4842-2683-4

Library of Congress Control Number: 2017955380

Cover image designed by Freepik

    Managing Director: Welmoed Spahr
    Editorial Director: Todd Green
    Acquisitions Editor: Aaron Black
    Development Editor: Jim Markham
    Technical Reviewer: Charlie Cruz
    Coordinating Editor: Jessica Vakili
    Copy Editor: April Rondeau
    Compositor: SPi Global
    Indexer: SPi Global
    Artist: SPi Global

Distributed to the book trade worldwide by Springer Science+Business Media New York, 233 Spring Street, 6th Floor, New York, NY 10013. Phone 1-800-SPRINGER, fax (201) 348-4505, e-mail orders-ny@springer-sbm.com, or visit www.springeronline.com. Apress Media, LLC is a California LLC and the sole member (owner) is Springer Science + Business Media Finance Inc (SSBM Finance Inc). SSBM Finance Inc is a **Delaware** corporation.

For information on translations, please e-mail rights@apress.com, or visit http://www.apress.com/rights-permissions.

Apress titles may be purchased in bulk for academic, corporate, or promotional use. eBook versions and licenses are also available for most titles. For more information, reference our Print and eBook Bulk Sales web page at http://www.apress.com/bulk-sales.

Any source code or other supplementary material referenced by the author in this book is available to readers on GitHub via the book's product page, located at www.apress.com/978-1-4842-2682-7. For more detailed information, please visit http://www.apress.com/source-code.

Printed on acid-free paper

*To my wife, Aghavni, and children,
Alen and Lana, the brightest lights of my life!*

Contents at a Glance

Contents

About the Author

Hagop Panosian Educated as an architect, Hagop understands the impact new technologies can have on an industry. He believes that the more advanced aspects of new technologies should be made accessible to non-tech professionals, especially given the changes technological advances are bringing to every aspect of life and the workplace.

To drive his vision, Hagop made a career shift from architecture to technology authorship and education. He currently advises app startups on topics such as pitching, fundraising and managing growth. He lives with his wife and two children in Yerevan, Armenia. Hagop can be contacted on his personal website, *www.hagoppanosian.am.*

About the Technical Reviewer

Charles Cruz is a mobile application developer for the iOS, Windows Phone, and Android platforms. He graduated from Stanford University with B.S. and M.S. degrees in engineering. He lives in Southern California and runs a photography business with his wife (www.bellalentestudios.com). Charles can be reached at codingandpicking@gmail.com.

Acknowledgments

This book is the product of effort on my part combined with inspiration and support from family and professional guidance and editing from the team at Apress.

I owe a debt of gratitude to my parents, who dedicated their lives to giving their kids a childhood that was better than theirs had been. They succeeded. In the mid-eighties, they invested in a computer for my brother and me when no one else where we lived thought it was important, which made self-driven, tech-savvy self-learners out of us. My brother contributed greatly to this book by making sure I didn't get into financial hot water while I took the time to write it, and also served as the main reader persona. I wrote this book with him in mind as my audience.

This book is also a product of the love and patience of my wife and kids, who are the force that drives everything I do every moment of the day. It's easy to believe in yourself when your family believes in you so much!

Finally, a big thank you to Aaron Black, Jessica Vakili, and everyone else at Apress who contributed to making a quality product out of my efforts. I'm inspired and humbled by their professionalism and look forward to working with them on new projects!

Introduction

"Innovation is change that unlocks new value."
Jamie Notter

Welcome to one of the most incredible technological innovations of the past decade.

The app industry was born on July 10, 2008, when Apple first "opened the doors" to its App Store to allow iPhone users to download apps onto their devices. According to *rewrite* (www.ca.com/us/rewrite.html), an online journal by CA Technologies and *Wired* magazine, within a space of just seven years, by 2015, the app economy

- grew into an industry worth an estimated $143 billion;
- created at least 627,000 jobs (just through the iOS App Store);
- created 54 percent job growth for iOS developers between 2012 and 2014;

- generated app downloads that are expected to grow to just under 300 billion by 2020; and

- generated annual app revenue that is expected to grow to $77 billion in 2017 and over $100 billion by 2020 through the iOS App Store alone.

The app revolution has created whole new sectors of the U.S. and global economies, with new markets, marketing channels, and professions that did not even exist just a few years ago. It has opened up new ways for vendors to reach and interact with customers and empowered and entertained billions of smartphone users. Most important, it has created a way for resourceful and ingenious entrepreneurs and people-next-door to make millions with their creativity and inventiveness by giving them access to a huge market. Without a doubt, there have been very few times in history when access to markets and wealth has been as easy as it is today for anyone with a good idea and marketing smarts.

The immensely transformative power of the app industry in its infancy was the reason I became interested in apps several years ago, when a friend suggested I put aside what I was working on and shift to developing apps. As a self-learner, I spent many months trying to learn how the app business works and how apps are built, combining tidbits of actionable information wherever I could find them.

Eventually, it became obvious that what was available out there to help self-driven outsiders like me learn app development could be grouped into two broad categories: tech books by techies for techies, and the "make millions overnight with no money down, no coding, and no effort" books that sold a dream with little actionable information. At the same time, there were countless bits of expert advice, tips and tricks, best practices, and insights spread across countless books, e-books, blog entries, and articles written by authors whose expertise was evolving alongside the industry itself. Clearly, there was a need for a book that combined the fundamentals and best practices of app design, development, and distribution to produce a one-stop shop for both insiders and outsiders that was more than just an introduction to the business—a book that would contain everything about the app-publishing industry a newcomer would need to know. That was the inspiration behind this book.

Who This Book Is For

There are, of course, many excellent books on app development, app design, the app business, and everything in between, but there was one thing that struck me: they were unlikely to appeal to, or meet the needs of, a very specific and quite large group of people who are very much interested in apps as an investment opportunity but (wrongly) believe it takes a great deal of tech savvy to succeed in the app business. They may also be frustrated by not having one place in which to find easily absorbable, straight-to-the-point, actionable information and guidance about how to navigate through the app jungle and be in a position to understand the market they will be competing in. They want to know how to make informed decisions about whether or not to invest in apps, how to pick the right type of app. They also want to know how to set a budget and create an investment plan, and how to measure the success of a project and get a return on their investment.

Eventually, the research for this book grew to represent value not just for investors pursuing returns, but for other groups of readers as well. While writing it, I've had a very specific list of potential readers in mind, as you will see later. Despite the differences between them, these reader personas share a common characteristic in that they have little interest in coding, either because they already are accomplished coders or because they plan to get others to code their apps. As a result, there is not a single line of code in this book. There are many great books on coding for apps already out there. This book is about everything else.

The reader categories that follow care most of all about understanding every aspect of the industry and knowing enough to make informed decisions instead of simply blindly trusting the experts. Some of them, like coders and digital marketers, care mostly about complementing what they already know and keeping up with the evolution of this amazing industry.

The Whiz Kid is a master of code. He knows everything about how to code iOS apps and has already coded a few basic games. He wants to be an app-distribution pro.

The Newbie knows next to nothing about the app business, except for the apps she uses, some of which she likes so much she's curious about how they're made. Plus, she's thinking about getting into app design.

The Investor is interested in apps as an investment opportunity and wants to know what returns he can expect from apps as compared to other investments. He also wants to decide whether to establish an app design company or work with one to create a portfolio of apps.

The Pro Coder is interested in improving his career prospects by going beyond the code to learn about app design and marketing, possibly as a prelude to becoming an independent app professional.

The Educator teaches students about the app industry from a design, coding, or marketing perspective and is looking for a book that contains both the basics and the latest in the industry.

The Researcher wants a book he can refer to for useful data and additional sources and information for his work, and as a way to keep up with the industry.

The Student is studying apps as part of a course on business, coding, or marketing and wants a book that succinctly explains the fundamental concepts and processes of each of these aspects of the business.

There is something for all of these groups in *Learn iOS App Distribution*, and despite their different viewpoints on the same subject, there is something common to all of them: the coding aspects matter less to them than everything else does. They either already know how to code or plan to outsource the coding part for their apps, or have other, great books on coding and don't feel the need for another one.

As the author, I felt that what was needed was a book about the big picture that is thorough enough to allow readers to go beyond the basics and make informed decisions about navigating their way to success.

Assumptions

This book assumes the following:

1. You know next to nothing about the app business or industry (so, we'll look at everything from the beginning).

2. You want straight-to-the-point knowledge that is condensed but easy on the brain and actionable.

3. You want to feel like an expert after you read this book, or at least earn respect from the experts when you talk to them.

These three elements have informed the content and tone of *Learn iOS App Distribution*.

What Is App Distribution?

What is app distribution exactly, and how does it differ from app development or app publishing?

For the purposes of this book, app publishing is the complete process of creating apps and releasing them onto the market. App development is the process that combines ideation, design, and coding. App distribution, as Apple defines it, is a very specific phase in the app publishing process that combines testing, submission, and release.

This is how Apple defines app distribution on its own online App Distribution Guide (https://developer.apple.com/library/content/documentation/IDEs/Conceptual/AppDistributionGuide/Introduction/Introduction.html):

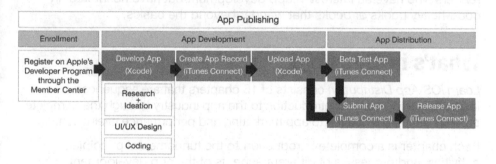

Although iOS app distribution is the main focus of this book, we will be looking at the whole app publishing process in detail, including what happens after app release.

What This Book Is

This book combines information from three main sources: my own knowledge, Apple's own guidelines, and best practices and content from respected developers and companies. Each of these sources contributes a very specific kind of knowledge that, when combined with the others, forms the best and most actionable information you can find anywhere.

I have put in this book everything that I wished was there for me to learn when I first started exploring the app business. I want this book to make you an expert literally overnight by giving you all the information you need to make informed decisions and make your mark in the app business.

What This Book Is Not

This is not a coding book. Coding is beyond its scope, and it is not a coincidence that there is not a single line of code in this book. Learn iOS App Distribution is designed to meet a different need.

This book is also not a "fast track to riches" guide designed to foster false hopes as a selling point. As far as I am concerned there is no fast track to riches in this or any other business. Only determination and commitment can produce an opportunity for wealth.

This book is structured to introduce readers to the app industry, allow them to talk comfortably with the experts overnight, and choose which corner of the industry works best for them. Learn iOS App Distribution is intended for readers who have an interest in app development but have no interest in code-heavy books or books that wander beyond the basics.

What's in This Book

Learn iOS App Distribution consists of 15 chapters that are sequenced logically, starting from an introduction to the app industry through the complete process of app distribution to app marketing and performance evaluation.

Each chapter is a complete introduction to the fundamental principles, activities, and processes of different aspects of the app development process. These chapters make sense when read in sequence, but the reader can also return to each of these chapters separately later on.

Chapter 1, "The Smartphone Landscape," is an introduction to the devices that host the apps we use. We'll look at how smartphones and iOS devices have evolved and how they are distributed worldwide. We'll take a closer look at what types of iOS devices are available and how many people use them all over the world.

In Chapter 2, "The App Landscape," we look at apps as entities: what they are, where they begin and end, and what the top apps in the app stores are.

Chapter 3, "The App Ecosystem," looks at who does what in the app industry, dividing them into three fundamental groups: those who influence an app before release, those who influence it after release, and appreneurs (app entrepreneurs) who develop and publish apps as a business.

Chapter 4, "App Economics," is about how apps make money, what the available and popular monetization models for apps are, and how return on investment is measured in the app world.

In Chapter 5, "Imagine Your App," we'll look at how app ideas are generated, what the most effective processes are, and where to find inspiration.

In Chapter 6, "Design Your App," we'll look at how apps evolve from concept to design. We'll also look at everything that affects the design of an app and at the basics of building a team to develop the concept.

Chapter 7, "Building Your App," is about turning a concept and design into a prototype, from the software you will need to creating storyboards and wireframes to building a team. We'll also look at how apps are assembled, their components, the platforms on which they are hosted, and everything that goes into a full-fledged app.

In Chapter 8, "Configuring Your App," we'll look at everything that needs to be done on Apple iTunes to configure an app for distribution.

In Chapter 9, "Testing Your App," we'll look at how iOS apps are tested on Testflight before they are submitted for approval.

Chapter 10, "Submitting Your App," elaborates on the submission process and looks at all the reasons why an app might get rejected and how to avoid them.

In Chapter 11, "Distributing Your App," we'll see how app distribution is managed after an app is approved and released on the App Store.

Chapter 12, "Marketing Your App," is all about how apps can be marketed, what channels are used to market apps, and the best practices that lead to successful marketing.

Chapter 13, "App Marketing Concepts," looks at the latest concepts and techniques marketers are using to give their products and value propositions an edge and make their campaigns as efficient and effective as possible.

Chapter 14, "Prepare for Success," will help you prepare for unexpected success in every fundamental way. The conclusion of the book looks at the biggest trends in the app world today and at the future of apps.

Appendix, "Online Resources," is a collection of available resources to help you access more information and improve your skills.

How to Use This Book

As you will have noticed, the chapters of this book are written in a logical sequence that optimizes the learning process for the newcomer to the industry, but each chapter can also be read separately should the reader want to focus on one aspect.

I wrote this book from the perspective of what I wished someone would have written when I was trying to learn app publishing as a total newcomer. I hope you'll enjoy reading it as much as I enjoyed writing it.

Chapter 1

The Smartphone Landscape

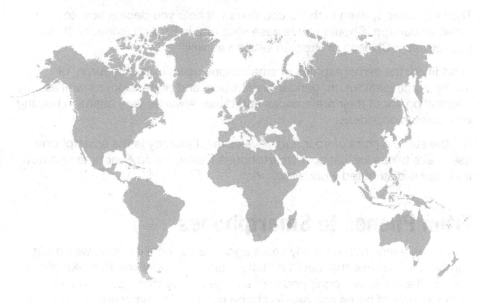

"The goal is to transform data into information,
and information into insight."

Carly Fiorina

© Hagop Panosian 2017
H. Panosian, *Learn iOS Application Distribution*, DOI 10.1007/978-1-4842-2683-4_1

To understand the evolution of the app industry, we need to first look at the evolution of the devices that host them: smartphones.

Smartphones, as well all know, are taking over the world, or have already done so. There are currently two billion smartphone users worldwide, each of whom has an average of 27 apps on their device and checks some of them between 35 and 75 times a day.

Apps are intricately tied to the capabilities and features of the devices that host them, and understanding the distribution of smartphones, tablets, and their platforms across the globe is crucial to knowing how to plan your app development project and your marketing campaign.

So, what insights can you extract from information about the global shipments and geographic distribution of smartphones? Shipment statistics will help you identify the markets on which you should focus—those countries that have the most smartphone users and widest smartphone use.

The languages spoken in these countries will help you decide how to localize your app. Should you release your app in English alone, or should you release a Chinese or Russian version as well?

In addition, the demographics of smartphone users in each country or market—age distribution, gender distribution, and profession, as well as information about their preferences and habits—will be very useful in helping you develop app ideas.

So, the starting point of your app development journey is the smartphone user. Let's take a look at how smartphones have evolved over time and how their use is distributed worldwide.

From Phones to Smartphones

There was a time not too many years ago when a mobile phone was a big, cumbersome device that could do little more than allow you to make phone calls on the go. It was equipped with a huge battery that lasted no more than a couple of hours and needed to be charged for many hours. The first screens could only support two colors, and the only "apps" on the first "smartphones"—meaning phones that could do more than make phone calls—were a simple calendar, a calculator, and a few primitive games.

The "Brick" and Simon

The first mobile phone was the Motorola DynaTAC 8000X (such a 1980s name, right?). It was first released in 1983, weighed around 2.5 pounds, and sold for an incredible $3,995—plus monthly fees. It was affectionately known as "the brick."

The very first "smartphone" was the IBM Simon, which turned 20 years old in 2014. It cost $899, and IBM sold around 50,000 units over six months. Besides making and receiving telephone calls, it could send and receive faxes and emails.

Competition

In the early years of the mobile phone, manufacturers were highly secretive about the inner workings of their devices, and all software development for them was done in-house as a very closely guarded trade secret. It was only in 2007 that Apple made the software for its devices open to all developers everywhere, setting off a boom in development. Today, open-sourcing is a very common strategy for improving software quality and creating a community around a product.

The Smartphone Market Today

In just a decade, the number of smartphones in use worldwide has grown to more than two billion devices. Many of these devices are built by pioneers like Apple, but a growing number are being built by companies that did not exist even a couple of years ago (Figure 1-1). Apple's operating system, iOS, runs only on Apple's devices, like the iPhone and iPad, but Google's operating system, Android, can run on any device designed to host it. As a result, there is a multitude of smartphone models that are designed for Android being built by more than one company, which has allowed Google to raise its share of the smartphone market to more than 80 percent today.

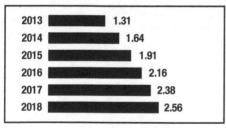

2013	1.31
2014	1.64
2015	1.91
2016	2.16
2017	2.38
2018	2.56

Total Number of Smartphones
in Use Worldwide

Android	1,164.3	81.1%
iOS	223.7	15.6%
Windows Phone	36.9	2.5%
Other	11.5	0.8%
TOTAL	1,436.4 million	

Smartphone Shipments
& Market Share Per OS in 2015

Figure 1-1. Smartphone statistics

Today, Android runs on the vast majority of smartphones in the market, including Samsung, Huawei, Xiaomi, and other brands. According to Gartner, Android had an 86.2 percent market share of the total number of phones sold in Q2 of 2016, with some 296.913 million phones, followed by iOS with a 12.9 percent market share and 44.395 million phones, Windows with 0.6 percent market share and 1.97 million phones, Blackberry with 0.1 percent market share and 400,400 phones, and other manufacturers with 0.2 percent market share and 680,600 phones.

Several Chinese smartphone manufacturers, like Huawei and Xiaomi, have emerged over the past several years to meet the fast-growing Chinese consumer demand for smartphones, while Apple devices remain popular in North America. According to *expandedramblings.com*, in 2016 the iPhone had a 41.9 percent share of the U.S. and Canada smartphone market but only an 8.2 percent share of the Chinese market.

Again according to Gartner, in Q2 of 2016 Samsung sold around 76.75 million phones for a 22.3 percent market share, followed by Apple with around 44.39 million for a 12.9 percent market share, Huawei with 30.67 million for a 8.9 percent market share, Oppo with around 18.49 million for a 5.4 percent market share, and Xiaomi with 15.53 million for a 4.5 percent market share. Other manufacturers sold a total of 158.53 million phones in Q2 of 2016 for a 46 percent market share.

Samsung is the world's top-selling smartphone maker with a 22.8 percent market share in Q2 2016 and 7.7 percent year-over-year (YoY) growth, driven mainly by the success of the Galaxy S7 and Galaxy S7 Edge smartphones. In Q2 2016, Apple registered a 15 percent YoY decline from Q2 2015, selling 40.4 million units. Apple's best-selling device worldwide is the iPhone 6s.

Smartphone Use Worldwide

China, India, and the United States are the three biggest consumers of smartphones and the only three that currently have more than 100 million smartphone users each. China is emerging as the big behemoth among the three, and not just in terms of numbers of smartphones in use. In late 2016, China overtook the United States in terms of iOS App Store revenue.

Figure 1-2, based on data from Gartner and eMarketer dated December 2014, shows the three countries and their projected numbers of smartphone users for 2015 and 2016.

Three Countries with More Than 100 Million Smartphone Owners in 2015–2016

(in millions)

UNITED STATES			
2	2015	184.2	
	2016	198.5	

CHINA		
1	2015	574.2
	2016	624.7

INDIA		
3	2015	167.9
	2016	204.1

Figure 1-2. *Smartphone users in United States, India, and China in (projected, 2015 and 2016), in millions*

Smartphone Users

Using the same data from Gartner and eMarketer, Figure 1-3 lists the world's top 25 countries ranked by the projected number of smartphone users in 2015 (based on information dated December 2014), along with projections for 2016.

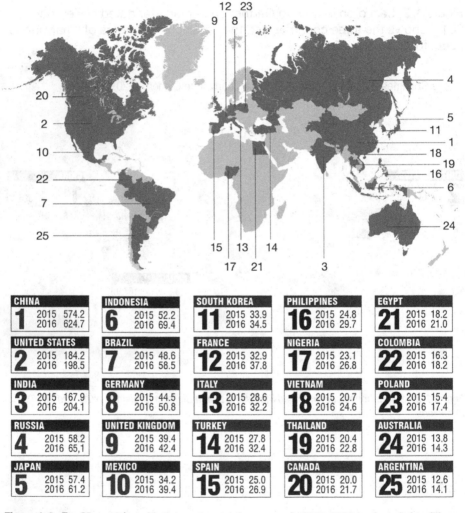

CHINA		
1	2015	574.2
	2016	624.7

UNITED STATES		
2	2015	184.2
	2016	198.5

INDIA		
3	2015	167.9
	2016	204.1

RUSSIA		
4	2015	58.2
	2016	65,1

JAPAN		
5	2015	57.4
	2016	61.2

INDONESIA		
6	2015	52.2
	2016	69.4

BRAZIL		
7	2015	48.6
	2016	58.5

GERMANY		
8	2015	44.5
	2016	50.8

UNITED KINGDOM		
9	2015	39.4
	2016	42.4

MEXICO		
10	2015	34.2
	2016	39.4

SOUTH KOREA		
11	2015	33.9
	2016	34.5

FRANCE		
12	2015	32.9
	2016	37.8

ITALY		
13	2015	28.6
	2016	32.2

TURKEY		
14	2015	27.8
	2016	32.4

SPAIN		
15	2015	25.0
	2016	26.9

PHILIPPINES		
16	2015	24.8
	2016	29.7

NIGERIA		
17	2015	23.1
	2016	26.8

VIETNAM		
18	2015	20.7
	2016	24.6

THAILAND		
19	2015	20.4
	2016	22.8

CANADA		
20	2015	20.0
	2016	21.7

EGYPT		
21	2015	18.2
	2016	21.0

COLOMBIA		
22	2015	16.3
	2016	18.2

POLAND		
23	2015	15.4
	2016	17.4

AUSTRALIA		
24	2015	13.8
	2016	14.3

ARGENTINA		
25	2015	12.6
	2016	14.1

Figure 1-3. Top 25 countries with the most smartphone users in 2015–2016 (projected), in millions

Smartphone User Growth

Smartphone markets can also be ranked according to fastest user growth. Using Gartner's data from December 2014, Figure 1-4 ranks the world's top 25 countries in terms of projected smartphone user growth in 2015.

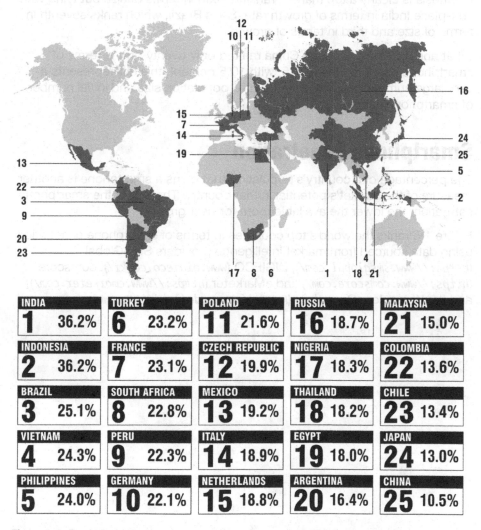

INDIA	TURKEY	POLAND	RUSSIA	MALAYSIA
1 36.2%	6 23.2%	11 21.6%	16 18.7%	21 15.0%

INDONESIA	FRANCE	CZECH REPUBLIC	NIGERIA	COLOMBIA
2 36.2%	7 23.1%	12 19.9%	17 18.3%	22 13.6%

BRAZIL	SOUTH AFRICA	MEXICO	THAILAND	CHILE
3 25.1%	8 22.8%	13 19.2%	18 18.2%	23 13.4%

VIETNAM	PERU	ITALY	EGYPT	JAPAN
4 24.3%	9 22.3%	14 18.9%	19 18.0%	24 13.0%

PHILIPPINES	GERMANY	NETHERLANDS	ARGENTINA	CHINA
5 24.0%	10 22.1%	15 18.8%	20 16.4%	25 10.5%

Figure 1-4. Top 25 countries with fastest smartphone user growth in 2015 (% YoY growth)

Top Markets

Looking at the country rankings in terms of both size and growth rate, you can identify the countries with the biggest potential for your app projects. India, for example, was third in terms of size but first in terms of user growth. Indonesia is clearly a top market, ranking sixth in terms of size but tying with first-place India in terms of growth rate. So is Brazil, which ranks seventh in terms of size and third in terms of growth.

What about China? Although China ranked only twenty-fifth in terms of smartphone user growth in 2015, with 10.5 percent, this still represents a very large number of users given China's population size and initial number of smartphone users.

Smartphone Penetration

The percentage of a country's population that owns a smartphone is another measure of the market's potential in that country. The higher the smartphone saturation, the lower the available room for user growth.

Figure 1-5 ranks the world's top countries in terms of smartphone penetration using data sourced from market intelligence providers SMSGlobal (*https://www.smsglobal.com/*), DIGIECO (*www.digieco.co.kr/*), comscore (*https://www.comscore.com/*) and eMarketer (*https://www.emarketer.com/*), and the Korea JoonGang daily (*koreajoongangdaily.joins.com/*).

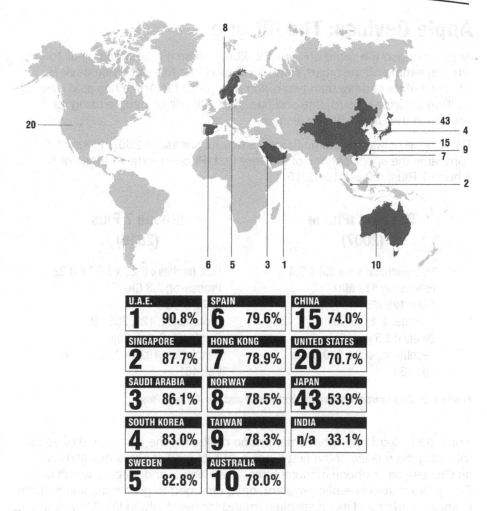

Figure 1-5. Countries with highest smartphone penetration in 2015, as percentage of population

Apple Devices: The iPhone

Apple changed the world on June 29, 2007, when it introduced us all to the iPhone, setting off the smartphone revolution that has put these devices into the hands of more than two billion people so far. Apple has sold over a billion smartphones to date and has over 100 million people using its devices in the United States alone.

The iPhone has evolved significantly since its release in 2007. Figure 1-6 compares the specifications of the very first iPhone model to those of the iPhone 7 Plus, released in 2016.

The First iPhone (2007)

Size (inches): 4.5 x 2.4 x 0.6
Processor: 412 Mhz
RAM: 128 MB
Storage: 4, 8, 16 GB
Display: 3.5 inch Color
Resolution: 480 x 320 pixels
Ppi: 163

iPhone 7 Plus (2016)

Size (inches): 6.23 x 3.07 x 0.29
Processor: 2.3 Ghz
RAM: 3 GB
Storage: 32, 128, 256 GB
Display: 5.5 inch Color
Resolution: 1920 x 1080 pixels
Ppi: 401

Figure 1-6. Comparison between the first iPhone and the iPhone 7 Plus

Apple had a lead over other smartphone makers in the first couple of years following the release of the first iPhone, but its market share has shrunk as Chinese smartphone manufacturers like Huawei and Xiaomi, which use Google's Android operating system, have emerged to grab a big share of the Chinese market and its insatiable demand for new tech. In Q2 2016, Apple had a 12.9 percent market share of smartphone sales worldwide compared to Android's 86.2 percent (source: www.gartner.com/).

Apple's smartphone operating system, iOS, has evolved alongside its devices. Figure 1-7 shows the compatibility of each iPhone release with different iOS versions.

2007	iPhone	iOS	2	3						
2008	iPhone 3G		2	3	4					
2009	iPhone 3GS			3	4	5	6			
2010	iPhone 4				4	5	6	7		
2011	iPhone 4s					5	6	7	8	9	
2012	iPhone 5						6	7	8	9	10
2013	iPhone 5s							7	8	9	10
2013	iPhone 5c							7	8	9	10
2014	iPhone 6 / 6 Plus								8	9	10
2015	iPhone 6s / 6 Plus									9	10
2016	iPhone SE									9	10
2016	iPhone 7 / 7 Plus										10

Figure 1-7. iOS version compatibility chart for iPhone models

Apple Devices: The iPad

Apple first released the iPad in January 2010, and by January 2015 it had sold more than 250 million of these devices. Some 300,000 were sold on the first day, and over one million were sold by May 2010. The iPad Mini was first released in 2012, the iPad Air in 2013, and the iPad Pro in 2015. Figure 1-8 shows the specifications of the various models.

iPad Mini 4

Size (inches): 8 x 5.3 x 0.24
Processor: 1.5 GHz
RAM: 2 GB
Storage: 16, 64, 128 GB
Display: 7.9-inch multi-touch
Resolution: 2048 x 1536 pixels
Ppi: 264 ppi
Camera: 1.2 MP, 8 MP

iPad Air 2

Size (inches): 9.4 x 6.6 x 0.24
Processor: 1.5 GHz
RAM: 2 GB
Storage: 16, 64, 128 GB
Display: 9.7-inch multi-touch
Resolution: 2048 x 1536 pixels
Ppi: 264 ppi
Camera: 1.2 MP, 8 MP

iPad Pro 9.7-inch

Size (inches): 9.4 x 6.67 x 0.24
Processor: 2.26 GHz
RAM: 2 GB
Storage: 32, 128, 256 GB
Display: 9.7-inch multi-touch
Resolution: 2048 x 1536 pixels
Ppi: 264 ppi
Camera: 1.2 MP, 8 MP

iPad Pro 12.9-inch

Size (inches): 12.04 x 8.69 x 0.27
Processor: 2.26 GHz
RAM: 4 GB
Storage: 32, 128, 256 GB
Display: 12.9-inch multi-touch
Resolution: 2732 x 2048 pixels
Ppi: 264 ppi
Camera: 5 MP, 12 MP

Figure 1-8. Specifications of iPad models

The Apple Tribe

Apple, as a software and hardware manufacturer, was the first to build devices, create software and operating systems that run on those devices, and also operate the marketplace through which the apps created for those devices are sold.

Apple also imposes strict standards and quality controls on the design, aesthetics, and functionality of iOS apps. All this allows the company to offer its customers a user experience that's consistent with the company's intended image.

Apple customers were known for their brand loyalty long before the advent of the iPhone and iPad, and the company has extended this relationship of trust to its smartphone and tablet customers as well (Figure 1-9). This is reflected in the willingness of iPhone and iPad users to spend money on apps and games through their devices. Despite Apple's overall smartphone market share of around 20 to 25 percent, its customers still outspend the users of smartphones running other operating systems.

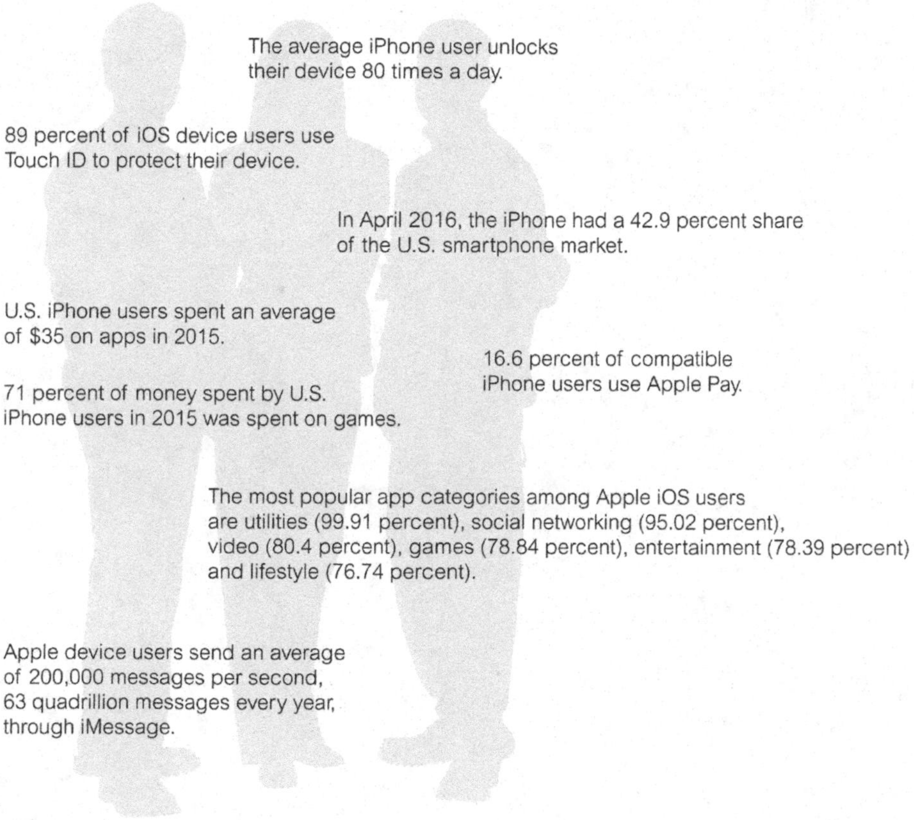

The average iPhone user unlocks
their device 80 times a day.

89 percent of iOS device users use
Touch ID to protect their device.

In April 2016, the iPhone had a 42.9 percent share
of the U.S. smartphone market.

U.S. iPhone users spent an average
of $35 on apps in 2015.

16.6 percent of compatible
iPhone users use Apple Pay.

71 percent of money spent by U.S.
iPhone users in 2015 was spent on games.

The most popular app categories among Apple iOS users
are utilities (99.91 percent), social networking (95.02 percent),
video (80.4 percent), games (78.84 percent), entertainment (78.39 percent)
and lifestyle (76.74 percent).

Apple device users send an average
of 200,000 messages per second,
63 quadrillion messages every year,
through iMessage.

Figure 1-9. The Apple tribe

Summary

Knowing how the smartphone market is evolving over time is the foundation
of a good app development and marketing strategy. Reliable and up-to-date
information about smartphone use, growth, and market penetration will tell
you which countries are the best bets, which languages should be on your
localization list, and where your app is most likely to reach sustainability
quickest. Later on in this book, you will combine this information with data
about app usage, user behavior, and spending habits to determine how to
design a competitive product for your target audience.

Chapter **2**

The App Landscape

"Never innovate to compete.
Innovate to change the rules of the game."

David O. Adeife

Software programs are also known as applications, or apps. Those that are
run on desktop computers are known as desktop apps, while those that are
run on mobile devices are referred to as mobile apps.

A mobile app is just a program, but one that was specifically designed to
run on your smartphone. Apps have transformed the way we interact with
software and how we use it to do the things we want to do. Supported by
the smartphones that host them, apps have created incredible possibilities

© Hagop Panosian 2017   **15**
H. Panosian, *Learn iOS Application Distribution*, DOI 10.1007/978-1-4842-2683-4_2

for communication. They have also made the creation of software for profit accessible to many people who were once far removed from programming and software development.

The Evolution of Apps

Apps have evolved alongside the devices that host them: the smartphone and the tablet. The first apps were primitive versions of what is built into new smartphones today: a calendar, contacts list, and a few basic games. Because the fundamental innovation of the first mobile phones was mobility itself, and since the technology was still in its infancy, all the software was built in. The concept of browsing the Internet, not to mention the idea of downloading apps, was still far away because the bandwidths that we are used to today were simply not there.

At a technology conference in Aspen in June 1983, Steve Jobs predicted that in the future software would be able to be bought over phone lines from a distribution center. As mobile phones became more and more ubiquitous in the 1990s, demand grew sharply for more and more features, and the mobile phone evolved into today's smartphone.

Laying the Foundation

Phones have evolved to meet demand for various features and capabilities, while phone manufacturers have retained only a limited number of built-in apps and allowed third-party developers to build the apps that users crave. This required that they grant developers access to the inner workings of the smartphones. In June 2007, Apple released the first iPhone, selling 270,000 units in 30 hours, and allowed developers to build Web 2.0 apps that were based on Apple's standards and could use its services.

The idea of open access is the foundation of today's app stores and app industry. When Apple first opened the App Store for the iPhone in July 2008, there were just 500 apps available for download. Ten million were downloaded in the first week. Just 60 days later, in September, there were more than 3,000 apps, and they had been downloaded more than 100 million times. Now, there are between 1.8 million and 2 million apps on the Apple and Google app stores available for the over two billion smartphones worldwide. Some 25 billion iOS apps and 50 billion Android apps were downloaded onto smartphones in 2015.

The first apps on the Apple and Google app stores were simply extensions of the mobile phone features that had come before them. Matthew Panzarino, co-editor of *TechCrunch* (*https://techcrunch.com/*) calls the first phase of smartphone apps the "information appliance" phase—apps that turned the phone into a device performing a single function, like a calculator or calendar. The next phase, according to Panzarino, was the "home screen" era, when every app fought to become the user's main app for everything.

The Boundaries of an App

An app is more than just the bit of software that is sitting in your smartphone's memory. Depending on what type of app it is and what features it has, it can communicate with a backend server over the Internet, talk to all the other instances of the same app on other smartphones, and benefit from an endless array of services related to its purpose. Generally, a fully developed app would have the following components:

- Icon – This is the "button" that you press to run the app on your smartphone.

- Splash Screen – This is the non-interactive screen that tells you the app is loading. It's usually just an image and a message telling you to wait.

- Key Features – Besides performing its main function, be it entertainment or utility or something else, a fully developed app will have features related to security, offline functionality, user support, update capability, ways to contact the app publisher to offer feedback or submit inquiries, personalization, device-responsive design, internal search, and integration with social media for sharing purposes.

- Analytics – Analytics are snippets of code that are inserted into an app to monitor, analyze, and predict user behavior inside an app.

- Backend – A mobile backend is software hosted on a server that the publisher of an app uses to keep in touch with all of its users, store relevant information, update the app's content, and supplement the app in different ways. The backend for an app can be hosted on a custom-made server; cloud servers like Amazon AWS, Google App Engine, or Windows Azure; or MBaaS (Mobile Backend as a Service) startups like Stackmob, Kinvey, Appcelerator, and Parse.

Apple's App Store

Apple opened the App Store on July 10, 2008, and hit the one billion download mark on April 23, 2009, hitting 1.4 billion in June of the same year. By November, there were 100,000 apps available on the App Store, and Apple hit the three billion download mark in December. In April 2010, there were 225,000 apps, and by June, those apps had been downloaded a total of five billion times. By November 2010, there were 300,000 apps.

In May of 2011, the number of apps on the App Store hit the half-million mark. As of May 2017, there were around 2.2 million apps available for download, which had been downloaded a total of 180 billion times by June 2017.

According to research by Appboy (*https://www.appboy.com/*) published in April 2016 (*https://www.appboy.com/blog/mobile-customer-99-stats/*), more than 50 percent of smartphone owners today have between 40 and 70 apps installed on their device, while 80 percent engage with their apps at least 15 times a day. Just 8 percent use more than ten apps per day, while 63 percent use between four and ten.

App Types and Categories

Every app falls into a certain category that describes its main function. Each app-publishing platform, like the Apple App Store or Google Play, has its own list of app categories that publishers use to classify their app to make it easy to find.

As of October 2016, the list of app categories on the Apple App Store was as follows: Books, Business, Catalogs, Education, Entertainment, Finance, Food & Drink, Games, Health & Fitness, Lifestyle, Kids, Magazines & Newspapers, Medical, Music, Navigation, News, Photo & Video, Productivity, Reference, Shopping, Social Networking, Sports, Travel, and Utilities.

Each category has its own subcategories. The Games category, for example, has the following subcategories: Action, Adventure, Arcade, Board, Family, Music, Puzzle, Racing, Role Playing, Simulation, Shopping, Sports, and Strategy.

For purposes of comparison, as of October 2016, Google Play has the following categories of apps: Android Wear, Art & Design, Auto & Vehicles, Beauty, Books & Reference, Business, Comics, Communication, Dating, Education, Entertainment, Events, Finance, Food & Drink, Health & Fitness, House & Home, Libraries & Demo, Lifestyle, Maps & Navigation, Medical, Music & Audio, News & Magazines, Parenting, Personalization, Photography, Productivity, Shopping, Social, Sports, Tools, Travel & Local, Video Players & Editors, and Weather.

The Most Popular App Categories

Some apps and app categories are more popular than others in terms of available apps and user engagement. According to statista.com, as of July 2017 the most popular Apple App Store categories by share of available apps were Games (25.08 percent), Business (9.83 percent), Education (8.47 percent), Lifestyle (8.33 percent), Lifestyle (8.33 percent), Entertainment (6.1 percent), Utilities (4.89 percent), Travel (3.93 percent), (6.31 percent), Books (3.02 percent), Health & Fitness (2.98 percent), Food & Drink (2.86 percent), Productivity (2.61 percent), Music (2.54 percent), Finance (2.23 percent), Photo and Video (2.22 percent), Reference (2.21 percent), Sports (2.18 percent), Social Networking (2.11 percent), News (2.11 percent), Medical (1.86 percent), and Shopping (1.29 percent).

Top Apps

According to digital marketing company Smart Insights (*http://www.smartinsights.com/*), as of 2013, adults in the United States have spent more time per day on mobile devices than on their desktop or laptop computers, and, in 2015, the average adult spent 2.8 hours (51 percent of the total time spent) on mobile per day. What kinds of apps did they spend their time on?

According to media analytics company comScore (*https://www.comscore.com/*), the app category users spent the most time on in 2015 was Social Networking (29 percent), followed by Radio (15 percent), Games (11 percent), Multimedia (6 percent), and Messaging (6 percent).

Apple App Store Top Apps

This is reflected in the Top App rankings on the Apple and Google app stores. App market data and insights company App Annie (*https://www.appannie.com/en/*) lists the top apps on the app stores on a day-to-day basis. Let's look at the App Store rankings for October 27, 2016.

Among free apps, the chart leaders were Facebook Messenger, Snapchat, YouTube, Facebook, Instagram, Ever, and Bitmoji.

Among paid apps, the leaders were Toca Life: Farm, Minecraft: Pocket Edition, Earn to Die, Heads Up!, Plague Inc., Enlight, and Bloons TD 5.

The top-grossing apps on the Apple App Store on October 27, 2016, were Pokémon Go, Mobile Strike, Game of War: Fire Age, Clash Royale, Netflix, Candy Crush Saga, and Clash of Clans.

Google Play Top Apps

Let's see the rankings for Google Play for October 27, 2016.

Among free apps, the chart leaders were Facebook Messenger, Facebook, Snapchat, Ever, Instagram, Pandora Studio, and Plants vs. Zombies.

Among paid apps, the leaders were Minecraft: Pocket Edition, Don't Starve: Pocket Edition, Toca Lab, Tamotions, Bloons TD 5, Mini Metro, and Reigns.

The top-grossing apps on Google Play on October 27, 2016, were Mobile Strike, Clash of Clans, Game of War: Fire Age, Clash Royale, Pokémon Go, Candy Crush Saga, and Candy Crush Soda Saga.

According to digital marketing agency Ironpaper (*www.ironpaper.com*), the following iOS apps had the highest market reach in June 2016, in descending order:

- Facebook, 68 percent

- YouTube, 60 percent

- Instagram and iBooks, 44 percent each

- Skype for iPhone, 40 percent

- Podcasts, 38 percent

- Twitter, 34 percent

- Facebook Messenger, 31 percent

Gaming: The Biggest App Category

Games outdo all other app categories in revenue. According to statista.com, total mobile gaming revenue in the United States from 2013 to 2016 in U.S. dollars was $2.03 billion in 2013, $2.61 billion in 2014, $3.04 billion in 2015, and $3.61 billion in 2016. Meanwhile, the top-grossing iPhone mobile gaming apps in the United States as of October 2016, ranked by daily revenue in U.S. dollars, were Clash Royale with $1,969,094, Pokémon GO with $1,562,029, Game of War: Fire Age with $1,226,442, Mobile Strike with $690,275, Candy Crush Saga with $478,159, Clash of Clans with $402,001, Candy Crush Soda Saga with $337,727, MADDEN NFL Mobile with $281,295, Toy Blast with $213,516, and Slotomania Free Slots with $186,724.

Developer Payouts

Developers of all types of apps have made a great deal of money through the Apple App Store. According to statista.com, by January 2014, Apple had paid developers a total of $15 billion. By January 2015, the number was $25 billion, while as of June 2016 the App Store had paid mobile app developers a cumulative total of $50 billion.

Top App Developers and Revenue

As of February 2016, there are around 400,000 developers registered on the Apple App Store, releasing around 1,000 apps a day. The best-performing companies are normally the game developers, with several registering sales of $1 billion or more.

According to Pocketgamer (www.pocketgamer.biz), the following companies made at least $1 billion in sales in 2015: Blizzard (U.S., $4.7 billion), NetEase (China, $3.5 billion), Tencent (China, $3 billion), Supercell (Finland, $2.3 billion), Mixi (Japan, $2 billion), King (U.K., $2 billion), Ubisoft (France, $1.5 billion), GungHo (Japan, $1.3 billion), Dena (Japan, $1.2 billion), and Machine Zone (U.S., $1 billion estimated).

The following companies made between $100 million and $1 billion in sales in 2015: CyberAgent (Japan), Netmarble (South Korea), Zynga (U.S.), GREE (Japan), Colopi (Japan), EA Mobile (U.S.), Elex Technology (China), Nexon (Japan), Square Enix (Japan), Kabam (U.S.), Com2uS (South Korea), Jam City (U.S.), Wargaming (Belarus), Gameloft (France), Disney Mobile (U.S.), Sega Networks (Japan), Glu Mobile (U.S.), IGG (Singapore), Scopely (U.S.), Rovio (Finland), Pocket Games (U.S.), Miniclip (U.K.), Gamevil (South Korea), and Etermax (Argentina).

The following companies made between $1 million and $100 million in sales in 2015: ZeptoLab (Russia), Seriously (Finland), TinyCo (U.S.), Wooga (Germany), Kiloo (Denmark), Space Ape Games (U.K.), IUGO Mobile (Canada), Bethesda Studios (U.S.), Hister Whale (Australia), Next (Finland), KetchApp (France), Super Evil (U.S.), Gram Games (Turkey), Everywear Games (Finland), and Mediocre (Sweden).

Apps have made a lot of developers and companies a great deal of money, but the latest trends suggest the early "Gold Rush" days of the app industry are nearing an end, and the "middle class" of app development is slowly giving way to a bipolar system consisting of a small number of companies raking in the profits and a large number of small developers scoring modest earnings, with a wide gap in the middle.

The big companies invest a great deal of money in developing top-notch games and apps. They use big marketing budgets and user-engagement skills and experience to get the users and keep them, making it impossible for smaller companies to find a gap they can exploit to thrive in. With user acquisition costs at around $3.50 per user and growing, developers need big budgets just to get the users they need to survive, and this makes for a strong barrier to entry.

This is not to say that there no room for newcomers. It just means that newcomers need to be well prepared before entering the business, with good, well-developed ideas, strong planning and budgeting, and a good understanding of what works and how to go about it.

Summary

Monitoring the popularity and financial performance of app categories and top apps will help you glean crucial insights during the design phase of your app, when your focus will be on positioning your product against competing apps in its category and creating a unique value proposition to differentiate that product from the rest. It can also help you identify niches where a product with a specific set of features can do well so you can design a product around those features.

Monitoring the app stores is something you will be doing constantly as an app developer, so finding multiple sources of accurate, up-to-date information you can rely on and use should be a top priority.

Next, we'll be looking at the app industry's ecosystem—who does what and who works with whom to produce the apps and games you love.

Chapter **3**

The App Ecosystem

*"No man will make a great leader
who wants to do it all himself,
or get all the credit for doing it."*
Andrew Carnegie

What happens in the space between the birth of an app as an idea and
its evolution into an appealing, fully functional product ready for you to
download from the app stores? And who influences that app as it evolves
from a concept into a product?

© Hagop Panosian 2017
H. Panosian, *Learn iOS Application Distribution*, DOI 10.1007/978-1-4842-2683-4_3

There are several stages an app goes through as it evolves into a finished product. Each stage defines the app's function, look, and feel in more and more detail, after which the first prototype is created and thoroughly tested before producing the final version for release.

As you become increasingly familiar with the app industry, you will notice that there are literally thousands of companies out there—many of which began as startups like yours—that supply services, resources, or products related to app publishing rather than publishing apps themselves, or that regulate the app publishing process or the industry or market in some way. More and more companies are founded every day, each targeting a specific part of the industry or a specific aspect of the app publishing process. You and the apps you publish will either benefit from their products and services or have to conform to the rules and regulations they set. They are the intermediaries between your startup's founding team and your app users.

Device Manufacturers

Device manufacturers are the companies that build the hardware—the smartphones, tablets, iPods, and other devices and accessories that host your apps and enhance their capabilities. This group also includes companies that build other devices and accessories, such as 3D cameras, 2D and 3D printers, and credit card readers that attach to your device and are managed by apps.

As we saw in the previous chapter, the main device manufacturers related to the app industry are Samsung and Apple, followed by Huawei, Xiaomi, Lenovo, and newcomers like Oppo. According to statista.com, Samsung had the highest smartphone market share in Q2 of 2016 with 22.4 percent, followed by Apple with 11.8 percent, Huawei with 9.4 percent, Oppo with 6.6 percent, and Vivo with 4.5 percent, while other manufacturers together had a 45.1 percent market share. Other companies that manufacture smartphones or have done so in the past include LG, RIM, Blackberry, HTC, Nokia, Motorola, ZTE, Sony, and Microsoft.

Any app that you design will have to take into account the specifications, features, and components of these devices, like the screen resolution, pixel density, available cameras (one or two) and their resolution and capabilities, GPS, accelerometer, processor speed, storage capabilities, and so on.

Many apps are built around using data from one specific component of these devices, like apps or games that use accelerometer data to function, location-based apps that use GPS data, or filter apps that use pictures taken with the camera. Your app will also use these components to gather information about your users, like using GPS data to segment your users by location.

Operating System Developers

Operating system developers like Apple and Google build the operating systems that help you manage your devices and run apps on them. In the case of Apple, the manufacturer of the devices (iPhone, iPad, iPod) and the developer of the operating system that runs on them (iOS) are the same company. Android, on the other hand, is an operating system built by Google that runs on a very long list of devices sold by a very long list of manufacturers that includes Google with its Nexus smartphone series as well as the vast majority of other manufacturers, especially Samsung, Huawei, and Xiaomi.

Operating system builders also set strict guidelines for the design of apps and their user interfaces. Apple and Google have strict design guidelines for apps' design and functionality and publish these guidelines on their websites for developers to follow.

App Distribution Platforms

As a rule, app distribution platforms are native to the mobile operating systems, as dictated by the integration of technologies. The biggest as of May 2017 are Google Play, with 2.8 million apps and Apple's App Store, with 2 million apps. Besides these two most popular platforms, there is the Windows Store with 669,000 apps, the Amazon Appstore with 600,000 apps, and Blackberry World with 234,000 apps. Just in 2017, apps have been downloaded over 180 billion times through these app stores.

App Marketing and Analytics Platforms

App marketing platforms are digital marketing facilitators that will support your marketing campaigns in several ways, as follows:

- They will provide market research and data to support decision-making.

- They will organize and standardize your marketing materials.

- They will help you test your designs and prototypes.

- They will automate your marketing campaigns and help you improve their effectiveness.

- They will supply feedback and analytics data about user response.

You can find a long list of app marketing platforms in the "Resources" section at the end of this book.

Regulators

Regulators set the laws that govern the manufacture, sale, and use of apps and the devices than run them. Regulators deal with issues like device safety and usability, data security, user privacy, standardization, fair competition, prevention of fraud and abuse, licensing for app stores, combating malicious software, enforcing real-name registration, and disclosing to users any in-app payments and information gathering, especially unauthorized charges made by children. They also resolve legal disputes resulting from the use of apps in a specific context, such as the conflict between the taxi service app Uber and local taxi drivers in countries where it is used.

Sometimes the design of an app is not affected by the regulation of its own industry, but by that of the industry for which it is intended. For example, apps for the medical industry have to adhere to strict regulations, mainly regarding the security of patient information gathered through apps and stored in records, the reliability of medical information disseminated through apps, and data-breach notifications.

Financiers

Financiers invest in promising apps at different phases of the lifecycles of app-based tech startups. An app startup's first sources of financing are likely to be personal savings, family, and friends. To grow beyond the first stage, they normally search for other sources of cash, either through loans or equity or from mentors, startup incubators, angel investors, venture capitalists, and banks, starting with what is known as seed capital. Another way an app startup can raise funds is crowdfunding through platforms like Kickstarter and Indiegogo.

Developers

Developers, as individuals or companies, are the people who will take an app concept and turn it into a working app. Developers can be part of your own startup, working full-time or part-time, or can be hired or outsourced based on your project needs and budget. They include coders, user interface (UI) and user experience (UX) designers, game designers, and web designers.

Developers will start with a concept and develop a project plan based on your specifications and intentions, the operating system, platform, and market for which you want to build the app, and your budget. Developers design the user experience and the user interface for a multitude of devices, screens, and user groups, optimizing the app's technical, experiential, and commercial performance. They will also test the app extensively before publishing it on the app stores. There are currently more than 13 million registered Apple developers worldwide.

Asset Producers

Assets are digital products that are used extensively in app design and promotion, such as images, sounds, game characters, or even bits of code that can be inserted into apps and games. Asset producers design and sell or share products like the following:

- Images – device and screen mockups for app promotion, backgrounds for games, standard screen layout types (like login screens, registration screens)

- Wireframes – pre-designed skeletal illustrations of various screens (or pages) common to apps

- Templates – user interface (UI) and graphical user interface (GUI, pronounced *gooey*) kits and templates that speed up the developer's design, iteration, and wireframing work

- Game assets - levels, characters, and objects such as weapons

- Code – pre-written bits of code that perform specific functions and save programmers time

Marketing and Advertising Companies

Marketers will help you maximize the exposure of your app and its chances of success through a variety of channels. Services range from simple e-mail marketing services to automate and manage communication with large numbers of subscribers, to full-range marketing planning and execution by professional app marketing agencies.

If you want to work with a professional marketing and advertising agency, it's wise to do so while your app is still in the development stage, or perhaps even before then. In the early stages of your app's lifecycle, before your app reaches the market, app marketing agencies will, among other things, do the following for you: analyze your competitive landscape, create a unique value proposition, identify markets and segments suitable for your app, make user response and revenue forecasts, test your app before release, launch early marketing campaigns to create interest around your app, design and produce optimized promotion materials, like app descriptions, screenshots, and videos for the app stores, and manage the app submission and approval process for you. Marketing agencies will also develop a focused post-release marketing and promotion plan and implement and manage it on your behalf.

Educators

These days, technology enables easy and affordable access to vast learning resources about every aspect of app development, from blogs, websites, articles, and forums to YouTube videos, where the curious can get all the help they need.

If you are committed to learning app development, there are online courses available on websites like Udemy, Udacity, Lynda, Coursera, Team Treehouse, Code.org, Code Academy, iTunes U, Khan Academy, Pluralsight, Skillcrush, Tuts Plus, Skillshare, and Sitepoint. There are also MOOCs (Massive Online Open Courses) offered by respected universities, like Harvard, MIT, Yale, Berkeley, Carnegie Mellon, the University of Texas, and other institutions.

Online tutors can teach you programming skills and can also advise you on any app development issues you may be facing. Search for mentors on CodeTutor, Chegg, Presto Experts, Tutor Universe, Wyzant, Tutors Live, eTutoring, and other sites. Tutoring companies also organize workshops on both broad and narrow themes related to app development. In these workshops, learning is done in groups. They can usually be found with a simple search. The most popular subjects are programming and app marketing.

If you are a passionate and motivated self-learner, there are books available in print or online on almost any subject related to app development. All the major technology book publishers, like Apress, McGraw Hill, New Riders, Wrox, and Wiley have hundreds of books on all aspects of app development, from programming to UI/UX design to marketing.

Online Job Marketplaces

One important aspect of the app publishing process you will need to manage is deciding which tasks to handle in-house and which to outsource or hire out as a service.

As an app publisher, you may decide to outsource part of the app development process, fundamentally to save money, and to avoid having to hire in-house for any reason, such as space restrictions or the small size of a project.

As the "gig economy" grows, hiring online has become very popular, especially for technology-related work. You will need to hire primarily for two types of work: design and programming. Designers will present you with app branding ideas and UI/UX designs, while programmers will code your apps.

The most popular online job marketplaces are Upwork.com, Freelancer.com, Guru.com, Elance.com, Toptal.com, 99designs.com, Fiverr.com, MatchList.com, Gun.io, Crew.co, LocalSolo.com, Onsite.io, Folyo.me, Crowdsite.com, GetaCoder, and PeoplePerHour.com.

This brings us to the most important player in the app publishing industry— the appreneur (app entrepreneur). That's you!

Appreneurs

If you are getting into the app industry with the intention of publishing one or more apps and building a business around them, you are an app entrepreneur, or appreneur. As we will see later, with few exceptions, going through the whole process of conceiving, designing, coding, and publishing an app on your own is not a smart way to go about app publishing for several reasons, the most important of which is that this strategy fails to maximize the app's potential for success.

You are unlikely to have honed all the skills that are needed to steer your app to success, not to mention the time constraints and the amount of work involved, so you are much better off creating a team that combines all the needed skills and distributes the tasks efficiently.

Why is building a team wiser than working on your own? The following sections identify the reasons.

Combination of Skills

As smart as you may be, you are unlikely to have mastered all the skills that are needed to make your app a success. Publishing an app requires the following skills: visual design, UI/UX design, coding, project management, accounting, financial management, business law and intellectual property protection, time management, marketing, customer relationship management (CRM), and so on. The members of a well-built team will bring together all the key skills that are needed for an app project and complement each other's strengths and weaknesses.

Time Management

Simply put, there are just not enough hours in a day for you to do everything on your own for a serious app project unless you're planning to take years to bring it to market, by which time the competition will probably have already saturated the market. Doing everything on your own will also force you to micromanage and possibly lose sight of the broader vision for your project.

Feedback

When you're working on your own, you are missing out on the opportunity for constant feedback from your teammates, which is so important to the efficiency and success of a project. It's not that you *can't* do it on your own—many do—but with a team, your potential and capability are so much greater.

Contacts

Besides their own personal contribution to a project, each member of a team will bring their own circle of friends, colleagues, and other contacts to a project, multiplying the project's visibility and likelihood of strong mentor support, especially at the beginning.

Credibility

Investors will rarely take a single-person team seriously. "I can do it all on my own; I don't need anyone else" is a sure way to kill your credibility and drive away investors. It suggests that 1) you don't understand the work involved and the separate tasks relevant to app publishing well enough; 2) you may be paranoid and may be obsessed or emotionally attached to your project, and thus do not want to share your idea with anyone else; and 3) you may be greedy and do not like the idea of surrendering equity to finance your project. All of these impressions about you send very bad signals that undermine your credibility as a founder and paint a picture of you as someone who is not mature enough to treat the project as a future business. Any serious app project will be built around a team, and a well-built team that combines the right skills, the right people, and the right networking potential becomes much more than the sum of its parts.

Let's take a look at the different members of a founding team.

The Founding Team

The founding team consists of three subgroups: the founder, the co-founder or co-founders, and the mentor or mentors (Figure 3-1). Each plays an important role in the launch and evolution of a company.

Co-founder   Founder

                                         Mentor

The Founding Team

Figure 3-1. *The founding team*

The Founder

Every project or business begins with the founder. Besides being "the one with the original concept" and the carrier of the vision, the founder is the driving force who keeps the project on track and moving in the right direction, especially if he or she is also acting as the CEO.

The Co-founder(s)

Co-founders contribute their skills, experience, and social networks to a startup and help send a positive signal to investors about how the founders are approaching their project.

Building the team begins with the founder. As a smart founder, you will first make a realistic and accurate assessment of what you can accomplish and the skills you have, identify the key skills that are lacking, and complement those skills by bringing in reliable and committed co-founders who understand and share your vision. People who would be indispensable for an app startup from the beginning are the best candidates for the founding team.

When building the founding team, however, you as a founder also need to make sure the founding team does not become too large, as having too many members would dilute ownership over the project or startup and raise the likelihood of conflict. The members of the founding team need to share your vision, and the likelihood of this shrinks as the size of the team grows. A small founding team that combines vision with management skills, financial skills, and technical skills will send the right signal to investors and raise your chances of success as you grow.

The Mentor(s)

Mentors are highly valuable contributors to an app project or startup. They may or may not be part of the original founding team, but the right mentors will contribute their experience, knowledge, and social networks, raising the credibility and visibility of your startup. They will offer guidance when the managing team sails into uncharted waters, and if you are new to app publishing, you will be doing that a lot.

Users

By far the largest group that keeps the app industry evolving is the users. There are more than two billion of them across the globe, armed with smartphones they check around 15 times a day on average. They will download your app, engage with it, review it, share their experience with it, and hopefully spend money on it.

Your relationship with your users is vital to the success of your app. Understanding who your users are, what they want, what they like, and what they expect from your app is the key to creating a successful app that is a perfect product-market fit and leads to money in the bank for you.

The most important thing to know about your users is that they are all different from each other. Ignore this fact at your peril. As you will see, users can be divided into different groups based on the characteristics they share, but each expects you to treat them as an individual, and each responds much more positively to anything that is marketed to them personally than to anything that is marketed generically. You will be automating your marketing efforts as you scale, but the closer you can get to what makes your users different from one another, the better you will understand what inspires them and makes them want to buy and, as a result, the more effective your marketing efforts will be.

So, how will you be interacting with your users through your app and your marketing campaigns? Your relationship with users has three aspects: gathering information, segmenting users, and relating/responding. Let's review them now.

Gather Information

Analytics software used in your app will gather all the information about your users they are willing to share. Analytics will gather three categories of information: user attributes, user preferences, and user behavior.

User attributes are what describes your user: location (city and country, and GPS data for location-based apps), age, gender, birth date, native language, number and types of devices used, and their operating systems.

User preferences are what the user likes and how they want you to relate to them. Depending on the type of app, analytics will tell you what social media they use, what their favorite types of content are, where they like to hang out, what they like to eat, how often they travel, and where they like to go on vacation. Your users will also tell you how they want you to relate to them—whether they like to be contacted through push notifications, their subscription to in-app services and content, the device settings they have enabled, and their social media connection status.

User behavior monitoring tells you what your users are doing and gathers statistics about their behavior to create a profile you can use to develop the next version of the app, as well as for marketing purposes to target them with the right offer.

User behavior information includes frequency and interval of app usage, duration of app visits, depth of app engagement, and financial information, such as average and total values of in-app purchases, frequency of purchases, last e-mail or push notification opened, which campaign they were converted from, and last action taken inside the app.

Segment Your Users

The first step to marketing to your users effectively is segmentation. Segmentation is the process of dividing a user group into smaller segments based on different characteristics, such as a age, gender, location, behavior patterns and preferences. However, segmentation is based first of all on your marketing goals. You may be trying to convert non-paying users to paying users, and would therefore segment users based on their financial data. You would isolate the non-paying users and try to make them an offer, possibly of new features you have designed for the most deeply engaged user group. You may want to strengthen retention by rewarding your most loyal users, those who use your app the most, and by marketing the rewards for loyalty to users who are active but not loyal to encourage them to be more engaged.

You may be trying to re-target users who have your app installed on their devices but rarely use it, if at all. They are known as lapsing or inactive users. In this case, you would isolate users who are the least engaged with your app and nudge them into returning to it. It's all a matter of what you want to achieve, but the more detailed your analytics data is, the more effective you will be in achieving your marketing goals.

One example worth noting is hyper-local marketing, which segments users depending on their proximity to a specific location that is relevant to a marketing campaign. For example, an automated marketing platform would display an ad for a restaurant, shop, or other establishment to all users located within one kilometer from that establishment using GPS data.

Relate and Respond

Once you collect and structure all the data you are gathering through analytics about your users, you can use that valuable knowledge to personalize your marketing in the following ways:

- Through content. You can design your marketing content to match a user's preferred subject.

- Through design. The history of their responses to marketing messages could provide information about the type of message and design they respond to best.

- Through timing. A user may respond positively if you catch them at a certain time of day, say, after working hours, while a message in the middle of the day will be ignored.

- Through the right offer. Tailor your offers to your target segment's profile, and you will be successful.

Summary

This chapter is all about the different people who determine how an app functions, its look and feel, and, ultimately, its fate. Amateur app publishers are likely to be deeply attached to their projects and see them as expressions of their own ideas and intentions, but more professional publishers understand that, like all products, apps are shaped by different people and are designed to meet the very specific needs of their users, with their success dependent on how well they perform in that respect.

An app is like a living entity that grows with its users. Through their response to your product, users will tell you what they want from you, and your mission as a publisher is to keep up with your users' evolving needs and expectations.

Chapter 4

App Economics

*"When money realizes that it is in good hands,
it wants to stay and multiply in those hands."*

Idowu Koneyikan

This chapter is all about money. It is the chapter where we ask (and answer) the five big questions that everyone interested in apps as an investment or a business wants an answer to:

1. How much does it cost to create an app?

2. How do apps make money?

3. How much money do apps make?

4. How can I measure the performance of an app?

5. How can I measure the ROI (return on investment) of an app?

© Hagop Panosian 2017
H. Panosian, *Learn iOS Application Distribution*, DOI 10.1007/978-1-4842-2683-4_4

Making an app profitable is a tricky affair and an evolving science. It is as much a matter of good design, marketing, and interaction with the customer through the mobile interface as it is of financial savvy, and therefore it relies on both rational thinking and intuition.

So, how should we look at apps from a financial perspective?

The revenue cycle of an app is illustrated in Figure 4-1.

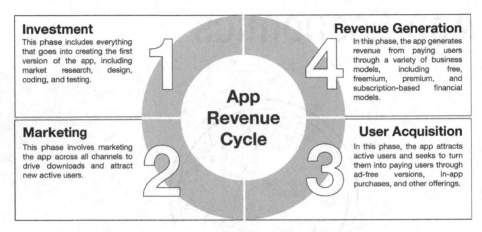

Investment
This phase includes everything that goes into creating the first version of the app, including market research, design, coding, and testing.

Revenue Generation
In this phase, the app generates revenue from paying users through a variety of business models, including free, freemium, premium, and subscription-based financial models.

Marketing
This phase involves marketing the app across all channels to drive downloads and attract new active users.

User Acquisition
In this phase, the app attracts active users and seeks to turn them into paying users through ad-free versions, in-app purchases, and other offerings.

App Revenue Cycle

Figure 4-1. The app revenue cycle

Although it may seem that the first phase, **Investment**, needs to be implemented just once to create the first version of an app, it's important to understand that each of these phases is constant once the app is online. You as a publisher will be constantly investing, constantly marketing, constantly acquiring users, and (hopefully) constantly generating more and more revenue. If you stop investing in your app once it's online, you'll eventually stop generating revenue as well.

It's also important to note that besides going to salaries and other operational costs, a part of the revenue your app generates will be invested in creating new versions, adding features, creating new in-app purchases (and levels, if your app is a game), and generally thinking up new ways to keep your existing users engaged and willing to pay.

Big Question 1: How Much Does It Cost to Create an App?

This question does not have a clear-cut answer, because the cost varies greatly depending on a number of factors. The cost of creating an app can range from close to nothing if you are a pro coder building a very simple game on your own to millions of dollars for the mobile version of a popular game with millions of users playing at the same time.

A simple standalone app can cost anywhere from a few hundred dollars (if you're designing and coding it yourself) to tens of thousands, depending on its size, complexity, and platform. Estimating the cost of an app also depends on how you are calculating the cost of the hardware and software you will need for the task, as well as the developer subscription costs involved. If you are developing multiple apps, such costs will be distributed among the total number of apps you have published. Location is an additional important factor: coding and testing and debugging for an app can cost from $10 to $20 per hour in East Asia to over $200 per hour in Europe and North America. A backend database can cost anywhere from several thousand to tens of thousands to create.

Social media integration for a medium-complexity app can also set you back several thousand, and so can an in-app purchasing system. An enterprise app can cost tens of thousands of dollars, while a complex game with great design, many levels, and in-app purchases can cost hundreds of thousands of dollars, or even millions.

The following sections will review the main factors that affect the cost of developing and publishing an app. Answering the questions in these sections will give you a good estimate of what it will cost to create the app you have designed.

App Type

What type of app do you want to create? Is it a simple standalone app or game that does not need a backend and can be downloaded and run entirely on a user's device without needing Internet access, like a flashlight app, for example? Is it a complex game with many levels, characters, and players? Is it a social media app, an enterprise app with a closed group of users, or something else?

App Platform

Which platform(s) are you developing for? Your app can be a native app, meaning it is designed exclusively for Android or iOS or another platform; it can be a cross-platform app, which means it will be built once to run on many platforms; or it can be a hybrid app, which means it's a web app (like a mobile website) inside a code "wrapper" that allows it to be downloaded and run like a native app.

Cross-platform or hybrid apps cost significantly less than native apps do, which have to be developed separately for each platform, but they also have their drawbacks, especially with regard to which services they can access. Native apps are designed specifically for the operating system that runs them, like iOS apps for Apple devices, and can therefore make full use of the capabilities of the device on which they are hosted.

As part of your strategy, you might decide to build native apps for each platform you have chosen, but you will want to start by building for just one platform first in order to test user response, and then build the second version for several platforms. This will have a major impact on your cost, as building for one platform at the beginning will cost much less than building for two or more.

Coding

Who will code the app? Do you plan to code the app yourself, hire an in-house coder, or hire online? How much testing and debugging will the app require?

Outsourcing coding on websites like Upwork.com or Freelancer.com can save you a lot of money compared to hiring in-house, and coding done in an East Asian or Far Eastern country may cost a fraction of what coding done in Europe or North America will cost, but there is a downside to it as well. Working with coders who are far away will have an impact on development speed, as it may have a negative effect on how fast changes and improvements are made and errors are fixed. You may find yourself getting exhausted with all the back-and-forth and frustrated by the difficulty of explaining what you want accurately over Skype or e-mail. There may or may not be language-related problems as well. All these things must be taken into account when you make your decisions.

Features

What features will the app have? Does it have a backend database or social media integration? Does it include separate accounts for users with login and content-sharing capabilities, which would require additional data privacy and security provisions? Does it have in-app purchases?

App features are individual components that your app may require, such as live chat, news feeds, content management features, code readers, and delivery or order tracking, depending on what kind of app it is.

UI Design

What kind of UI (user interface) will the app have? Is it a simple, standard, pre-designed UI bought over the Internet or a custom-designed UI with unique design elements created exclusively for you? Will you require a logo design, and, if you will, who will design it? Will you hire a professional designer to brand your app, or do you plan to hold a quick design competition on Freelancer.com?

Graphics

How graphics-heavy is the app? Will it require extensive and continuous design work, like levels and characters for a game, or many priced images, like a news app? Three-dimensional worlds and game characters can cost a lot to create and maintain, but so can constantly buying images or creating your own as content for your app.

Marketing

Are marketing costs included in your cost estimate? How do you plan to promote and market your app? What budget have you set aside for marketing purposes, and do you have a well-thought-out and budgeted marketing strategy?

For example, if you plan to market your app so it reaches the top ranks of its category, you will have to take into account that finding and attracting paying users is an expensive investment. One of the most important calculations you will make is determining how much money on average you will spend for every user you acquire compared to how much money you expect to make on average from that user over their lifetime as a user. We will look at this in more detail later on in this chapter.

Content

Does your app have unique content? What type of content is it? Is it information, music, news, movies, or images? Who creates it—the employees of the app, paid writers, or the users themselves? How much does it cost to create the content?

Updating

How often will the content of your app be updated after launch? Is it unchanging, like the content of an e-book app, or updated constantly, like the content of a news app?

Operational Costs

What operational costs are involved in managing the app? Do you have salaries to pay, office space to rent, taxes to pay, and content that needs to be hosted on servers?

The answers to these questions will also help answer another important question: *how long does it take to build an app?* A basic standalone app may take around two months to complete. An app that requires a backend server and database may require another two months. App development times vary from one platform to another. Android apps take longer to build than iOS apps do. Graphics-heavy apps like games will take up to a year or more to design, code, and debug before release.

Big Question 2: How Do Apps Make Money?

Apps generate revenue through business models that are based on the combination of four different components, as shown in Figure 4-2.

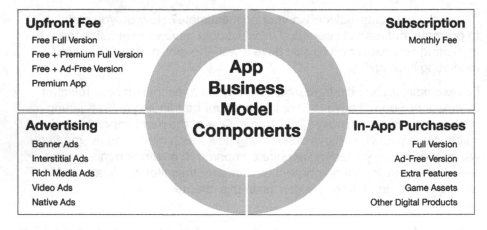

Figure 4-2. App business model components

Let's look at each of these components closely.

Upfront Fee

Deciding whether or not to charge a fee upfront is essentially a marketing and growth decision. In general, you should have a good reason for charging a fee upfront, because the vast majority of apps are free to download, and if there's a free app competing with yours, you don't stand a chance.

Normally, in the period immediately after your app's release, you will likely be focusing on growth and on building a large-enough user base. A large user base is essential to the sustainability of an app as a business, even if the vast majority of those users will never pay you a dime, because in that base of users there's the group of potential paying users you are looking for. This means giving your app away and looking for other ways to generate revenue.

There are four options in this component of your business model:

1. You can give away your app for free. This is by far the most popular model, and is usually combined with revenue-generating options like ads and in-app purchases. These will also be an essential part of your strategy if you are focused on growth at the beginning of your app's lifecycle.

   If your strategy is focused on growth first and revenue later, giving your app away for free is the right way to go. Later on, once your user base is large enough and you shift to revenue generation, charging an upfront fee will be irrelevant, as you will be using other ways to generate revenue, like in-app purchases.

2. Give your app away and charge for a full version. This method allows users to try out the app before committing to the paid version. This model is known as the freemium (free + premium) model.

3. Give your app away and charge for the ad-free version. This is also known as freemium. In this option, you give away the full app with all its features for free, but free users get the ad-laden version and have to pay for the ad-free version. In this way, you can make money from all your users—ad revenue from free users and a fee from paying users.

4. You can charge a fee upfront. It's usually very difficult to convince users to pay any money upfront in the app business because users will only pay for certain apps, like popular games or professional utility apps. When you charge a fee upfront, you are essentially asking people to commit to your app, even if the fee is small, and users don't like to commit to an app before trying it out.

Some apps combine an upfront fee with in-app purchases for certain features, but this is probably the most difficult to implement without losing users. Apply this option only for specific types of apps.

Subscription

One alternative to the upfront fee is the subscription-based app, which creates a revenue stream that can support the future growth of your app and development costs for updates and new versions.

This revenue-generation method is becoming increasingly popular, as it creates a revenue stream and generates more revenue than other models. Why only charge $1 upfront when you can charge $1 every month? However, to convince users to sign up, you must either have the right type of app with renewable content, like a music service or magazine app, or provide a consistently great user experience, like a game with new levels or challenges every month.

Advertising

Mobile ads come in different sizes and formats and use different methods to reach the user. The five basic types are shown in Figure 4-3.

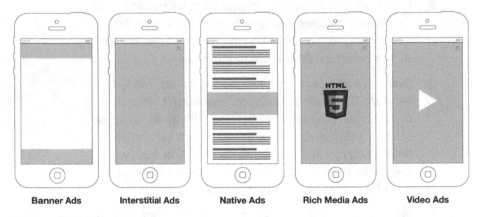

| Banner Ads | Interstitial Ads | Native Ads | Rich Media Ads | Video Ads |

Figure 4-3. Mobile ad types

Banner Ads

Banner ads are the most popular and common ad format. A banner is a narrow horizontal strip at the top or bottom of a screen that displays different ads. As there is little space in a banner, such ads contain very short, simple messages and rely on visual impact to influence the user.

Interstitial Ads

Interstitial ads take up the entire screen, giving the user a choice of either clicking on the ad or closing it to return to the current app screen. Interstitial ads need to be used carefully because they tend to disrupt the user experience and could irritate and alienate users instead of generating revenue.

Interstitial ads appear at times and on events set by the publisher, such as on app launch or exit, or when a specific screen is visited for the first time, or at specific intervals, like every third launch.

Native Ads

Native ads are embedded in app content and are designed to be as unobtrusive as possible. They work well with specific types of apps that display content, like news apps.

One big perceived advantage of native ads is that they are not affected by ad blockers, which can block all other types of ads. This is not true, however, as ad blockers can block native ads as well.

Rich Media Ads

Rich media ads come in different sizes and combine text and all image and video formats.

Video Ads

Video ads display clickable full-screen videos. Video ads are an expensive but compelling way to draw user attention and increase engagement.

Ad Blockers

Ad blockers do exactly that—block ads. The most popular means of blocking ads are ad-blocking mobile web browsers and downloadable content-blocking apps. If an app user has ad blockers installed on their smartphone, your app will not be able to display ads, and your ads will not produce revenue.

Ad blocking has spread like wildfire among smartphone users since 2015. According to a study by PageFair and Priori Data, more than 419 million smartphone users in the spring of 2016 had ad blockers installed on their smartphones, and 22 percent of smartphone users worldwide were blocking ads while surfing the mobile web.

In-App Purchases

The list of what you can market to users from inside your app is endless and will change radically depending on the type of app it is and your own revenue goals. Here's a short list of sample in-app purchases you can offer your users:

- games market power-ups
- boosters
- weapons
- new levels
- virtual currency
- new characters

Other types of apps market special features or ad-free versions or other offers unique to the app.

In-app purchases can also be added or removed depending on your revenue goals. You can, for example, create special offers for the holiday season or bundle several offerings together with a discount. The only limit is your imagination and strategy.

Studies suggest that among the monetization models available to app publishers, subscriptions produce significantly more ARPU, or Average Revenue per User, over other options like in-app advertising, paid downloads, in-app purchases, and the freemium model. This model, however, may not be suitable for your app. Choosing the right monetization model, or combination of models, for your app depends on both the kind of user experience you are offering and how you plan to charge for the value you are offering your users.

Creating a Solid Monetization Strategy

The four sources of app revenue we just looked at—the upfront fee, subscriptions, advertising, and in-app purchases—will be the main options available to you as you develop a monetization strategy for your app. A solid monetization strategy is built above all on a thorough understanding of your user and your app's value proposition.

What can your app do for your user? What part of that value proposition will you offer for free to capture the user's attention and loyalty, and which features will you offer at a price? Will your user be willing to pay the price for in-app purchases?

The truth is, app publishers that have excellent marketing, engagement, and monetization strategies make a great deal of money, especially game makers. We'll look at app revenues next.

Big Question 3: How Much Money Do Apps Make?

The immediate answer to this question is "a lot." Successful apps make lots of money, especially games. Apps made a total of $25 billion in 2014, and will make an estimated $46 billion in 2016. Much of that revenue originates from games. For example, according to statista.com, the top-grossing iPhone game in the United States as of October 2016 in terms of daily revenue is Clash Royale, with $1,969,094, followed by Pokémon GO, with $1,562,029, Game of War: Fire Age, with $1,226,442, Mobile Strike, with $690,275, Candy Crush Saga, with $478,159, Clash of Clans, with $402,001, Candy Crush Soda Saga, with $337,727, Madden NFL Mobile, with $281,295, Toy Blast, with $213,516, and Slotomania Free Slots, with $186,724.

Also according to statista.com, total mobile gaming revenue in the United States has grown from $2.03 billion in 2013 to $2.61 billion in 2016. Total mobile gaming revenue worldwide has grown from $9.1 billion in 2012 to $24.4 billion in 2014 and $35.6 billion in 2016, and it is projected to grow to $44.6 billion in 2018.

Mobile Gaming Spend per Player

Here's a look at game revenue from another angle: according to a study by Slice Intelligence, spend per player in 2015 on the top 25 mobile games ranged between $549.99 (yes, $549.99 per player) for Game of War: Fire Age and $6.50 for Minecraft. In between were $272.41 for Summoners War, $232.67 for Big Fish Casino: Free Slots, $202.26 for Castle Clash, $156.20 for Brave Frontier, $127.77 for Marvel: Contest of Champions, $126.82 for DoubleDown Casino: Free Slots, $117.91 for Boom Beach, $116.25 for Covet Fashion, $112.99 for Clash of Clans, $100.15 for Gummy Drop, $83.93 for Family Guy: The Quest for Stuff, $80.81 for Hay Day, $80.15 for Kim Kardashian Hollywood, $72.14 for The Simpsons: Tapped Out, $70.19 for FarmVille 2 Country Escape, $67.52 for Cookie Jam, $66.24 for Candy Crush Soda Saga, $65.76 for Hearthstone: Heroes of Warcraft, $61.49 for Candy Crush Saga, $57.08 for Madden NFL Mobile, $55.67 for SimCity BuildIt, $55.21 for Farm Heroes Saga, and $38.55 for The Sims FreePlay.

Developer Revenue

It's estimated that over 37,000 developers made more than $10,000 in 2015. In the same year, 17,024 developers are estimated to have made more than $50,000, and 11,273 developers are estimated to have made more than $100,000.

In that year, 6,000 developers are estimated to have made more than $250,000, and 3,525 developers are estimated to have made more than $500,000.

Still in 2015, 1,887 app developers are estimated to have made more than $1 million, either in iOS or in Android, and 132 who developed on both iOS and Android are estimated to have made more than $1 million.

Forty-five percent of app store revenues will go to developers outside the top 100, who made $2.3 billion in Q2 of 2015 alone. Seventy-eight percent of millionaire developers will have made their money in games.

Mobile Payments

It's not all about games, though. Financial transactions over mobile are growing very fast year on year, which is an indication of growing user confidence in the reliability and security of mobile transactions. App users are increasingly willing to make payments over mobile. The challenge for you is coming up with ways to develop a product that can capture some of those paying users. The effort, however, is worth it. According to statista. com, annual mobile payment transaction value has literally exploded over the past several years and looks set to continue to do so, having grown from $4.93 billion in 2014 to $22.74 billion in 2015 and $74.29 billion in 2016, and it is projected to grow to $163.47 billion in 2017 and $745.12 billion in 2020.

Unicorns

Apps can be successful not just in terms of daily revenue, but in terms of value as well. There are startups built fundamentally around mobile that have valuations larger than the Gross Domestic Product of small countries. Some produce significant revenue, but others don't, and their valuation is based on other factors, such as their domination of their niche, ability to create disruptive innovation in their sector, and expected future monetization potential.

Below is a list of app-based startups that had investment valuations of more than $1 billion in 2015. Such startups are known as unicorns, and you are likely to have their apps on your smartphone:

> Uber (U.S., $41 billion)
>
> Snapchat (U.S., $15 billion)
>
> Pinterest (U.S., $11 billion)
>
> Dropbox (U.S., $10 billion)
>
> Airbnb (U.S., $10 billion)
>
> Spotify (SE, $8.4 billion)
>
> Square (U.S., $6 billion)
>
> Lyft (U.S., $2.5 billion)
>
> Ola Cabs (IN, $2.4 billion)
>
> Evernote (U.S., $2 billion)
>
> Tango (U.S., $1.1 billion)

Big Question 4: How Can I Measure the Performance of an App?

How do you measure anything related to how your app is doing? The performance of an app can be measured from a technical, financial, or user-engagement perspective, and the data is provided by what is known as analytics.

Analytics information is produced by software that is inserted into the code of your app and constantly monitors everything that is happening in the app and how individual users are interacting with it. Performance measurements are known as metrics and KPIs, or key performance indicators.

App Metrics and KPIs

Metrics and KPIs related to the performance and success of an app can be grouped into five broad categories:

1. Performance Analytics

2. User Analytics

3. User-Engagement Analytics

4. Financial Analytics

5. Marketing Analytics

The first four categories produce measurements made from inside the app and are tied directly to the app itself. The fifth category, marketing analytics, is produced partly from inside the app (from in-app advertising) and partly from outside (your own campaigns in print, social media, and other channels) and measures the effectiveness of your own marketing efforts.

Although these analytics look at app performance from five perspectives, they all measure how well your app is doing and are closely interconnected.

There are literally thousands of metrics and KPIs you can use to measure the performance of an app from these different perspectives, and analytics software allows you to customize your analytics reports depending on what questions about your app's performance or your users' behavior and preferences you want to answer.

Metrics and KPIs also differ based on the type of app involved. Games, enterprise apps, and commercial apps will set their own benchmarks for user engagement, profitability, and virality on social media, will use very different metrics to measure success, and will monitor user behavior from very different angles. Metrics and KPIs also differ within a single app based on your own evolving strategy goals. When you are focused on rapid growth, the metrics you will be using to measure how well you are doing will be different from the metrics you will be using if you are focused on maximizing revenue.

Basic App Metrics

These app metrics are the most fundamental and most common. The following form the basis for creating more detailed metrics and will give you a quick assessment of how your app is doing:

- **Average Download Rate** – This metric tells you how many times your app is being downloaded over a set period of time, like 500 downloads a week, or 150,000 downloads a month.

- **Retention Rate** – The number of users an app is keeping over a set period of time. Retention is the difference between the number of new users an app creates within a set period and how many users have interacted with the app after another set period. For example, if an app gets 500 new users in June, and 75 of them have used the app in July, the app has a retention rate of 75/500, or 15 percent, for this user segment.

- **Churn Rate** – The number of users an app is losing over a set period of time. The churn rate is the opposite of the retention rate, and the relationship between them is as follows:

  - Churn rate = (100 - Retention Rate). For example, if the app just mentioned has a retention rate of 15 percent, its churn rate is 85 percent. That's the percentage of the app's users who are "churning."

  - It's difficult to measure the number of users you are losing over a set period of time, because users may have lost interest in an app but kept it on their device. What counts as a "lost" customer depends on you: is a user who hasn't opened your app for a month but is still keeping it on their device a "lost" user? Some users like to keep certain apps on hand in case they need them, but may not use them regularly.

  - As a result, for some publishers a more accurate basis for creating metrics would be to focus on active users who interact with an app frequently, especially if they are looking to measure engagement and financial performance.

- **DAU—Daily Active Users** – This metric is closer to the actual number of users who are actively using your app. DAU is the number of users who launch your app at least once a day. They may be using your app a dozen times a day, but they count only once because you are counting them as an individual, not as the number of sessions they spend interacting with your app, which is another metric.

- **Daily Sessions per DAU** – This metric will tell you how many times a day your app is being used by your daily active users. To get this number, you will divide the average number of daily sessions by the number of DAUs. If your app is being used an average of 150 times a day by a DAU of 75, your daily sessions per DAU is two, or, in other words, your users are each interacting with your app twice a day.

- **MAU—Monthly Active Users** – This metric is similar to DAU, except it measures the number of users who used your app at least once in a given month. Note that MAU would include someone who used your app just once in a month.

- **Stickiness** – This is how consistently users are interacting with your app, or how deeply users are engaged with your app.

  On its *Relate* blog, app marketing firm Appboy calculates stickiness as DAU divided by MAU. The higher this percentage is, the "stickier" your app is.

  Another app marketing firm, Localytics, defines app stickiness differently, as the average of an app's Power Users and Loyal Users, Power Users being "the percentage of users who launch an app at least 10 times a month," and Loyal Users being "the percentage of users who return to an app within 3 months of their first session." Power Users represent engagement, and Loyal Users represent retention.

  Localytics publishes an App Stickiness Index every quarter, according to which app stickiness hit an all-time high of 26 percent in Q1 2015.

- **Customer Acquisition Cost (CAC)** – This is the cost of acquiring a customer, also known as CPA, or cost per acquisition.

  To measure CAC or CPA, divide your marketing campaign costs over a set period of time by the number of new users your marketing campaigns produced within that period. You can also use the same method to measure the effectiveness of a specific marketing campaign, like your holiday season campaign, or a specific channel, like social media or print ads.

  The rising cost of customer acquisition is a big issue these days, especially given that the money spent to acquire a user will be wasted if that user does not stick around for very long. In Q4 2015, it stood around $2.80. It is generally accepted that an app will retain just 10 to 20 percent of its users over time, so the cost of acquiring users is partly a recurring one, and maintaining a steady and high-enough number of users will cost a lot more than $2.80 per user.

  Conclusion: Strong user engagement will have a very big impact on your customer acquisition costs and your app's profitability, as you will spending less on replacing lost customers with new ones and more on building a truly large customer base. User engagement and loyalty are key to achieving success in the app world.

- **Average Revenue per User (ARPU)** – This is the average revenue generated by active users within a specific period of time. If your app had 1,000 active users in the month of March, and they generated $1,000 of revenue in the same month, your ARPU for March is $1. ARPU helps publishers monitor how revenue is changing and take action accordingly.

- **Average Revenue per Paying User (ARPPU)** – This is the average revenue generated within a specific period of time by paying users. As the number of paying users is much smaller than the number of active users, ARPPU is naturally significantly higher than ARPU.

- **Customer Lifetime** – This is the average amount of time your app users will retain your app before abandoning it. A customer's lifetime is inversely proportional to the churn rate. For example, if your churn rate is 20 percent, then your average customer lifetime is 1/0.2 = 5 months.

- **Lifetime Value (LTV)** – This is the amount of money an average customer will spend on your app throughout the time they use it. It's also known as CLTV, or Customer Lifetime Value.

One way to measure LTV is by multiplying the average value of a financial transaction generated by your app by the number of transactions within a set period, then by the duration of an average customer's lifetime. For example, if your gross margin on an average transaction is $2, and the average customer makes four transactions a month, and the average lifetime of a user is three months, then your LTV is 2 × 4 × 3 = $24.

The tricky part, of course, is accurately measuring the customer's lifetime, especially if your app is new and you have no past experience you can apply. The way to measure a customer's lifetime is to use the inverse of churn, or the number of customers your app loses in a set period of time.

The formula for measuring monthly churn is as follows: Divide the number of customers lost over a given month by the number of customers you had at the start of that month. The inverse of the churn rate will be the expected customer lifespan. If you are losing 50 percent of your users every month (which is quite normal, by the way), your churn rate will be 50 percent, and your customer lifetime will 1/0.5 = 2 months. You can then multiply that number by the value of the average transaction and the number of transactions an average customer will make in your app, and you will have the LTV.

LTV is usually compared to CAC as a measure of the financial sustainability of an app. If an average user spends more on your app over their lifetime than it costs you to acquire that user (i.e., LTV is higher than CAC), that's usually a sign your app is doing well and can scale.

Again, like in the case of CAC, user loyalty will greatly affect the value of LTV, because as a multiplier, a longer lifetime will push your LTV value very high. In the preceding example, increasing the lifetime duration from three to four months will increase LTV by 33.3 percent, from $(2 \times 4 \times 3) = \$24$ to $(2 \times 4 \times 4) = \$32$.

■ **Payback Period (PBP)** – This is the time it takes for total ARPU to match CAC, meaning the money spent on acquiring a customer is recovered from revenue produced by that customer.

Figure 4-4 below depicts the relationship between key financial metrics.

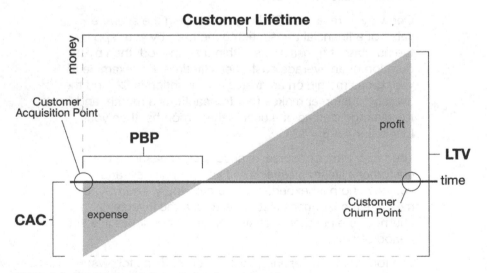

Figure 4-4. The relationship between key financial metrics

Performance Analytics

Performance analytics measure the technical performance of your app, such as how long it takes to load and how often it crashes.

The loading time of your app may seem relatively unimportant, but it will affect how much users enjoy using it and how many of them will abandon it in frustration.

Fast, efficient, and reliable performance is a key component of strong user engagement.

Types of Performance Metrics and KPIs

App performance metrics and KPIs include the following:

- **App Throughput** – the number of requests an app can handle over a set period of time

- **Application Latency** – the time it takes for an app to respond to a request

- **API Latency** – the response time of an API to a request

- **App Load per Period** – the time it takes for different types of requests to load in the app

- **App Crash Rate** – how often an app will crash for a set number of activations

- **App Load Time** – how long it will take an app to load after the icon is pressed

- **End-to-End Application Latency** – the time it takes between the moment a button is pressed in an app and the moment the results of that request reach the user

User Analytics

User analytics provide information about the users who are interacting with your app. It will tell you in which countries and cities your users live, how old they are, what their native language is, what devices they are using, how often they are using your app, and how much time they spend on it on average.

Types of user metrics include OS Version Distribution, Geographic Location Distribution, Age Group Distribution, Gender Distribution, Device Type Distribution, and User Native Language Distribution.

User-Engagement Analytics

User-engagement analytics supply information about how users are interacting with your app. It can tell you how many people have downloaded your app and how many have kept it (retention rate) or deleted it after a day, week, or month (churn rate). User-engagement analytics also create what are known as session recordings. As you interact with an app, everything you do in your "session" is "recorded" and aggregated with everyone else's session recordings to produce actionable information for the app publisher.

User-engagement analytics can also tell you which parts of your app's content users like the most and which they ignore, which icons or buttons they are clicking on the most, what they are sharing, and how often they are sharing. Detailed information about users helps you tailor your app to their tastes and improve their engagement with the app.

Event Tracking

Event tracking is an aspect of user engagement analytics that monitors specific actions users are taking inside an app rather than what they are looking at. Event tracking is used to count how many users, for example, are answering a question or clicking on a specific button, and it can be used to test how well specific app features are working. Event tracking is implemented over a set period and changes depending on your design, interaction, and marketing goals.

Touch Heatmaps, Cohort Analysis, and Session Playbacks

Tools like touch heatmaps, user journey recordings, session playbacks, and real-time reporting can help you understand how your users are interacting with your app, which buttons or icons they are pressing, and which parts or features of your app they are ignoring.

By supplying accurate real-time information about whether your users are interacting with the app the way you want them to, touch heatmaps will help you identify and correct UI problems that are frustrating users, optimize the user experience, and maximize your app's revenue potential.

Cohort analysis classifies users into various groups based on different factors to monitor user behavior and measure the effectiveness of features and offerings.

Session playbacks supply "recordings" of what a specific user did inside an app to create a picture of how users are navigating the app and identify pain points that need to be fixed.

Types of User Engagement Metrics and KPIs

User engagement metrics and KPIs include the following:

- **Daily Sessions per DAU** – the number of times a day a Daily Active User launches an app

- **Average Visit Time** – the average time a user spends in an app per visit

- **Screen Views per Visit** – the average number of screens viewed in a session

- **App Session Intervals** – the average time gap between a user's sessions

- **Download Count** – the total number of times an app has been downloaded

- **Number of Active Users** – the number of users who are considered to be active users

- **Goal Completion Rate** – the number of app users who have completed a specific goal you have set

- **Number of Sessions in First Week** – the number of sessions a new user launches in the first week after download

- **Peak Usage Times of Day** – the times of day when the number of users who are using the app is at its highest

- **Session Frequency** – the timespan between a user's first session and the next one

- **Depth of Visit** – the number of pages a user visits during an app session

- **Organic User Growth Rate** – how fast the number of app users is growing without active marketing

- **Number of New Users per Month** – the number of new users who are downloading the app in a given month

- **Permissions Granted** – the average number of permissions an app user is giving the app

- **User Lifecycle Duration** – the timespan between the moment a new user discovers and downloads an app to the moment they abandon it

- **Customer Support Response Times** – how long it takes for Customer Support to respond to inquiries

- **Net Promoter Score** – the likelihood that a given user will be willing to refer others to your app

- **Opt-In and Opt-Out Rates** – the percentage of app users who opt in for, or opt out of, a given offer related to an app

Financial Analytics

Financial analytics provide information about your app's commercial performance and will tell you how much money your users are spending on your app, who is spending the most money, and which channels are your best sources of revenue.

The types of financial metrics and KPIs are as follows:

- **Total Revenue per Period** (Hour, Day, Week, Month, Year)

- **Total Revenue per Period per Source** (Ads, In-App Purchases, etc.)

- **Revenue Distribution per Period** (Day of Week, Day of Month)

- **Shopping Cart Abandonment Rate**

- **Brand Awareness Rate**

- **Total Revenue from Acquired Users**

- **Average Revenue per Transaction**

- **Peak Transaction Times**

- **Number of Items in Shopping Cart**

- **Transactions per Second, Hour, or Day**

- **Days from Signup to First Payment**

Marketing Analytics

Marketing and advertising analytics show how effective the money you spend on marketing really is. Marketing analytics tell you how well your marketing dollars are being spent, how efficient your advertising strategies are, and which marketing channels are bringing in the most users. It's very easy in the app business to spend a lot of money and get next to nothing in return because of a bad strategy that targets the wrong users, has badly written ad copy, or involves expensive campaigns that fail to attract new users. Campaign analytics measure the effectiveness of a specific marketing campaign, or a specific ad type, over a set period of time.

Marketing metrics and KPIs include the following:

- Pay per Click (PPC)
- Cost per Click (CPC)
- Cost per Loyal User (CPLU)
- Cost per Thousand Impressions (CPM)
- Cost per Install (CPI)
- Customer Acquisition Cost (CAC)
- Average Revenue per User (ARPU)
- Cost per Install (CPI)
- Effective Cost per Install (eCPI)
- Fill Rate
- Click-through Rate (CTR)
- Viral Coefficient (K)
- Number of Shares
- Number of Product Likes
- Conversion Rate
- Number of Subscriptions/Registrations
- Number of User Likes
- Percentage of Mobile Influenced Customers
- Paid Conversion Rate
- Percentage of New Leads
- Organic User Growth Rate
- Push Notification Open Rate

- E-mail Open Rates

- E-mail Click-through Rate

- E-mail Click-to-Open Rate

- Campaign Conversion Rate

App Analytics Tools

The following tools will produce analytics for your app. Visit each website separately to find out more:

Flurry Analytics (*https://developer.yahoo.com/analytics/*)
Google Analytics (*https://analytics.google.com/*)
App Annie Analytics (*https://www.appannie.com/en/*)

AppsFlyer (*https://www.appsflyer.com/*)
Localytics (*https://www.localytics.com/*)

Countly (*https://count.ly/*)
MixPanel (*https://mixpanel.com/*)

Swrve (*https://www.swrve.com/*)
Kochava (*https://www.kochava.com/*)

Upsight (*https://www.upsight.com/*)
Tapstream (*https://www.tapstream.com/*)
Appsee (*https://www.appsee.com/*)

Appboy (*https://www.appboy.com/*)
Apsalar (*https://apsalar.com/*)
Taplytics (*https://taplytics.com/*)

Game Analytics (*www.gameanalytics.com/*)
AppAnalytics (*appanalytics.io/*)
AppDynamics (*https://www.appdynamics.com/*)

HeapAnalytics (*https://heapanalytics.com/*)
MoEngage (*https://www.moengage.com/*)

Understanding what your app analytics data is telling you is not easy for a newcomer, but over time your investment in information about your users will pay off. As a skilled reader of analytics, you will save yourself a great deal of money and effort by making wiser marketing decisions.

Big Question 5: How Can I Measure the Return on Investment of an App?

Once you understand metrics and KPIs, monitoring the financial performance of your app is not very hard. Improving the financial performance of your app is a mix between an art and a science, a combination of design and good planning.

If you own an app publishing business or have published more than one app, each of your individual apps will produce its own return on investment. Using the income projections for each app, you can also calculate the Internal Rate of Return (the interest rate at which the net present value of all the cash flow in an investment is equal to zero) and Net Present Value (the present value of a future cash flow) for your investments and your app business as a whole.

ROI calculations differ depending on the type of app you are developing and the goals associated with it. The goal of a mobile game will be easily measurable as revenue from ads and/or in-app purchases, while the goal for an enterprise app will also include measuring the financial impact of increased workplace efficiency and the benefits of replacing an outdated technology with a mobile solution. The benefits of a mobile enterprise app can include reducing the duration of business cycles, cutting communication costs, improving customer satisfaction and customer service, automating business processes, and reducing human resource requirements. All of the net benefits and impact of an enterprise mobile solution have to be taken into account when calculating the value and return of the investment.

Basic ROI

The ROI for an activity or product is a function of money invested and revenue produced. The metrics that go into the calculation of ROI for an app are shown in Figure 4-5.

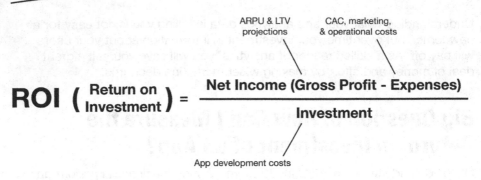

ARPU & LTV projections

CAC, marketing, & operational costs

$$\text{ROI} \left(\begin{array}{c} \text{Return on} \\ \text{Investment} \end{array} \right) = \frac{\text{Net Income (Gross Profit - Expenses)}}{\text{Investment}}$$

App development costs

Figure 4-5. Measuring app ROI

Net Present Value

Net Present Value is a function of projected future cash flows, both positive and negative, and a discount rate, usually the cost of capital or another rate acceptable for the investor. The metrics that go into the calculation of NPV for an app are shown in Figure 4-6.

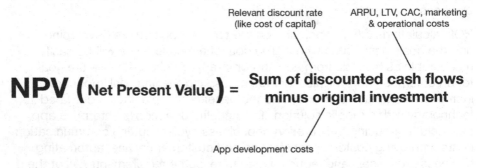

Relevant discount rate (like cost of capital)

ARPU, LTV, CAC, marketing & operational costs

$$\text{NPV} \left(\text{Net Present Value} \right) = \begin{array}{c} \textbf{Sum of discounted cash flows} \\ \textbf{minus original investment} \end{array}$$

App development costs

Figure 4-6. Measuring NPV

Internal Rate of Return

The IRR of an investment in an app can easily be calculated using the same metrics as an extension of NPV. The metrics that go into the calculation of IRR for an app are shown in Figure 4-7.

$$\textbf{IRR}\left(\text{Internal Rate of Return}\right) = \text{Discount rate that makes the net present value (NPV) of all cash flows from an investment equal to zero}$$

Figure 4-7. Calculating IRR

Measuring the ROI of an app accurately is a tricky affair and depends on the goals behind the release of the app. For example, measuring the profitability of a standalone game with in-app purchases will be done differently than measuring the financial impact an enterprise app has on a company.

In general, however, the return on investment for a mobile app is the result of the relationship between how much money is spent as an initial investment and the ongoing cost of acquiring users, compared to the revenue those acquired users generate for the developer over their lifetime as customers.

What Can I Do to Keep an App Profitable?

Once you are tracking user behavior and producing analytics, you are in a position to identify weak points in your app's design or in your marketing strategy that are undermining your profit potential. Many of the resources listed at the end of this book will help you compare the performance of your app to industry benchmarks so that you know where you stand. So, what are your goals for key metrics? See Figure 4-8.

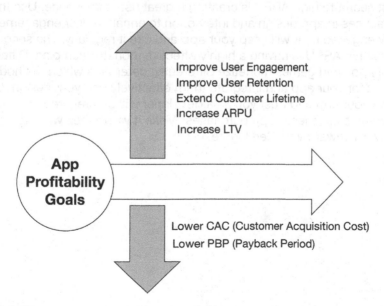

App Profitability Goals

Improve User Engagement
Improve User Retention
Extend Customer Lifetime
Increase ARPU
Increase LTV

Lower CAC (Customer Acquisition Cost)
Lower PBP (Payback Period)

Figure 4-8. What to do to make an app more profitable

As a rule, you always want to keep your customer lifetime value, LTV, higher than CAC, which essentially means you expect to make more money from your users than what you pay to acquire them. Experts recommend keeping LTV at least three times higher than CAC in order to keep your project in the black.

So, your monetization goals are to reduce CAC, reduce PBP, increase ARPU and ARPPU, and raise LTV.

Reducing CAC

The lower your CAC, the higher the ROI. How do you minimize CAC?

Acquiring users will inevitably cost money, but there are ways to maximize the acquisition capability of your app. As in the case of increasing ARPU, the secret is in the design of the app. Give your users every opportunity to share what they are doing in your app with their friends, and your users will act like free marketing machines for you. Sharing is the most powerful channel for user acquisition, and it's free!

Increasing ARPU

The higher the ARPU, the greater the ROI. So, how can ARPU be maximized?

The first secret to high ARPU is creating a great user experience. Use the best practices in app design and interaction to enhance user engagement. A highly engaged user will keep your app and use it regularly. The second secret to high ARPU is having a highly effective monetization plan. Different types of apps and games monetize differently; determine which methods work best for your app and integrate them effectively into your design. Users who love your app and trust you as a developer will be prepared to pay for good features or other in-app purchases. Make it worth their while to pay, and they will reward you. See Figure 4-9.

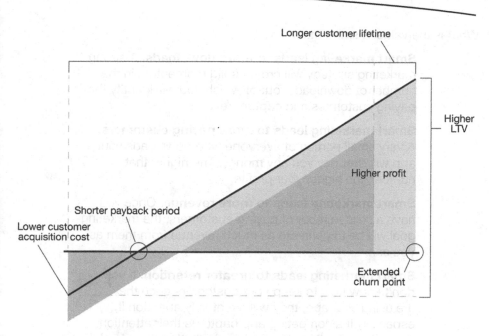

Figure 4-9. The positive impact of higher user engagement and retention

This brings us to the Golden Rule of App Publishing Success:

If you want your app to be enormously successful and profitable, master user engagement and app marketing.

In short, Great User Experience + Smart Marketing = Money in the Bank

What is the value of strong user engagement?

- **Strong user engagement means higher retention and lower churn.** This means your customers are keeping your app longer than average. A low churn rate means a higher customer lifetime, and this produces a higher LTV.

- **Strong user engagement means lower customer-acquisition costs.** With users sticking with your app longer, you will be spending less on retaining existing customers and more on acquiring new ones.

- **Strong user engagement means greater virality rates.** Strong user engagement increases the virality of an app, or the likelihood that a user will recommend it to others or share information about it on their networks. If each user convinces one other person to download your app, your customer acquisition cost will shrink by 50 percent.

What is the value of smart marketing?

- **Smart marketing leads to more downloads.** A strong marketing strategy will create solid momentum in the number of downloads, out of which you will identify the paying customers and capture revenue.

- **Smart marketing leads to more paying customers.** A very small portion of everyone who downloads your app will ever pay you any money. The higher that number, the higher your profits.

- **Smart marketing leads to more revenue.** Once you have a solid number of paying customers, the marketing goal will be to generate as much revenue from them as you can.

- **Smart marketing leads to greater retention.** If you don't know how to keep your customers once they are using your app, they will eventually abandon it, especially if a competing app captures their attention. Keeping your existing users is a marketing domain of its own, especially given that keeping an existing customer is much cheaper than replacing a lost customer with a new one.

The Most Important Question for an App Business

When preparing to publish an app and developing your marketing strategy, the most important question you have to answer is the following:

How many paying customers do I need in order to make my app business sustainable?

To answer this question, you need to know the following:

- Your operational expenses. How much money will you spend on your app business every month, including marketing costs and CAC? This will vary greatly depending on the type and size of app you have, and it will also vary over time as your app draws more and more users.

- Your projected ARPU and ARPPU.

- The projected percentage of your users who will be paying customers.

Let's make a very basic calculation based on the following assumptions:

- You plan to spend $10,000 per month on your app business, including salaries, marketing, and other operational expenses.

- 5 percent (1 out of 20) of your users will be paying customers, and they will generate an average of $2 ARPPU (average revenue per paying user) each and every month.

This means you will need 5,000 paying users (10,000 divided by 2) to generate the $10,000 per month needed to sustain your business. If 1 out of 20 users are paying users, you will need to have at least 100,000 (5,000 multiplied by 20) users, paying and non-paying, in total to generate the same revenue. In this situation, your ARPU would be $0.10 (10,000 divided by 100,000). If the market benchmark for CAC is $3, you would need to invest $300,000 to grow your users to 100,000.

Now, if you were to raise user engagement and retention, say through improved marketing and a redesigned UI, and the portion of paying customers grew from 5 percent to 10 percent, and the ARPPU grew from $2 to $4, how would that change your app's financial performance?

First, you would now need only 2,500 paying users (10,000 divided by 4) to generate the $10,000 per month you need to sustain your business. Second, now that 1 in 10 of your users are paying users, you would need far fewer paying and non-paying users, just 25,000 (2,500 multiplied by 10), to generate the same revenue, and your ARPU would be $0.4 (10,000 divided by 25,000). With CAC at $3 per user, you would need to spend much less, $75,000 (compared to $300,000) to grow your user base to a sustainable level for your business.

These figures clearly show the impact that improved user engagement and retention can have on an app's financial performance. Raising the number of paying users from 5 percent to 10 percent, and raising ARPPU from $2 to $4, may not sound like much at first glance, but it shrunk the minimum sustainable level for your app business from 100,000 users to 25,000 and shrunk your marketing budget from $300,000 to $75,000, a 75 percent reduction.

Summary

In this chapter and the preceding three chapters, we looked at the app publishing industry worldwide, including its evolution, scale, and basic economic structure.

In the coming chapters, we will look at how app ideas are generated and turned into full-fledged apps.

Chapter 5

Imagine Your App

"It is better to have enough ideas
for some of them to be wrong,
than to always be right
by having no ideas at all."

Edward de Bono

© Hagop Panosian 2017
H. Panosian, *Learn iOS Application Distribution*, DOI 10.1007/978-1-4842-2683-4_5

Welcome to the business of app development.

By now you should know much more about the app development industry than you did before you picked up this book. Having absorbed the information in the preceding chapters, you are now in a position to launch your app publishing career by making informed decisions about everything related to your app, from its name, size, color-coding, and content to the marketing strategy you will use to promote it.

The app world is full of stories about accidental millionaires who built an app just for the fun of it only to see it turn into an overnight sensation that generated a fortune. These stories are largely responsible for the fascination people have with the app industry and the "Gold Rush" aura that surrounds it, especially among complete outsiders. A quick online search can produce hundreds of links to books, courses, videos, blogs, and other resources that exploit this "Gold Rush" aura and claim to show you how to build and publish an app in minutes that can make you rich overnight with little effort on your part.

However, as the market matures, taking the app stores by storm and making a quick fortune has become an increasingly thin possibility. Today, those who have a real chance of succeeding in the app stores are those with the most thorough understanding of what makes an app successful: great design, high user engagement and retention, and solid and skillful marketing. Furthermore, as users become increasingly picky about what they expect apps to do for them and abandon apps at the slightest glitch, grabbing the attention of users and keeping it long enough for them to commit to the app and spend money on it is becoming a challenge that demands a professional approach.

Before you take your first step as an app publisher, what you need to do is get into the professional app publisher frame of mind. This involves putting aside myths and misconceptions that create unreasonable expectations and making a conscious choice to rely on solid knowledge and skills. In this frame of mind, you will never be in the dark about where your app is headed, where your money is going, and what returns you should expect on your time and effort. You will not waste your time on irrational expectations or your money on misguided marketing campaigns, and you will never waste your time by neglecting important steps only to realize you should have done certain things much earlier.

Let's look at what it means to be in the professional app publisher's frame of mind.

The Right Frame of Mind

The professional app publisher's frame of mind combines the mindsets of the inventor and the investor. As an inventor, an app publisher directs his creativity toward generating solid app ideas with good prospects for success, as well as toward solving design, development, and marketing problems in unexpected ways that give him an edge over the competition. He keeps himself open to new ideas and stays flexible in order to adjust to new concepts and approaches to app design, development, and marketing. This allows him to stay on top of the market as it matures and evolves.

As an investor, an app publisher realizes that he is putting a great deal of time, effort, and money into turning an idea into a profitable business. He realizes that a great idea is worth little without effective implementation and is a waste of time without strong returns, and as a result he focuses on making good use of resources like time and money, on managing a development team well, and on marketing his product well.

By combining the creativity and intuitiveness of the inventor mindset with the methods, knowledge, and managerial skills of the investor mindset, you will start off on the right foot, apply your assets and resources wisely, and maximize your chances of creating a big hit in the app stores. You will also resist getting distracted by the get-rich-quick mentality and the four big myths of app development that are propagated to support that mentality, which we will look at next.

The Four Big Myths of App Development

There are four big myths about app development that are quite popular among people who see app publishing as a means of getting rich quickly without investing time, money, or effort. This perception is also supported by actual cases of amateurs who did become unexpectedly successful beyond their wildest expectations, but if you take a closer look at how success happened for them, you will see that none became successful by sitting back and doing nothing. No one has ever just sat back to count the money as it rolled in. On the contrary, these successful app publishers reacted quickly to the strong user response to their app or game, changed their outlook and lifestyle very quickly, hired the right people to complement the skills they lacked, and built real businesses around their successful ideas. You must be prepared to do the same should it happen to you.

There are four popular myths attached to app development that create incorrect expectations and can lead you in the wrong direction.

Myth 1: You Need a Big Idea

We already looked at this earlier. This is the biggest misconception among app enthusiasts who want to get into app publishing. Why is this a misconception?

Well, for one thing, almost anything you can think of has probably already been done, many times over. With millions of apps and games available in the app stores, the likelihood of coming up with something completely new or something no one's seen before is close to nil. There are exceptions, of course, but the vast majority of games, for example, are built around already existing game concepts or physics simulation principles.

The vast majority of games are not original in their concept, but this does not mean that there is no originality or inventiveness in app design. It just means that this originality and inventiveness usually lies elsewhere. For example, successful apps can easily stand out and attract users by offering a new take on an already popular app or game. Candy Crush and Angry Birds are perfect examples of hugely successful games that are not original in their concepts but are highly addictive and successful because of the quality of the experiences they provide and the clever ways they retain users. Other apps build their success by offering new features or combining features from several apps to create a new value proposition.

Myth 2: Making Apps Is Very Easy

Making an app may be easy or hard depending on its function, size, and complexity, as well as the skills of the person producing it. An experienced programmer who buys an existing simple game that is fully functional without a backend and is small enough to be downloaded onto a smartphone, changes the game's look and feel, and releases it under a different name in a matter of days will tell you that yes, making apps is easy. On the other hand, a professional app development company that is working on a personal banking app that allows users to check their bank account balances, move money from one bank account to another, and perform other personal banking functions will tell you that developing an app of this kind is far from easy, as it requires an advanced backend of the right size and complexity, very strict security systems, a customer relationship management (CRM) system to keep the bank's customers happy, a user experience design that is consistent with the bank's image and goals, and a team of programmers on hand to manage the app and respond very quickly to problems that can occur.

The purpose of the "easy" myth is that it helps amateurs overcome their fears and the feeling of intimidation inspired by the seemingly daunting aspects of app development, especially programming. The important point here is this: an app that is worth your time will take some effort. What's the point of making an "easy" app that goes nowhere? Why should app development be any easier than any other profession? Would it be a good thing if app development were so easy that absolutely anyone could do it, and everyone did?

Myth 3: You Can Do It for Free

This is another myth told to amateurs that exploits the "Gold Rush" image of the app industry, but this time it takes advantage of the fear of financial risk. It is indeed possible to use a basic app template posted on a website, populate it with your own content, and publish it. It is possible to do this when creating an e-book app, your personal wedding app, or other simple app projects that rely on ready-built templates. However, because these templates are generic and are not customized for your app's particular needs, the apps you can publish with these templates will have extreme limitations and will lack many of the features standard in full-fledged apps, like a backend for updates and content management. They will also advertise the creator of the free app template, which means you lose out on much of the profit opportunities, and the producer of the template will promote themselves and their paid services through your app.

The truth behind this myth is this: in the long run, what you will get for free will be worth exactly what you paid for it.

Myth 4: You Can Make Apps Without Writing Code

This is the last of the four myths that offer to give you a taste of the app publishing universe without any real commitment or effort on your part. Again, the myth involves ready-made app templates you can fill in with your content and publish on the app stores without writing a single line of code.

Yes, it is possible to publish an app, probably on your own, by getting a hold of a template online and filling it with your own content, but this is relevant in only a small number of cases where the app has limited use and its content cannot be changed after publishing.

If you want to build a full-fledged app, you will need programmers to build a backend to allow you to update and manage your content. You will need code that integrates social media APIs so your users can share content, code for analytics inserted into your app to track user behavior, and code to manage the advertising space in your app. These are just some of the basic features of apps that cannot be made available to users without programmers' writing custom code.

Furthermore, if your app is not single-use, like a wedding app, for example, you will inevitably want to update your app and release a new version of it, and inevitably you will need programming skills to do it.

Get Serious

These four popular myths are propagated to create the impression that success in the app stores is possible without risk. The truth, however, is that anything worth investing in entails some degree of risk, and the only real way of mitigating risk is by being committed to a professional approach that relies on thorough knowledge and best practices in order to produce something users will love.

If you want to approach the app business like a professional, do not rely on the "free, quick, and easy" approach, because it will lead nowhere. Instead, rely on great design, skillful marketing, and an excellent value proposition to propel the adoption of your app forward.

The Most Important Principle of App Publishing

If there is one principle that must always be on your mind as you design, develop, and distribute apps, it's this:

Marketing is everything, and everything is about marketing.

Let's look at the first part of this sentence: marketing is everything. This suggests, first of all, that in the pre-development phase, relying on your idea alone to sell itself to investors will never lead anywhere. No idea is good enough to sell itself, and investors will care little about your idea if they do not feel you can carry it through to completion. Similarly, no matter how well it is designed, no published app will succeed on its own without help from you.

Whatever app you may be distributing, you will have to work very hard and be very smart, and have a solid understanding of the market and your users, to steer it to success. Marketing is everything when it comes to an app's success, and without solid marketing it will linger forever at the bottom ranks of the app store. So, be ready to commit to the marketing effort and learn what you need to learn to do that job well.

Marketing begins long before the launch of your app. This is because the first days and weeks that follow the launch of your app are crucial to its success, and there can be no traction without a community of fans waiting for the release, without magazines waiting to publish reports about it, and so on. This means you have to start building your community of fans long before you actually release the app itself. If you begin marketing the moment you release the app, it's probably already too late.

The second part of the sentence, everything is about marketing, means everything that is happening in the app development process, and every part of your app, is designed for marketing purposes. Besides the obvious, like the design of the app icon, the App Store page, and your own marketing campaign, the speed at which your app loads, the level structure, the content, the color coding, the sharing capabilities for social media, the levels structure (if it's a game), the services it uses, and the functions it performs—every single aspect of your app—all revolve around making sure your users love it, use it obsessively, and help you market it.

Internal and External Marketing Tools

Let's face it—app users are highly fickle consumers. They will abandon your app at the slightest glitch or pesky ad or delayed response. This brings us to another important point: the best marketers for your app are your users. No one will promote your app like happy users sharing their views. This means you have to be ready at launch time to keep your users happy after they have downloaded your app. This includes forums where they can ask questions and get user support. For example, if your app analytics identifies a point in the app where many of your users are abandoning the app or failing to complete their customer journey, you can start a discussion to find out what's wrong. Is it a technical glitch, a design problem, or something else? This feedback loop will be invaluable in helping you fix problems fast so as to keep your users happy.

This also means giving your users every chance you can for them to share their experience of your app with their social circle. Remember, users are like advertisers who promote your app for free. Incorporate functions like posting on Facebook, Google Plus, and so forth into key points in your app, like when a game user breaks his or her own record, for example, or passes a difficult level. This is a powerful marketing system that you should not make the mistake of ignoring. Asking users to rate your app is another strategy.

In general, keep in mind that there are two main marketing mechanisms at work in any app. There is the internal promotion mechanism, like sharing functions, posting, content sharing, and app ratings and reviews. Then, there is the external marketing mechanism, which involves your own marketing activities, like promotions, Google AdWords, magazine ads, online advertising, and so on.

So, what does this all mean? It means that you have to incorporate the items covered in the next few sections when you start designing and building your app, and not just think about translating your idea into an app.

Feedback Support, Internal Promotion, and Revenue-Generation Strategy

If you start thinking about all these things only after you've completed your app design, you've wasted your time, because you're only going to have to go back and incorporate them. If you understand and incorporate these principles into your mindset and design approach from the beginning, you're already on your way to building a well-designed app that has the ingredients for success.

Determine Your Marketing and Revenue Strategy Early On

You have to have a good idea about your marketing strategy from the beginning, as soon as you conceive your app. In fact, the very nature of your app (such as what kind of game it is or what kind of content it produces) will to a great extent determine the marketing, advertising, and monetization strategies you use because these strategies have already been optimized for each type of app.

A game app, for example, will rely a great deal on in-app purchases for revenue, but will also combine interstitial ads, banner ads, and video ads and sell an ad-free version of itself for a fee.

A magazine app, on the other hand, will publish some of its content for free, and will focus on convincing users to subscribe to the full version for a monthly fee, with limited or no in-app ads.

Why is all this important? Because these factors will affect the layout of your app, level hierarchies if it's a game, the type and price of in-app purchases, the content structure of a content-based app, and nearly every design or technical detail.

How to Generate App Ideas

Everything starts with an amazing idea. — or does it? If you are just getting started in app development, you are likely to believe that to be successful in this business you need to start off with an incredible idea no one else has thought of before that will change the world and make you very rich overnight. Or, at least, this is more or less what you're hoping will happen, because it has already happened to others more than once.

However, so that no time is wasted chasing fantasies, it would be wiser to put aside this Internet "Gold Rush" fantasy and get accustomed to the notion that the difference between success and failure has little to do with how great your idea sounds when you're talking about it over lunch with your friends, and everything to do with determination and smart decisions.

It's very much realistic to enter the app publishing industry without that amazing idea and expect to do very well. Success is less about changing your life overnight and more about understanding the app industry and market well, understanding users and their behavior very well, finding the right niche for a product, creating a well-designed value proposition and an app to deliver it, and tracking the performance of the app while tweaking your marketing strategy to build up momentum until it sustains itself financially and brings in profit.

In other words, lots of hard work and smart decisions.

This is what will make the difference between success and failure: commitment, "sweat equity," and smarts. As you begin your app publishing journey, you need to start thinking less and less like a magician and more and more like an investor. You will be investing a great deal of time, effort, and money into your projects, so it pays to approach things like a professional.

In that sense, the app business is like any other business. The app industry does indeed offer incredible potential to create a product and make it available to the whole world with little investment compared to other, more traditional industries, but there is no guarantee of success, and you are likely to be wasting your time if you believe otherwise. If this is not what you had in mind, you might as well keep your day job, because an app built only around what you think is a great idea will not survive the brutal competition for people's attention. This brings us to an important point:

Don't become obsessed with your app idea.

Resist becoming enamored with your app idea. It's a waste of time, and it's dangerous. It's dangerous because when you're deeply attached to your idea, you will refuse to abandon it even when it fails. You will keep pouring resources into it because you "just know it'll work," and will drive yourself into the ground.

The app world does indeed have its charm, and just the idea of becoming an app publisher may be giving you stars in your eyes, but an app is just an app, and an idea is just an idea. It's just a product for a market, and it will need a product-market fit to work, so treat it as such and focus on making that work. If it's not working for any reason, or does not have a unique feature or value proposition that sets it apart, it has little chance of grabbing user attention or surviving the competition.

So, Where Do I Start?

Is it even possible to "generate" app ideas? Don't they just pop into your head on their own at random? Well, sometimes, but most of the time, they don't. There are highly rational, objective, and reliable ways to generate ideas for apps, and rational, objective, and reliable ways for you to test how sustainable they are and how likely they are to succeed rather than relying on "I just know it'll work."

There are two main starting points for the process of generating app ideas through the rational method: 1) start with the user and 2) start with the app store. First, though, let's take a look at the intuitive method.

Method 1: Brainstorm

Brainstorming is an activity during which you create a chance for the "bolt of lightning" effect to help you. The objective is to bring creative minds together so as to benefit from their imagination and experience in the hope of generating unexpected ideas through spontaneous insights. You can brainstorm on your own, of course, but doing so with a group is more likely to generate interesting ideas through the opportunity for interaction.

If you decided to create a brainstorming group, don't make the group too big or too small. Brainstorming in small groups misses the point and lacks variety, and groups that are too big tend to move off subject and become chaotic. Groups of five to seven people are usually recommended as optimal.

A group brainstorming session can easily sway off track without guidance, so make the conversation productive by maintaining focus on your objective. The key is to find a balance between facilitation and control. Too much guidance kills creativity, and too little leads to chaos, and both will make your brainstorming session a waste of time. Keep your group on track but create room for the spontaneous and unexpected in order to make the most of your session.

Brainstorming can also be done individually, but it lacks the variety of insights created by the group. In a group, the flow of creative energy is primarily through conversation, but when you're alone it is not there. How can you create a positive flow of creative energy when no one else is around? The trick is in finding ways to stimulate the imagination by surrounding yourself with objects, text, images, audio, and other material relevant to the problem you are trying to solve. Naturally, it's good to have pens and lots of paper around for sketching or writing down anything that pops into your head.

Tip The value of sketching or writing down your ideas cannot be overstated. Do it liberally. Think of the flow of creativity as water flowing through a pipe and out from a tap. Trying to hold onto an idea in your head without putting it down on paper is like closing the tap, and the creative flow slows down or stops completely. By putting what pops into your head on paper, you free your mind from the burden of accurate recall and keep the creative flow going.

Note With brainstorming, you can generate a large number of ideas, but not all will be worth pursuing. Follow the brainstorming sessions with a thorough assessment of each idea's potential, and then narrow the list of truly good ideas until you decide which one is a worthwhile investment.

Brainstorming is a means of generating app ideas through intuition and informal interaction. The other means of generating app ideas is the rational path that relies on analysis.

The rational path has two main starting points. You can start with your intended users, analyzing their professions, habits, preferences, and daily rituals, or you can start with the app stores, analyzing trends, finding niches you can dominate, and exploiting the weaknesses or strengths of other apps. Let's start by taking a look at the user-centered method of generating app ideas.

Method 2: Start with the User

One good way to start generating ideas is by targeting a specific group of users. The more clearly that user group is defined, the easier it will be to deliver a positive user experience to them through your app.

Building an app for everyone is like trying to make everyone happy. It can only fail. Targeting a specific group of users who have a very specific need that your app fulfills efficiently is much more likely to meet with a positive user response.

Personas and Scenarios

A great way to start the process of generating ideas is to pick a user group for which you want to build an app. Your target user group can be broad (like creating a simple game, which targets as many people as possible) or narrow (like an education app for children, a magazine app for women, a productivity app for doctors, and so on).

Once you have picked the user group you want to target, create as detailed a profile as you can of members of that user group. Create a portrait of a typical member of the group. Gather as much information about them as possible. Ask relevant questions, such as the following:

- Who are they?

- Where do they live?

- What age group do they belong to?

- What do they do for a living?

- What are their shared habits?

- What is their education level?

- What is their gender profile (what percentage is male, what percentage is female)?

- What are their core values?

- What do they like to do in their free time?

- What do they like to do for entertainment?

- How do they get information (Internet, television, app, etc.)?

- What are their eating habits?

- Where do they go on vacation?

- What are their favorite pastimes?

- What is their predominant relationship status (single, married, etc.)?

- What is their income profile?

- What are their general character traits?

Then, ask questions about how your app will deliver value to these users, such as the following:

- How will these personas use your app?

- What is their goal or purpose for using your app?

- What are the problems they are trying to solve with your app?

- How will your app solve these problems?

- What would cause these users to reject your app?

Next, ask yourself questions about how you would market your app to these users, such as the following:

- How will these users find you? Which channels are they likely to use?

- How will you pitch your app to them? What benefits will you advertise?

- How will you defeat the competition to reach your users?

- How much will your users be willing to pay for your app?

Combine all the answers to these questions into a typical profile, or user persona, of your intended user. The more detailed your knowledge of your target user group is, the better your value proposition will match the needs of that group or fix a problem for them. Users want apps to do exactly what they need them to do, and that's usually something very specific (watch videos, play music, get a taxi, order food, etc). Matching the design of your app to a very detailed definition of what your users need the most is a guarantee that your app will be quickly accepted.

The pricing strategy of your app is something that will also benefit greatly from a detailed understanding of your users, especially their income levels and likelihood of spending money inside an app, which is a metric that varies greatly among user groups and platforms.

Equally important, the better you know your user group, the more effective and personalized your advertising or push messaging or marketing campaigns will be. For example, if you want to design an automated advertising campaign (called programmatic advertising) using push notifications sent to your app users, you want to know what time of day and what day of the week are the best to send those notifications out so that your users will be likely to read them and respond. Not knowing the optimal times to reach your users will lead to lots of money and time wasted on failed advertising campaigns.

Creating a User Persona

Creating a detailed user persona is key to your app's success. It involves analyzing human behavior and talking to your future users.

Analyze Human Behavior

After choosing a user group you want to target, start observing the behavior of members of that user group as they go about their day. Focus on identifying patterns and pain points. Ask yourself what problem you could solve or process you could facilitate through an app that would save them time or money or effort, or allow them to do something with your app they could not do before that improves their lives in some fundamental way.

Talk to Your Future Users

Go from passive observation to active interaction. Interview members of your intended user group so that they can tell you what they need in an app. Maybe they already use a particular app for a specific purpose, but wish it had additional features that are important for them. Talking to your users is invaluable for generating ideas, as they will save you a great deal of time by telling you what to build for them instead of your having to spend so much time and effort trying to find out on your own.

A user persona is a description of the intended user of your app, and that description needs to be shared with everyone on the design, development, and marketing teams so that everyone works in the same direction and for the same target user (Figure 5-1).

Figure 5-1. Typical user persona characteristics

In many cases, you will have several user personas because your product might work for several categories of users. If that is the case, then the whole team must again have all of these personas in mind when developing the app. Negative personas are also useful, namely who will *not* be interested in your product, so that the team knows which design and marketing methods to leave out of the development strategy.

Your app development team will apply this knowledge about the user persona everywhere, from design to marketing. You will identify keywords that appeal to the persona as well as design and layout styles, color codes, marketing approaches, and a unique selling proposition intended specifically for that persona.

Creating a User Scenario

While a user persona is a description of who your user is, a user scenario is a description of how your typical user behaves while pursuing a specific goal, and how they carry out a specific task as a sequence of steps. Again, observing your users and talking to them is the right method for developing user scenarios.

Building user personas and scenarios with these methods should be giving you not just abstract ideas for apps, but also a detailed understanding of how your app can offer them value as well.

Apply the user personas. They will help you design the app and its content for your users much better and will help you tailor your advertising and marketing strategies to their demographic characteristics and habits.

Optimization Through Localization

Localizing an app begins with internationalization, which allows the app to display different screens and different languages depending on the user's location and spoken language. A localized app has content in several languages and displays the appropriate language for the user. This is a very important aspect of app development that raises adoption rates significantly. An English-language app, no matter how well designed, will not do as well in a country like China, for example, as a Chinese version would do. There are more than 150 countries on the Apple Store, and English is spoken widely in only about half of them.

When it comes targeting a specific user group, the importance of localization cannot be overstated. Localization is generally about publishing your app in different languages, but cultural factors also play a role, or should play a role, in adapting an app to different markets. Even if your target user base is very broad, effectively targeting a group in one country or culture will differ radically from targeting the same group in another country or culture. Teenagers in the United States think and behave differently than teenagers in India or Japan do, and a small business startup in an African country will have different concerns than a startup in Germany.

Another aspect of localization is marketing. If you want to target your app users with push notifications when they are off work, in Spain you can do it in the early evening. During summer months in the United Arab Emirates, sending push notifications late at night, when most people are out enjoying themselves and escaping the daytime heat, is a good strategy.

Finally, localization is also useful as an App Store Optimization strategy. Translating your app name, description, keywords, images, and videos, publishing it as a separate app, and creating a custom App Store page in the target user's own language in a local App Store can help your app climb the charts fast, especially if the local store has fewer competing apps. Having a top-ranking localized app in another country, no matter how small, will give your original app a powerful marketing boost. How many times have you seen an app advertised as "Number one in Croatia!" or "Top App in its Category in Vietnam!"? This is achieved through localization. The following parts of an app can be localized for different countries and languages to help propel your app upward: the app's name, content, date and time formats, keyboard, units, App Store description, keywords, images, text on screenshots, and videos.

Localization costs money, and the scale and complexity of localization should be taken into consideration when you are generating app ideas and developing your marketing strategy. Localization is part of the game no matter what you are designing or for whom. It applies to all types of apps and to all user groups, so give it the attention it deserves.

Now, let's take a look at two other interesting user-centered methods for generating ideas: improving a profession and improving a process.

Improve a Profession

This is another good starting point for generating app ideas. Pick a profession, possibly your own, that you want to improve through an app. Analyze in detail the tasks and procedures that form the practice of that profession. Identify processes that suffer from bottlenecks, delays, or complications that an app could fix or eliminate. Design an app to deliver this solution as efficiently and effectively as possible. Think of your app not just as a tool to make a profession more efficient, but also as a potential game changer that could totally overhaul the profession you are targeting.

Improve a Process

Outside our professional lives, our personal and working lives also consist of different processes and rituals of varying lengths and complexity. Each of them is open to analysis and rethinking: ordering a pizza, paying a bill, buying a plane ticket, getting a plumber, monitoring a patient's vital signs, finding the closest drugstore, checking your bank account balance, changing money from one currency to another, sending someone a photo from your camera, learning a new language, and so on.

Method 3: Start with the App Store

The third main source of app ideas is the app stores themselves, where all the competition and some of the marketing are happening. Apple has one main App Store, as well as local app stores for more than 150 countries. Apps are constantly moving up and down the popularity charts, fighting for position and the attention of users.

Each app has its own individual path in the various app store charts, and there are short-term and long-term overall app store trends. Watching these trends and closely following the performance of apps can produce countless app ideas if you know how and where to look.

A good starting point is the iTunes app charts, where at any point in time you can see the top free apps, the top paid apps, and the top-grossing apps. You can view the most popular apps in different categories, like Games, Social Networking, Lifestyle, Utilities, Education, Photo & Video, Productivity, and Travel. You can also narrow down your search further, like App Store ➤ Games ➤ Puzzle.

However, it's crucial to remember that the app charts display results based on the country in which you are located, so it's impossible to use it to follow global trends. For global trends, which are probably more important, one great source of information is App Trace (www.apptrace.com), which gathers and displays statistics about how iOS and Android apps are doing around the world. You can see the top 300 apps overall on iTunes or Google Play, or the top 300 apps in a particular category, and even search by specific dates, which can help you identify trends over time or follow an specific app's path.

For example, if you are targeting the Education category, it's interesting to discover that the median price for education apps on iTunes on September 21, 2016, was $2.99, and that just 16.2 percent of apps in that category on that date were free apps, compared to 64.7 percent overall. As you can see, with just a simple scan App Trace can help you make key decisions about your app, in this case its pricing strategy.

App Annie (www.appannie.com) publishes detailed information about nearly every aspect of app store monitoring, including app rankings and app store trends, which allow you to monitor which apps are doing best, follow a single app's rankings and downloads over time, or find out how individual keywords are trending using the Keyword Explorer tool. It even has a video that introduces subscribers to the basics of monitoring app store trends.

Identify a Profitable Keyword Niche

Finding a profitable keyword niche is a good approach to generating app ideas that have a higher chance of success, because of the high demand–low supply relationship. It involves locating an area of the app business that gets a lot of attention from users but where the available offerings are less than the demand. To do this, you will need to use keyword tools to find what are known as long-tail keywords (Figure 5-2).

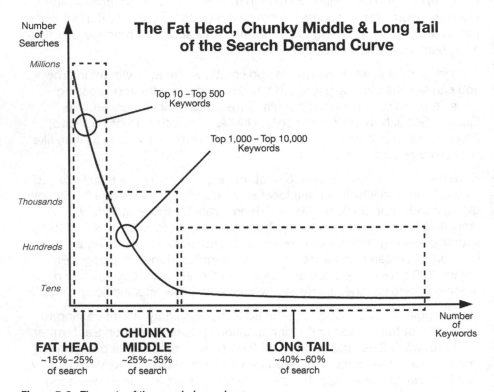

Figure 5-2. *The parts of the search demand curve*

A long-tail keyword is a longer and more focused keyword that web and app users use to search for the products they want. For example, the keyword "car" is a short keyword, while "used car parts stores for Ford Mustangs in Alabama" is a long-tail keyword.

The term "long tail" originates from the shape of the distribution graph of search terms. Short, general keywords form the "head" of the dragon. However, despite the fact that there are a very large number of searches using short keywords, the overwhelming majority of searches are made using long-tail keywords; in other words, the long tail is very long indeed. According to Wordstream (www.wordstream.com), head keyword searches account for just 10 to 15 percent of the total number of searches over any period of time. Medium-length keywords account for another 15 to 20 percent, and long-tail keywords account for at least 70 percent of searches over any period of time. That's a very large number.

Long-tail keywords are important because they give you an opportunity to rank very high in a specific area, rather than struggling to attract attention in a very broad niche with far too much competition. By focusing on long-tail keywords, you narrow the niche for which you are targeting users, which may seem counterintuitive, but you also create a big opportunity for yourself to dominate that narrow niche.

Furthermore, focusing on a narrow niche has the added advantage of targeting those users who are looking for precisely what you want to offer, which means they are far more likely to be paying customers if you make them the right offer. So, the difference between short, broad keywords and long-tail keywords is the difference between quantity and quality: is it better to reach a thousand customers who are unsure about what they want or to reach ten who want precisely what you have to offer?

Another advantage of long-tail keywords is that online advertising costs are lower because competition in a narrow category is much lower as well.

Not all long-tail keywords, however, are profitable niches. There are long-tail keywords for which a market of users does not exist. The secret to success with a keyword niche is to find a very specific area where there is significant demand but limited supply. In other words, there are many searches with a certain long-tail keyword (proof of demand), but very few good products that cater to it (proof of market). When you find such a keyword, the next step is to build an app around it.

How Can I Find a Good Long-Tail Keyword?

Start with a short term in the subject you are considering, such as "recipe" or "car." Use a keyword tool to generate the top long-tail keywords in that category. There are a number of online keyword generators, including free, freemium, and subscription-based ones, that can do it for you. Keyword tools will generate keyword niches, or groups of related keywords that can be used to build apps and promote them. Good keyword tools will also publish information about the level of competition and the total number of searches related to a long-tail keyword, which you can use to identify the low competition–high demand niche you can target. Here's a short list of some options:

- Google Keyword Planner
- Google Trends
- Wordstream's Free Keyword Tool
- Yoast Suggests

The same keywords that you used to build your app will also be used for ASO, or App Store Optimization, to maximize the chances of an app's standing out and being found by its targeted users.

Compare, Improve, or Flip Apps

This approach to developing app concepts focuses on existing apps and uses their features, strengths, weaknesses, and position in the app store rankings as a starting point to developing improved versions that benefit from existing and proven demand.

When looking at different apps, you may come across one that's doing relatively well but lacks an important feature that would give it a bigger edge over the competition. This can be the basis for a new app concept, as the success of the original app suggests there is strong demand for it, and an improved or enhanced app could draw many of the original app's users.

In fact, one great strategy for developing an app concept is to group all the successful apps in a specific category, analyze their key features and weaknesses, and develop a new app that combines all the great features and eliminates the weaknesses. This a surefire way to end up with an app concept that has a strong prospect of success.

To apply this approach, you need to become an obsessive app downloader and tester. Pick an app category, find the best performers in that category, and download as many of them as you need in order to make thorough comparisons between them. Use a highly analytical process to identify what makes each of these apps successful. If there are more than a few apps in a category that are successful, this suggests that each of them has a specific feature that users love and don't want to do without. This screams opportunity. Identify these features, combine them into a new app with great UI/UX design, and you have a winner.

An alternative approach to benefiting from the strengths of popular apps is to benefit from the weaknesses of apps that are doing badly. The bottom ranks of the app store are full of apps that are built around good concepts but are unsuccessful because of specific weaknesses in design or gameplay, or a missing feature or two, or a bad marketing strategy. This is a good playground on which to find a potential winner by taking an unsuccessful app that has a good concept or set of features and building a new app that eliminates the weaknesses that are holding the original back.

App flipping, or app reskinning, is quite fun and is a quick way to enter the app business and make your first buck. It is based on the same principle as house flipping and doesn't require an original or any other kind of overall idea at all.

To flip an app, you first buy the source code of the original app, normally a game, modify the look and feel (colors, content, images, characters, levels), maximize the advertising space, and release it under a different name. One popular app-flipping tactic is to pick a game that is already relatively popular, find the source code for a similar game, change the look and feel, and release the app under a name similar to that of the more successful game. This allows you to not just publish an app at a relatively low cost, but also to capitalize on the success of the other app.

Other Sources of Inspiration

Finally, a third domain from which you can extract app ideas is that of external sources, which are sources other than your potential users and the app stores. This domain is limitless, as anything can be an inspiration for an app idea.

As an app publisher, focus on becoming a keen observer of everything happening around you, from global events to your immediate environment, and look at things from an app publisher's perspective. You will find that inspiration is not far away. Social media—for example, Facebook, Twitter, Pinterest, and so forth—are a great source of information about upwardly mobile trends because the reaction to events on social media is very quick.

The secret to doing this successfully is responding quickly so as to exploit any global or local trend in the form of an app, and also picking a trend that is not likely to fizzle quickly and looks set to be relevant long enough for you to exploit it. This means having a team around you that is ready to get to work quickly, to grab market share from the competition and maximize the gains from a trend before it fizzles. Here are a few examples of events and trends that can serve as the source for app ideas:

- The growing popularity of a tourist destination
- Sudden media frenzy around an app (like the Flappy Bird craze)
- New government regulations that change the way an industry functions
- New technologies that are set to give birth to a whole new generation of apps (like robotics, drones, and self-driving cars)
- Political events like elections and sports events like the Super Bowl or the Olympics

How to Assess and Validate App Ideas

The app concepts you have developed based on the strategies we have looked at are still just concepts, and they have to go through a thorough evaluation to determine how strong their prospects for success really are before you invest in them. At the very least, especially if you are new to the app business and are not ready to develop several apps in parallel, it's wise to narrow your list down to the best concepts, prioritize them in the order in which they will be developed, and start with the best.

To find the winner on your list, ask the following set of questions and assess the answers:

1. Does your app fulfill a need, a want, or both? A "need" differs from a "want" in that a need is something your user feels they cannot do without, while a want is something that is non-essential but highly desirable. How well does it fulfill that need or want on a regular basis for the user?

2. Does your app offer a feature, service, or experience that sets it apart from other apps in its category, especially the most popular ones? Is this feature, service, or experience enough to attract large numbers of users and keep them engaged?

3. How will you structure the user experience to keep your users engaged? Are you prepared to invest more time and money after the app is published to keep your users engaged and retain them in the long run?

4. What is the niche that this app will target? How broad or narrow is it? Have you accurately estimated market size for your app?

    This is an important question, and the answer will determine many things about the final product. For example, an app that targets a broad niche, like teenagers, for example, will focus on driving large numbers of downloads with a free version and then sell extra features in the app to make a profit. An app that targets a narrow niche, like doctors, for example, is more likely to be a paid app with a very specific purpose and set of features tailored to a user base willing to pay for them.

Knowing the size of your target market is also important if you are seeking external financing. It's also important to make sure that the market you are targeting is a growing market, or at least a stable one. You don't want to be climbing onto a sinking ship.

One important point worth mentioning here is that many successful apps have not targeted an existing market, but rather have themselves created completely new markets and dominated them. Apple essentially created the smartphone market, and Uber created the taxi app market.

5. Can your app concept be successfully monetized? Is this niche prepared to pay for your app or its in-app purchases, or will you rely on ad revenue? How likely are you to make a profit, how many users do you need to do so, and how should you structure your offering to maximize your revenue?

    In short, to make, say, $10,000 (before the app store takes its cut), will you get one million users to pay one cent, or get 10,000 users to pay $1? What income group do your users fall into, and how easily do your users part with their cash for apps and in-app purchases?

6. What is your break-even point? How much will you be investing in your app, and what will be your operating costs? Do you anticipate enough revenue to recover your original investment and cover your operating costs?

7. If your app develops traction and grows a strong user base, are you prepared to invest more money and build a business around it?

The answers to these questions will produce a great deal of information about how your app should be designed and how it needs to function in order to make your users happy and make you a profit. If the answers are thorough enough, it's safe you say you're halfway to publishing your app, because from this point on you will be very clear about what you want, what works or doesn't work, and where to start. You will do what you need to do from the beginning of the design process to make sure you get the final product you want.

The conclusions you reach from the answers to these questions will help you design your app around the feature or experience that sets it apart, identify the pricing strategy that will maximize your user base and your revenue, and efficiently market your app to its target niche.

Validation

When you are assessing app ideas in terms of their prospects for success, it's very helpful to have some way of knowing that there is demand for your app before you commit to it. Validation is a way of confirming your projections and expectations before investing in your app concept. By validating your app concept, you ensure that there is enough demand for your app to make it successful and that you are not wasting time and resources on a dead-end project people are no longer interested in.

Validation, of course, is not an exact science, and no matter how good you are, there are never any guarantees that your app will be adopted in large numbers. Accurately forecasting adoption is very difficult, if not impossible, but there are ways to at least make sure that your app is likely to be positively received and that there are enough people who want the product you are planning to build.

All the methods listed next are accepted ways of validating an app idea. Ideally, you would use all, or at least most, of them to generate as much useful information about your intended user group's response to the upcoming app release.

Method 1: Create a Basic "Coming Soon" Website and/or Social Media Page for Your App

Create a basic website landing page about your upcoming app, with analytics built into it. The purpose of this website is not to advertise the app, but to gather information about your prospective users' reactions to it. Describe your app and why you think it will be a success, and include some form of call to action that will gauge visitors' reactions, such as asking them to sign up for a newsletter or sign up to be notified when the app is about to be released, asking them to share the page, or asking them to offer some feedback. You can also ask them questions like "Would you download this app if it were available?" For users who answer they wouldn't, ask them to tell you why not. It may be because there is already some stiff competition and they see no need for another app in that category, or it may be because they see a flaw in your design, or something else entirely.

You can also build a Facebook page and use Facebook ads to test your concept with the public and build an audience for your product.

A landing page is not useful just for you. It is also very useful as proof of concept if you are planning to raise money for your app or your startup. The number of likes on your page and the analytical data will go a long way toward proving that demand for your concept is big enough to justify investment.

Now, start promoting the app website. Advertise in ways that allow you to target those users who form your desired market. Analytics embedded in your website will supply you with a wealth of information about your users. Combine this information with the responses to the call to action and you will generate a great deal of useful information about how your future users are likely to respond to your app and how likely they are to download it.

According to Apptentive (www.apptentive.com), getting a positive response on your app idea is a good thing, but is not worth that much in terms of validation. The key to effective validation is to determine whether your visitors are prepared to pay for your app, and this is the key to determining how financially sustainable or profitable your app is likely to be.

If you want to use your website to build up buzz about the app's release, include a blog and/or newsletter and ask people to sign up to receive the newsletter or notifications about the latest blog entries. That way, when it's publishing time for your app, your audience will be waiting.

Method 2: Find Out How Many People Are Searching for Apps Like Yours

Using keywords related to your app idea, use a keyword tool to determine how many searches are done for these keywords. Apply both broad keywords and specific keywords. If the number of searches for your chosen keywords is high compared to the number of available offerings on the app stores, this is a clear sign that there will be a market for your app if it's built around that specific keyword.

Method 3: Find Out How Apps Similar to Yours Are Doing

This comparison process has two aspects. One involves looking at how apps in your category are doing on the app stores, how many downloads they have, how fast they are climbing or falling, and how overall demand for them is changing over time. This will tell you whether you are in a growing market, a stable market, or a shrinking market. It will also tell you how many downloads you should reasonably anticipate over time.

The second aspect involves looking more closely at the main competitors in your market, especially user reviews, feedback, and conversations about these apps on forums and blogs. Use this information to determine where your competitors are making mistakes or what users say these apps are lacking so as to determine how your app should adapt to attract as broad a user base as possible.

Method 4: Check Demand for Keywords Related to an App Topic

If you have an idea for an app that is based on an external trend, topic, or event, like the Olympics, an election, Black Friday, the Christmas shopping season, Mardi Gras, and so on, use keyword tools to check how terms related to that idea are doing in search, how many apps are trying to respond to demand in that search area, and how well these apps are doing. If your app cannot differentiate itself from other apps enough to stand out, and these competing apps are not doing well, your app is also unlikely to do well unless you modify it sufficiently.

For the Serious Appreneur: MVP Publishing for Beta Testing

If you are committed to your app idea, one good way to test it and generate a great deal of useful information is to release an MVP, or Minimum Viable Product, to a small group of testers and get their feedback. As an app, an MVP will contain the core functions of your intended final product without any of the frills. The point is to determine how the beta testers are using the app, where they are having problems, and what they dislike about it. This will also keep you from wasting your time on features users do not care about.

By building an MVP, you are already halfway there as an app publisher, and you have a product your target market (or at least part of it) is already using. There is really no other way to see in real-time how your intended users are interacting with the app. You might even find out that your users are interacting with your app in innovative and unexpected ways! Releasing an MVP is an app-validation information gold mine!

Summary

Get it right! Approach the process of generating app ideas rationally and methodically. Use the method you like most or, better yet, use all the methods listed in this chapter to generate a reasonably large first set of app ideas.

Use keyword searches and other methods to paint a fairly accurate picture of demand and supply and anticipated profits. Narrow your list to the idea that has the best chances of success. Next, validate your app idea. Commit to it.

Chapter **6**

Design Your App

"Design is not what it looks like and feels like. Design is how it works."

Steve Jobs

Every app has a lifecycle, a journey that begins with an idea and matures into a fully functional app available for download in the app stores.

But what happens in between? What process does an app go through as it becomes more than just an idea?

There are several stages to an app's evolution into a finished product. Each stage defines the app's functions, look, and feel in more detail, after which the first prototype is created and tested thoroughly and the final version is produced for release.

© Hagop Panosian 2017
H. Panosian, *Learn iOS Application Distribution*, DOI 10.1007/978-1-4842-2683-4_6

Getting to launch day, however, is only half the story. There is a great deal of work to be done after launch, including marketing, performance monitoring, and making adjustments. In fact, as your app picks up momentum and downloads increase, your involvement with it will inevitably grow as you seek ways to improve it, overtake competitors, and monetize it.

Apps are much more than just code. In this chapter, we will look at how apps are assembled, what their important parts are, what standards are used to design and code them, and what principles app designers must adhere to if they want to have a great product that will be successful in the app stores.

At this stage, you are defining what is known as the user experience, or how a user will interact with your app.

Before Launching the Design Process: Know What You're Doing

Now that we have looked at popular myths about app development (see previous chapter), let's take a peek at what apps are really made of and what we have to keep in mind while developing them. A realistic and thorough understanding of what goes into building an app will help you ensure your apps are professionally built from the start.

Choosing a Platform

Before you begin developing an app, choose the platform you want to develop for first, most likely iOS or Android. Each has its upsides and its downsides.

The upsides of developing for iOS first are the relatively small number of devices, the faster time to a product, higher levels of user loyalty, and a system that is kept safer from malware.

The downsides are stricter standards and the longer time for app approval. In terms of monetization, Apple has a smaller number of customers than Android has, but these customers are known to pay more on average.

The upside of developing for Android first is the much larger market of potential users (around 80 percent of devices worldwide). Other key advantages of Android include fast app approval and ease of distribution.

A downside is the very large number of devices, screen sizes, and resolutions your app needs to cater to. Developing for Android is also known to take longer than developing for iOS.

iOS Native Apps: 13.9 Percent of Smartphones (in 2015 Q2)

iOS native apps run on Apple devices and are developed with the Objective-C or Swift programming languages using Xcode software, which is free to download and use on Apple computers for registered developers who have paid the annual fee.

Android Native Apps: 82.8 Percent of Smartphones (in 2015 Q2)

Android native apps run on all devices that use the Android operating system. Hundreds of different smartphone brands run on the Android system, including Samsung, Huawei, Lenovo, Xiaomi, and HTC. Android apps are developed with the Java programming language using free software like Google's Android Studio, Eclipse, NetBeans, JEdit, and other Java programming tools.

Windows Native Apps: 2.6 Percent of Smartphones (in 2015 Q2)

Windows native apps run on devices that use the Windows Phone Operating System. Windows apps are developed with the C++ and C# programming languages and the .NET framework using free software like Microsoft Visual Basic.

Hybrid Apps

Hybrid apps, also known as cross-platform apps or universal apps, are apps that are developed once using web development languages like HTML, CSS, and JavaScript and are then given a "shell" that allows them to be deployed on the Android, iOS, or Windows operating systems.

The upsides of developing a hybrid app instead of several native apps are the significantly lower cost, the faster time to release, and their much easier maintenance needs. The downsides are that hybrid apps can lack the sophistication of native apps and make more limited use of the capabilities of the various devices than native apps do.

Hybrid apps are developed with services like PhoneGap, Appcelerator Titanium, and Telerik. Most sites that allow users to build apps for free or without coding skills build hybrid apps.

Optimal Strategy

The first version of any app almost always needs improvement. If you want to develop native apps, develop on one platform first to keep costs down and your learning curve short, then publish the new version on all platforms. Or, if cost is the biggest challenge, start by developing a hybrid app.

Clarify the Concept

This stage in your app's lifecycle is the first step your idea will take toward becoming a full-fledged app. The key activity in this stage is to narrow your focus, put together the information you gathered and decisions you made in the previous chapter, and describe your idea in terms that can be used to build a prototype for a product.

Your idea will now go through a clarification process with regard to the following:

> **Type** – What kind of app are you building? Is it a game, socialization app, utility app, or another kind? What category would it fall under in the app store?
>
> **Purpose** – What is the app's main function? What are users supposed to do with it?
>
> **Features** – What other things can it do? Do these capabilities support the main function, or are they secondary functions a minimum viable product can do without, but that are good to have because they bring added value?
>
> **Market** – Who is it for? Who are its main users? Are you targeting a narrow niche or a broad audience of users?

The answers to these questions will guide you as you design the structure of your app, its look and feel, and its details.

Clarify the Scale and Cost

There are also a number of related questions that will define how big and complex your app will be, and therefore how long it will take to build. To further develop the app concept, you need to answer the following questions:

> **Size** – What is the size of your app? Is it a small standalone app that can be fully downloaded and run on a smartphone even without an Internet connection, or a larger app that will require a mobile backend to manage it?

Content – What will the app's content be? If it is a game, that content would be game characters, levels, images, sounds, and so on. If it is a news app, then the content would have to be constantly updated, and in some cases automated or user-generated.

Will you be creating the content, or will your users be sharing it between themselves? Will it be curated, or will it have to be sourced from different places at a cost to you?

Data Gathering – Will you gather information about your users through analytics? This question may not seem important at this early stage, but it's highly relevant because your approach to gathering information about your users will inform your app's design, especially the responses that you will solicit from your users at different points in the user experience.

Monetization Model – How will your app make money? This question is closely related to the design of your app and is not something unrelated that you simply apply to your design later on.

Many apps are designed around a specific monetization method. For example, small games that look like copies of other games are copied precisely to benefit from the success of the original game and are offered for free to maximize downloads. They are stuffed full of different types of ads to benefit from clicks. These apps use interstitial (full-page) ads each time you open or close the app, every time you switch from one level to another, and every other chance they get. They are designed purely for the purpose of making money without effort.

Other apps, like more sophisticated games, have a fully-functioning free version and charge for in-app purchases and additional functions or levels. This model is known as freemium.

Certain types of apps are subscription-based. This monetization model is suitable for magazine or video apps, which can logically charge a certain fee every month for their content, and is growing in popularity because of its ability to produce a steady stream of income for publishers.

What type of monetization model do you want to use for your app? An ad-based monetization model will not have a profound effect on design except to occupy permanent screen space (and possibly irritate your users), but a model based on in-app purchases will affect the very core of how your app will function and engage and retain its users.

Graphics – How design-heavy is your app, and how much design work will it need to function? A simple game will not require much in terms of visuals, but some apps, especially sophisticated games, will require constant work on graphics. You will have to decide whether you will have to produce visuals on a regular basis.

The Parts of an App

When designing an app, keep in mind that what you're designing is not a finite bit of software with a fixed user interface confined to a mobile phone (although it might be, if the app is a tiny game). It's a lively entity that extends beyond the mobile phones that host it, and, depending on what type of app it is, it will regularly change its content and feel while constantly gathering data about its users and their behavior. There will be database administrators and content managers working together somewhere to maintain the app and keep users engaged with their product, as well as a customer relationship management team responding to user inquiries and feedback. As Figure 6-1 shows, an app has several groups of standard components, each of which must be managed separately to make for a successful app. Each of these will be discussed.

User Interface

Assets	Images, icons, sounds, backgrounds, textures, game characters, and levels.
Informational Components	Tooltips, icons, progress bar, notifications, message boxes, and pop-up windows.
Navigational Components	Icons, sliders, scrollers, search fields, tags, and buttons.
Input Controls	Checkboxes, radio buttons, dropdown lists, list boxes, buttons, toggles, text fields, date and time fields, dialogs, and pickers.

Backend Server

User Database	Information about all the app's users, including demographic and behavioral data.
Content	The regularly updated content of the app.
Analytics	Reports on app usage patterns.

Code

Main program

Code Snippets	Code for social media integration.
	Code for analytics.
	Code for advertising.
	APIs (Application Programming Interfaces) for delivery of content to the user.

Commercial Package

Visuals	App icon, screenshots, and images and videos for ad content and marketing.
Text	App description for app store, keywords for SEO and ASO, and marketing copy.

Figure 6-1. Standard app components

The User Interface

This is the part of the app that interacts with the user, receiving commands and displaying content. It normally defines the user experience using the following elements:

> **Assets** are files that an app uses, like images, sounds, game characters or textures, and icons.
>
> **Informational Components** are visual elements that communicate information to the user, like tooltips, icons, progress bars, notifications, message boxes, and pop-up windows.
>
> **Navigational Components** help the user find their way through the app, like sliders, scrollers, search fields, tags, buttons, and navigational icons.
>
> **Input Controls** allow an app to receive input from the user through user interface elements like checkboxes, radio buttons, dropdown lists, list boxes, buttons, toggles, text fields, date and time fields, dialogs, and pickers.

The Backend

This is where the app publisher hosts and manages the content an app displays and the data it gathers. The backend normally consists of the content of the app, which is modified or updated at relevant intervals by the publisher, the user database, which contains demographic and behavioral information about the app's users, and the analytics component, which delivers that information and creates reports for the publisher.

Code

The code that runs an app has different components depending on programming language and platform, but all relatively complex apps have the following parts: the main program of the app, code snippets for analytics inserted into the main program, code snippets for social media sharing of app content, code snippets for ads to be displayed in the app, and APIs (Application Programming Interfaces) that allow an app to deliver content to the user.

Commercial Package

The commercial package of an app contains everything that will be used to market the app on the app store and online: images of the app icon, screenshots, images of videos for ad content and marketing purposes, and text, like the app description for the app store, keywords that will be used for SEO (Search Engine Optimization) and ASO (App Store Optimization), and marketing copy.

The Goals of App Design

Design, as Steve Jobs said, is not about what it looks and feels like, but how it works. Beyond looking nice and performing well, however, design also serves different purposes at different levels of user involvement.

Your app will be competing with millions of other apps for attention, with users spending no more than a few microseconds deciding whether an app icon and short description are worth a closer look. So, your design strategy and quality better be good, or your app will flop.

As shown in Figure 6-2, your app will have to steer users through four levels of interaction: discovery, engagement, retention, and monetization.

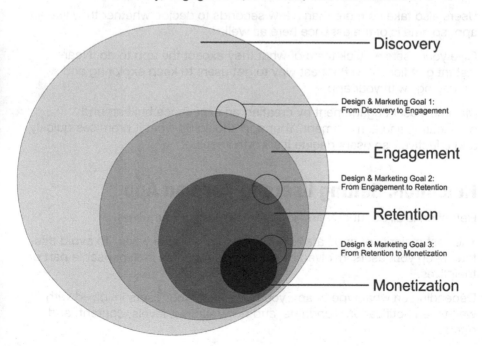

Figure 6-2. Goals of app design

At each of these levels, design is crucial to maximizing your app's potential. Ultimately, a very small percentage of users who see your app will download it, and a tiny percentage of those who download it will ever spend any money. Design goes a long way toward maximizing that number, which means good design leads to strong revenue and a solid return on your investment.

Discovery: Getting Users to Find an App

App discovery is mostly about effective marketing, but does design also play a role in app discovery?

Yes, it does! With so many competing apps, your app's name, icon, screenshots, videos, and description page on the app store need to be designed to catch the eye and to create the right kind of visual impact so as to convince the user to try out your app.

Users take no more than a couple of seconds to decide whether an app is worth downloading, so use them well.

Engagement: Getting Users to Like an App

Users also take no more than a few seconds to decide whether they like an app, so time is of the essence here as well.

Give your users a quick taste of what they expect the app to do. Near-instant gratification is the best way to get users to keep exploring and "engaging" with your app.

Maximize user engagement by creating an experience built around gratification and achievement. Your app should do what it promises quickly and effectively so users decide it's worth keeping.

Retention: Getting Users to Keep an App

Retention is all about creating long-term value for your users.

The vast majority of apps are abandoned after about a week. To avoid this fate, keep your users involved by making your app an indispensable part of their lives.

Depending on what type of app you have, keep your users involved with well-timed notifications, updates, and new features, levels, content, and offers.

Monetization: Getting Users to Spend Money

The ultimate goal, of course, is creating value and profit. Money will be made by offering additional value to users who are the most highly engaged with your app and are prepared to pay for that additional value.

This extra value is normally sold in the form of in-app purchases, like new features, a pro or full version of a free app, or new levels, characters, or weapons, in the case of games.

In-app purchases can be offered as single transactions or as a monthly or annual subscription.

Transition Points

Once your app is up and running, many of your additional design and marketing ideas will revolve around the three transition points between the phases of a user's relationship with your app. You will be modifying your app's design and your marketing content to push users from discovery to engagement, from engagement to retention, and from retention to monetization. Each transition is different in its nature and will require different approaches and techniques.

Mobile App Optimization

Mobile app optimization is the process of making small, incremental changes to your app to gauge user reaction until you arrive at the optimal design that brings in the maximum amount of profit.

The first version of an app is highly unlikely to be a perfect match for its users' desires when it's released. It's likely to have "teething problems." At the same time, it's very difficult to tell exactly where the problems are. How can you solve this problem?

This is where incremental changes come in. Start by identifying the actions that a user is expected to take at specific points in your app—open a file, send a message, share their experience, create content, and so on. Then, look at the paths that a user will take to get to that action. These paths are known as funnels (Figure 6-3).

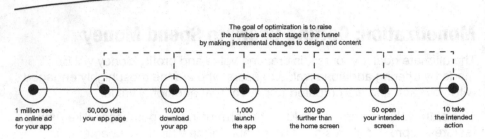

Figure 6-3. *Funnel for app optimization*

Time to Value

One measurement of an app's power to engage users is known as Time to Value. This is a business term that measures the time between when a request is made for something that's defined as a value (a business goal) and when that value is delivered to the customer.

In an app, this would be the measure of how long it takes a user to reach the point where the app serves its primary function. If the app is a messaging app, for example, Time to Value is a measure of how quickly a user can actually compose a message, identify a recipient, and send it.

Users like apps to be an extension of their intentions. If you want to send a message, you don't want to go through too many steps before getting to the point of pressing "Send." If Time to Value is too long, then the user is likely to see the app as too cumbersome or complex. Time to Value is not the same for all apps. As a process, it differs from app to app depending on what the app's primary function is.

It pays to recall, however, that Time to Value is not the single aspect of your app's design that will determine its value to a user.

Start with a Great App Design

Great app designs consist of several constituent aspects, each with its own essential components (Figure 6-4).

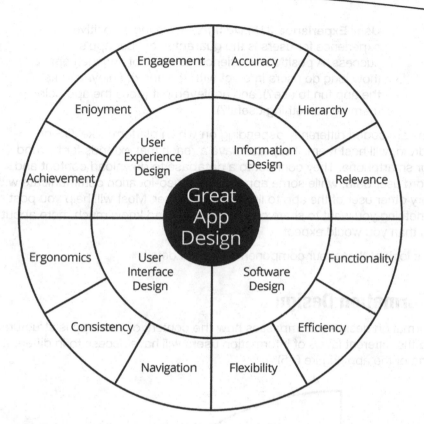

Figure 6-4. Components of a great app design

Specifically, there are four fundamental aspects that combine to increase the likelihood of a positive response from users:

Information Design – The content of your app needs to be useful, relevant, accurate, and properly structured so users can easily find what they want. Also, make sure to update your content regularly so users will keep coming back.

Software Design – The software that runs your app needs to work efficiently so that it does not crash and can handle new functions and a fast-growing number of users.

User Interface (UI) Design – A well-designed UI is key to user approval and takes into account ergonomics (can the app be used with one hand or just the thumb?), navigation (is it intuitive and quick?), and consistency (are icons and navigation buttons consistent and coded by color, shape, and sound throughout?).

User Experience (UX) Design – Creating a positive experience for users is the guarantee of your app's success. A positive experience consists of engagement (how long do users interact with the app?), enjoyment (is the app fun to use?), and achievement (does the app help them do something useful?).

Apps are coded differently depending on which platform, like iOS or Android, will host them. They also have a reach that extends far beyond your smartphone. They connect to a database to download content and record user data, while some apps that use geo-location communicate with every other user of the app to link users together. Most will help you post something you want to share on social media and know much more about you than you would expect.

Let's look at these four components in more detail.

Information Design

Information design encompasses how the content of your app is structured and the different levels of information users will have access to in different parts of the app (Figure 6-5).

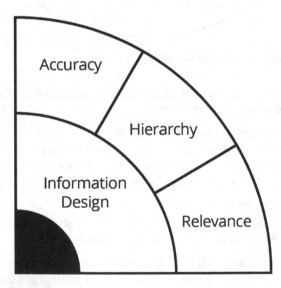

Figure 6-5. Information design

The structure of the information contained inside your app depends on two main considerations. One, the nature of your content: is it about images, video, text, or a combination of all three? Two, your user engagement considerations: how much of your content do you want to reveal at first glance, and how much do you want to keep deeper inside; how much do you want to concentrate on a single page, and how do you want to point to deeper content from that page (Figure 6-6)?

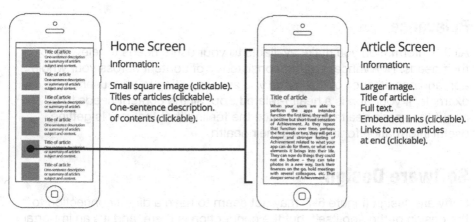

Figure 6-6. Information design

For an information design to be successful, the information you use needs to have three characteristics: accuracy, hierarchy, and relevance.

Accuracy

This is the most fundamental characteristic of all the information you will ever publish in your app, and it is particularly important if you intend to update your content regularly. Always make sure any information published in your app is accurate.

This is especially true of apps like news apps or magazine apps that publish a great deal of regularly updated content. Checking the accuracy of published information, or making sure the information you use is from respectable and reliable sources, is something that needs to be part and parcel of your content-creation system.

Hierarchy

The hierarchy of information in your app decides how much users get to see at first glance, and how deep they need to travel to access the rest. This structuring of information is determined by the need for consistency of navigation and your monetization strategy as well. For example, users can read short summaries of articles for free, but need to subscribe to access the full articles.

Organize the information you plan to publish logically and create a hierarchy that suits your needs. If you want to draw users into your app, you have to decide what to publish on the home screen or another key screen, like "All our blog posts," for example, to get the user to explore further and read your blog posts.

Relevance

All the information you make available to your users needs to relevant to their needs. Relevance is about consistency of content across your whole app and consistency of the image you are projecting to your users. For example, if your app is a health-related app, all the content needs to be about the user's health and enhance the feeling that the user is getting useful information for improving their health.

Software Design

Software design (Figure 6-7) may not seem to have a direct connection to the design of the app itself, but the connection is there, and it's an important one: if your software fails to deliver, your app doesn't stand a chance.

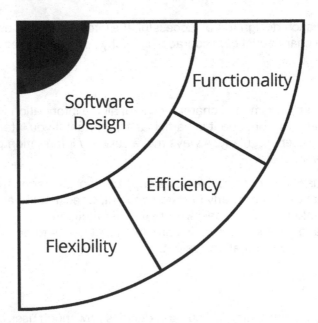

Figure 6-7. Software design

In terms of how it's designed, the software for your app needs to adhere to three principles: functionality, efficiency, and flexibility.

Functionality

Your code should work, period. No crashes, no bugs, no dead-end navigation. It should deliver what it's supposed to deliver to the user without fail. It's your responsibility as the publisher to thoroughly test your app, eliminate crashes, and fix bugs before release.

Note: The term "functional" in this context means "working" and is unrelated to the term "functional programming," which represents a different concept altogether.

Efficiency

Having efficient code means delivering value to the user with the least possible effort. Inefficient code, even if functional, will make an app feel burdensome and slow. A good example is your app's load time. If your app takes longer than an instant, 1 to 2 seconds, to load its primary interface or at least a splash screen, you've already got yourself a frustrated user.

Flexibility

Flexible software is designed from the outset for scaling. It takes into account any projections of how your app is likely to grow in the future and is already structured to make that evolution process as smooth and quick as possible.

User Interface Design

The user interface is the user's space of interaction with the app (Figure 6-8).

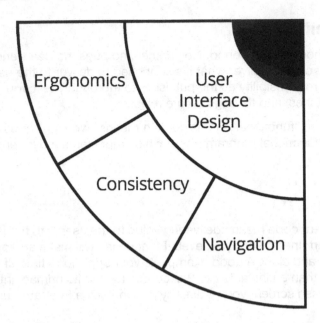

Figure 6-8. User interface design

To function properly and deliver a positive experience, the user interface should be built around three principles: ergonomics, consistency, and navigation.

Ergonomics

Ergonomics takes into account human factors in the layout of a user interface, like the size of the human hand and the thumb's circular motion. Can your app be used with one hand without frustrating the user? Can both adults and children use it with one hand? Are you avoiding placing buttons in uncomfortable-to-use locations on the screen? These are signs of carefully considered ergonomic design.

Consistency

Consistency means meeting a user's expectations of where everything should be. If you place a navigation button in a corner on one screen, it should stay in the same corner on every other screen on which it's used, as the user will expect it to be there.

Consistency also applies to your app's responses to hand gestures on the screen. A press, long press, small swipe, or large swipe should produce identical results every time.

It creates familiarity, and familiarity enhances the user experience by maximizing the user's comfort and confidence when using your app. When the user is not confused, they use the app much faster, their finger movements speed up, and the app becomes much more of an extension of their intent and a tool to do something efficiently, thus building the user's attachment to the app and the likelihood of long-term adoption.

Navigation

Clear communication of navigation means the user is always intuitively aware of where they are, how to get back, and how to return to the starting point if they decide to. Clear navigation supports the positive user experience by never allowing the user to feel lost in the app.

User Experience Design

Giving your users a positive experience is one of the most effective methods of marketing your app (Figure 6-9).

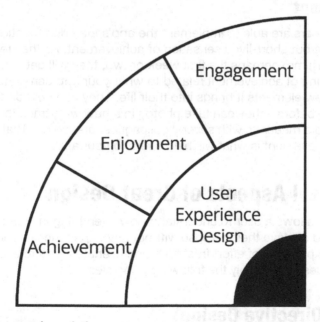

Figure 6-9. User experience design

A crowd of users raving about how great your app is is an unbeatable marketing tool, and building that crowd depends on your ability to deliver the following levels of interaction and sentiment: engagement, enjoyment, and achievement.

Engagement

A positive user experience has three levels. The first is engagement. An engaged user has already responded positively to their first impression of your app. They like it and want to explore it further. They are curious about its features and capabilities.

Enjoyment

Once your users have become familiar with your app, they will move to Enjoyment. They are having fun with the app, and the feeling of enjoyment is stronger and deeper than the feeling of engagement.

Achievement

When your users are able to implement the app's intended function, they will get a positive but short-lived sensation of achievement. As they repeat that function over time, perhaps the first week or two, they will get a deeper and stronger feeling of achievement related to what your app can do for them, or to what new elements it brings into their life. They can now do things they could not do before—they can take photos in a new way, track their finances on the go, hold meetings with several colleagues, and so on. That deeper sense of achievement is what will bind users to your app.

Additional Aspects of Great Design

Great design allows a user to understand how everything in your app functions and achieve their purpose without any experience of undue effort. Any experience of effort frustrates and alienates, and to avoid it user experience designers apply the following principles.

Clarity (Directive Design)

Clarity involves the consistent use of colors, shapes, and text to quickly inform the user about what the app does and the options that are available at any point inside the app.

The point of directive design is to make sure the user is never confused about where they are, where they need to go, or what they need to do to get what they want.

The Value of Intuitive Design

To make your app appealing to users, the visual design and navigation need to be as intuitive as possible. This means that the user should find everything they are looking for precisely where they expect it to be. In other words, an intuitive design is a precise match between a user's expectations and their experience. Intuitive suggests that there is little or no rational thinking; a user does not ask himself "What do I do now?" when interacting with your app. Rather, whatever they decide to do, the buttons they need to press to get it done are right in front of them. This makes a user comfortable with your app and helps them seek a deeper user experience. Problems with navigation will always prevent your user from engaging deeply with your app and will do everything to drive them away.

To make an app design intuitive, you need the following:

- **Core path** – The path a user takes to use the app's core functions should always be directly visible and accessible.

- **Directives** – A directive is a "command" from you that asks the user to do specific things at different points in your app. Icons that say "open," "send," "copy," or anything else are essentially giving the user directives to do what you want them to do or asking them to choose from a set of options you are creating.

- **Anchoring** – Any icon that performs a key navigation function across the app should always be in the same place and should not be moved around depending on how your content changes or at random. If you create an expectation at the launch of your app that a specific button is in a certain place, the user will always expect to find it there when they need it. The Home button on an iPhone is not just visually anchored, but physically anchored as well. As a result, the user always knows how to get back to the home screen whenever they want. Anchoring is particularly useful for key functions like returning to the home screen, leaving an app, and so on (Figure 6-10).

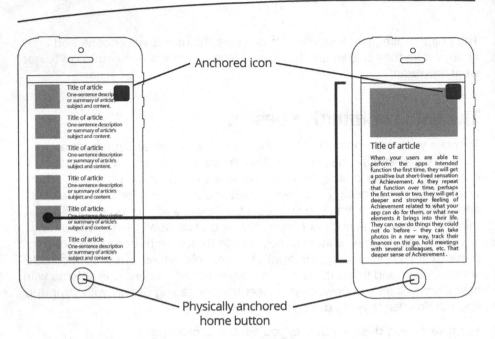

Figure 6-10. Anchoring: Consistency of icon placement

■ **Familiarity** – App publishers are always looking for ways to make their app designs stand out and differ from everyone else's. While pursuing originality and uniqueness is generally a good idea, there is one thing you should never mess with, and that is the symbolic power and familiarity of the icons you will use. There are many styles available for the same icon—square, round, shadow, no shadow, color, black and white, and so forth—but the meaning of an icon remains the same, and you should never mess with it, because you will risk losing its symbolic meaning.

■ **Simplicity** – Always resist the temptation to complicate your designs. This is truer for smartphone screens than for anywhere else. Smartphone screens keep getting bigger, but they still represent very limited visual real estate for you to use.

Cramming more and more functions onto a screen is a sure sign that you don't understand your app, what its core function is, or what needs to be directly accessible and what can be placed on the side.

Simplicity, however, is something that needs to be achieved, and with some effort. That effort usually involves understanding your user and how your app is structured to meet that user's needs. As Steve Jobs once said, "Simplicity can be harder than complex. You have to work had to get your thinking clean to make it simple. But it's worth it in the end because once you get there, you can move mountains."

In your search for the simplest solutions to the design problems at hand, you will be getting a lot of help from design guidelines, which are created to ensure the minimum required levels of ergonomics and functionality.

App Design Standards and Guidelines

App design standards and guidelines are created by the companies that build the platforms on which apps are run. These standards and guidelines are based on an understanding of human ergonomics and best design practices. They are designed to ensure apps function properly, to give users the necessary quality of experience, and to create a consistent aesthetic that is harmonious with the image platform manufacturers like Apple and Google want to create.

By complying with these guidelines in the design and layout of your apps, you ensure that the app is much more likely to be approved for publishing and that users will find the app appealing and easy to understand, navigate, and use. You can also save a great deal of time by downloading and using UI kits and templates that are built using these guidelines.

Platform Guidelines

Platform guidelines are design guidelines set by the companies that build the platforms on which apps are run.

Apple human interface guidelines can be found at:

https://developer.apple.com/design/

Android human interface guidelines can be found at:

http://developer.android.com/design/index.html

Windows human interface guidelines can be found at:

https://dev.windows.com/en-us/design

Apple

For companies like Apple, the application of its human interface guidelines in app design is essential to an app's being approved for release. The company has detailed human interface guidelines for iOS, macOS, watchOS, and tvOS.

Tools and Resources

The following sections discuss some tools and resources you may find helpful in designing an app.

Patterns

Design patterns are standardized solutions to user-interaction issues that can be used over and over again. There are collections of thousands of patterns available online and in print that can solve almost any interaction design issue you might have. For example, design patterns for iOS, Android, and other platforms suggest the best ways to design dialogs, tips, invitations, demos, transparencies, popovers, sidebars, notifications, photos, tab bars, signups, walkthroughs, videos, charts, widgets, shopping carts, comments, posts, events, filters, empty states, grids, home screens, and much more.

For iOS design pattern inspiration, visit iOS Patterns (http://ios-patterns.com/) or Pttrns (http://pttrns.com/ios-patterns/).

From a Sketch to an App

Now turn your ideas into sketches, sketches into designs, and designs into a coded app.

Turning a concept into a design involves looking at it from different perspectives. You can draw a flowchart to illustrate your concept as a sequence of steps, or do some layout sketches to illustrate your concept as a collection of app screens. The following sections discuss different approaches and tools.

Pen and Paper

Nothing brings ideas forth like doodling on paper. On a clean sheet of paper, you can draw anything, from icon designs to screen layouts to flowcharts or anything else that comes to mind, and this freedom to doodle and move between ideas and options before moving on to digital tools is important for the creative process.

User Flow Charts

User flow diagrams look at the app design from the user's point of view. They illustrate the user's journey through an app and the decisions they have to make and input they have to submit at key points of interaction.

With the flow charts and decision tree in hand, the next step is usually to design the screens for each part of the flow chart.

App Design Templates

To make your screen designs more accurate, use templates to set the icons, buttons and other visual assets in proportion. You can also use special app-design sketchpads with smartphone templates and dot grids for a very quick and accurate visualization of your designs. The templates suggested here are available to download for free in .pdf and .png formats.

Free and premium design templates and sketchbooks are available on interfacesketch.com, sneakpeekit.com, ideatoappbook.com, dotgrid.co, appsketchbook.com, popapp.in, uistencils.com, and smashingmagazine.com.

Stencils

Stencils work great with templates to produce accurate layouts. They contain the most common buttons and visual elements that are used in app design. Free and premium stencils are available on uistencils.com, mobilestencil.com, and elsewhere. Stencils are also available in digital formats, like Basiliq (https://castle.co/design/basiliq).

Wireframes and UI Kits

Wireframes are detailed designs of screen layouts in your app. They show the layout of different elements on the screen and the connections between different screens. They tell you that pressing a button on one screen will take you to another screen or activate a certain function. They also show you the total number of screens your app has and how each of them looks.

Given that many app features are similar and are governed by design standards and guidelines, collections of standardized screen layouts, known as wireframe kits, can be downloaded from various graphic design websites in different formats, such as for Photoshop, Illustrator, and Sketch.

UI kits and templates are fully designed user interface collections used to speed up the design process. They come with their own sets of elements like icons, buttons, sliders, fonts, backgrounds, and textures, as well as pre-designed layouts for activities like e-commerce or chat.

Many kits have names, like Helium UI Kit, Flat UI Kit, and Universe UI Kit, and come in various formats suitable for graphic design software like Adobe Photoshop, Adobe Illustrator, and Sketch. They can easily be found online on speckyboy.com, sketchappsources.com, wireframes.tumblr.com, and elsewhere.

App development companies also create their own UI kits to create a consistent aesthetic and visual language for their own products, while digital artists create and sell UI kits that can be downloaded and used in the layout and wireframing phase of an app project.

The following sections present some popular app wireframing and design tools.

Adobe Photoshop, Illustrator, InDesign, Experience Design (www.adobe.com)

Adobe has a suite of design tools that are applicable to app design, including Photoshop for image manipulation and app layouts, Illustrator for vector-based graphics, and InDesign for layouts. Adobe also has other Creative Cloud tools for HTML-based apps, like Edge CC and PhoneGap Build.

Adobe Experience Design is what Adobe calls its all-in-one tool for designing websites and mobile apps, while Adobe Digital Publishing is a content management system that works with Experience Design to deliver content over mobile.

Omnigraffle (https://www.omnigroup.com/omnigraffle)

Omnigraffle is part of a suite of digital design tools for user-experience design geared for Apple devices.

Sketch (https://www.sketchapp.com)

Sketch is a vector-based graphics editor designed specifically for the Apple Mac and won an Apple Design Award in 2012.

More App Wireframing and Prototyping Tools

UXPin (www.uxpin.com)

FluidUI (www.fluidui.com)

UXPin (www.uxpin.com)

FluidUI (www.fluidui.com)

Balsamiq (www.balsamiq.com)

Visio (www.visio.com)

Pidoco (www.pidoco.com)

JustinMind (www.justinimind.com)

Gliffy (www.gliffy.com)

FluidUI (www.fluidui.com)

HotGloo (www.hotgloo.com)

Solidify (www.solidifyapp.com)

Mockups.me (http://mockups.me)

Protoshare (www.protoshare.com)

Invision (www.invisionapp.com)

Flinto (www.flinto.com)

Build an App on Your Own

Before answering this question, you need to answer another one: do you know how to code for iOS or Android, the main app platforms?

If you have the needed coding skills, building an app on your own will be much easier. If you lack coding skills but plan to build an app on your own anyway, there are platforms that can help you do that (see the list in the "Resources" section at the end of the book).

If you plan to build an app on your own, in order to expect a reasonable measure of success you will need the following skills:

- Coding in the Swift and Java programming languages for iOS and Android apps, respectively.

- Web design and graphics. You will need to make icons for your apps, visuals like screenshots for your app's page on the App Store and on Google Play, and ads of different sizes and formats to promote your apps. You may also need video production skills (and software) if you plan to promote your app on YouTube or Vimeo. Finally, you will need web design skills for your app's website.

- Marketing skills. You will need skills like knowing how to identify the best keywords for App Store Optimization, how to write keyword-rich advertising copy, and how to design and write marketing emails and online ads.

The Time Factor

Building an app on your own will naturally take much longer than it would if you were working as part of a team or outsourcing the work. The time it will take to produce a finished app must be taken into account when working alone.

The Cost Factor

Developing an app on your own naturally costs much less than it would if you were to work with professionals. However, the opportunity cost of developing the app on your own must also be taken into account: can you afford the time?

The Quality Factor

If you want to develop an app on your own, you need to make sure you are able to insert key components like social media sharing capabilities or analytics code that are crucial to the success of your app. Can you realistically develop a high-quality app with no help from the pros?

The Next Step

Once you have a complete wireframe, you just need the following to build your app:

- The app design wireframe, with the screen layouts, active and interactive elements like buttons and forms, and connections between screens.

- The app content, namely anything in text form that will be a permanent part of the app (as opposed to regularly updated content like news), from button names to game instructions, disclaimers, and app documentation. This also includes updatable content that will be part of the app when it's first downloaded.

- All the assets, like icons, images, videos, sounds, backgrounds, and game characters that the app will reference.

- All necessary access information. For example, if you are registered on an analytics platform, but your programmers are in another location, you will have to give them your username and password so that they can set up analytics for your app based on your requirements.

You can then hand over this package to the programmers who will be coding the app. The more thorough and detailed the wireframe is, the quicker and cheaper the coding process will be. Getting stuck in coding glitches because of bad design is a highly frustrating situation for everyone concerned and is very time-consuming to fix. It can also push your development costs up, so investing the time and effort to create a thorough and well-thought-out design and wireframe will pay off several times over in the coding phase.

The Apple Way

If you're developing for iOS, Apple provides a complete app design and development environment that you can use to both design and code your app at the same time. The development environment, Xcode, is also fully integrated with iTunes Connect, Apple's content management system. You will use iTunes Connect to submit the app for review and, if approved, to publish it on the App Store. In the next chapter, we will look at how to do all this.

Summary

The design phase of an app is when your concept will gradually take shape as a unique product with its own value proposition. This is when you will make all the key decisions about how your app will look and function. What you are pursuing in this phase is a well-thought-out design that is built on a thorough understanding of the user, is capable is scaling easily as its user base grows, and has a smart monetization strategy that will make the most of attracting your users' dollars.

Good design is about more than just coming up with a good-looking product. Your app will probably go through several design iterations before you achieve a good product-market fit. More than anything else, good design is about adaptability without the loss of core identity, as it takes into consideration the future success of your app from the start so that you'll be ready and able to adapt quickly when it happens.

Chapter 7

Building Your App

Once you have a complete design for your app, you can proceed to the building phase. Before building an app for iOS, you must first register as a developer with Apple and build a development team. Each member of your team will have their own status and levels of access, depending on their role. Once the team is ready and roles have been assigned, you can start to shape your design as a storyboard or wireframe. But first, let's look at what makes the Apple system unique.

© Hagop Panosian 2017
H. Panosian, *Learn iOS Application Distribution*, DOI 10.1007/978-1-4842-2683-4_7

Develop with Apple for Apple: A Complete System

From the hardware to the software, from the programming language and operating system to the online marketplace, Apple has a complete proprietary system in place for developers to design, develop, and publish apps for Apple devices (Figure 7-1).

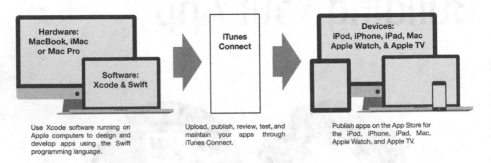

| Hardware: MacBook, iMac or Mac Pro | iTunes Connect | Devices: iPod, iPhone, iPad, Mac Apple Watch, & Apple TV |

Software: Xcode & Swift

Use Xcode software running on Apple computers to design and develop apps using the Swift programming language.

Upload, publish, review, test, and maintain your apps through iTunes Connect.

Publish apps on the App Store for the iPod, iPhone, iPad, Mac, Apple Watch, and Apple TV.

Figure 7-1. Develop with Apple for Apple

This is fundamentally different from Google's system, where the operating system, Android, is hosted on literally hundreds of device models built by almost as many manufacturers and uses a very popular programming language, Java, which means apps can be built with any Java-based tools. Google also manufactures its own devices, like the Nexus and Pixel, and has its own app-buildings software, Android Studio, but in no way does it exercise exclusive control over how the apps that are hosted on Google Play are designed and built.

Let's look at the components of Apple's app development and publishing system.

iOS (http://www.apple.com/ios/ios-10/)

iOS is an operating system developed by Apple to power its mobile devices, including the iPhone, iPad, and iPod Touch. All apps that are hosted on Apple mobile devices are iOS apps.

The latest version of the operating system is iOS 10. As of November 2016, 92 percent of all apps available on the App Store are designed for either iOS 9 or iOS 10.

Swift (`https://developer.apple.com/swift/`)

Swift is a programming language developed by Apple specifically for its operating systems, namely iOS, macOS, watchOS, tvOS, and Linux. Version 1.0 was first released in September 2014, and the latest stable release as of April 2017 is Swift 3.1.1. Before Swift, Apple's operating systems were written in Objective-C, which is itself based on the C programming language. Swift retains many Objective-C concepts but is designed to be safer, more concise, and simpler to use. In 2016, Apple introduced Swift Playgrounds, an iPad app that teaches Swift programming through an interactive, game-like interface.

Xcode (`https://developer.apple.com/xcode`)

Xcode is Apple's IDE, or Integrated Development Environment, designed for storyboarding, wireframing, and prototyping apps for the iOS system, including macOS, iOS, WatchOS and tvOS. In other words, developers can design and code their iOS apps with Xcode and then directly submit their completed app through Xcode to Apple for review and approval.

The App Development and Distribution Process

Before you begin, get the right equipment. You will need one or more iMacs, Mac Pros, or MacBook computers on which to develop. Then, to build apps for Apple devices, follow the steps outlined here and illustrated in Figure 7-2.

1. Enroll in the Apple Developer Program.

2. Build a development team. Everyone on the team is given a relevant status, with proper IDs and appropriate certificates.

3. The development team designs and develops apps on Xcode, from storyboarding and wireframing to prototyping, using Xcode's parallel visual design and code interface.

4. When the beta version of the app is ready, upload it onto iTunes Connect, then build a team of internal and/or external testers.

5. Use your testers' feedback to debug the app and improve the design.

6. When the app is ready for release, submit it to Apple for review.

7. When the app has passed review and is approved for release, publish the app on iTunes Connect.

In this chapter and Chapter 8, we will look at the first three steps. In Chapter 9, we will look at the testing phase; in Chapter 10, at the submission process; and in Chapter 11, at the distribution process. The complete process is shown in Figure 7-2.

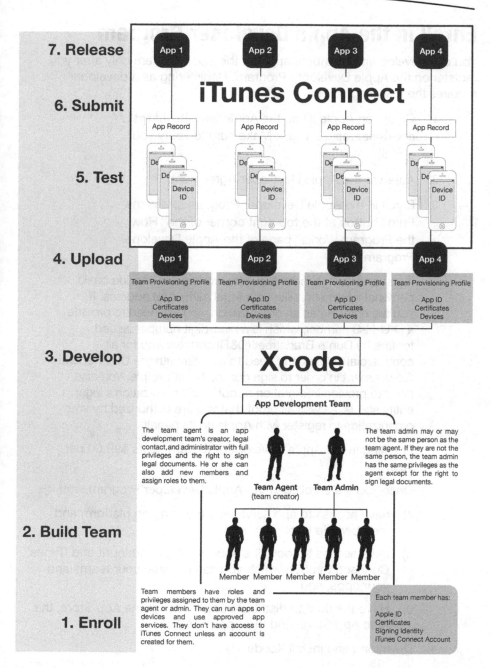

7. Release

App 1   App 2   App 3   App 4

iTunes Connect

6. Submit

App Record   App Record   App Record   App Record

5. Test

Device ID   Device ID   Device ID   Device ID

4. Upload

App 1   App 2   App 3   App 4

Team Provisioning Profile   Team Provisioning Profile   Team Provisioning Profile   Team Provisioning Profile

App ID
Certificates
Devices

App ID
Certificates
Devices

App ID
Certificates
Devices

App ID
Certificates
Devices

3. Develop

Xcode

App Development Team

The team agent is an app development team's creator, legal contact, and administrator with full privileges and the right to sign legal documents. He or she can also add new members and assign roles to them.

The team admin may or may not be the same person as the team agent. If they are not the same person, the team admin has the same privileges as the agent except for the right to sign legal documents.

Team Agent
(team creator)

Team Admin

2. Build Team

Member Member Member Member Member

Team members have roles and privileges assigned to them by the team agent or admin. They can run apps on devices and use approved app services. They don't have access to iTunes Connect unless an account is created for them.

Each team member has:

Apple ID
Certificates
Signing Identity
iTunes Connect Account

1. Enroll

Figure 7-2. The app development and distribution process

Enroll in the Apple Developer Program

You can develop and distribute apps on the Apple system only after you register on the Apple Developer Program. Registering as a developer requires the following steps:

1. Create an Apple ID on the Apple website (`https://developer.apple.com/`). Make sure to verify your e-mail.

2. Agree to the Apple Developer Agreement.

3. Enroll in the Apple Developer Program (press the Enroll button at the top right corner of the "How the Program Works" page of the Apple Developer Program.

   If you enroll as an individual, you will need to provide basic personal information like your legal name and address. If you are enrolling as an organization, you will need to provide a D-U-N-S number, which is a nine-digit number issued for free by Dun & Bradstreet (D&B) and required for all commercial entities that need to register with the U.S. Federal Government in order to sign contracts with Apple. You also need to provide information about your organization's legal entity status, as well as proof that you are authorized by your organization to register with Apple on its behalf.

   Enrolling in the Apple Developer Program costs $99.00 per year.

   Once you are enrolled in the Apple Developer Program, you

   a) have access to app services depending on platform and membership level;

   b) have access to tools like your developer account and iTunes Connect, through which you can manage your teams and your apps; and

   c) Have the right to distribute apps through the App Store, the Mac App Store, and the Apple TV Store.

4. Download and install Xcode.

Adding Your Apple ID to Xcode

As you may remember from the previous chapter, Xcode is a complete software package for designing, building, testing, and publishing apps on the Apple system. If you have wireframed your app design using a different software tool, your design will have to be transferred to Xcode. One great feature of Xcode is that you can start your project from scratch with Xcode, do your layouts, wireframes, and storyboards directly within it, and translate them into code as you assemble your app.

To download Xcode, press the Download button at the top-right corner of the Xcode page on the Apple Developer website (https://developer.apple.com/xcode/). The latest version as of April 2017 is Xcode 8.3.2.

Follow the instructions. Once you have Xcode running, add your Apple ID to it so that you can start building apps as a registered Apple developer. You can add your ID to Xcode by pressing the + button at the bottom right of the Accounts interface in Xcode, choosing "Add Apple ID," and signing in to iCloud with your Apple ID. Follow the steps in Figure 7-3 to add your Apple ID to Xcode.

(1)   Launch Xcode.

(2)   Choose "Preferences."

(3)   Click "Accounts."

(4)   Click "+" button at bottom right corner.

(5)   Click "Add Apple ID" in pop-up menu.

(6)   Enter Apple ID and password in pop-up dialog.

(7)   Click "Sign In" button.

Figure 7-3. Adding your Apple ID to Xcode

Build an App Development Team

As a developer, you may be part of more than one team, either as a leader or a member, with different roles and levels of access. You can view your teams under your Apple ID information.

As the creator of a team, you are known as the **team agent**. You can invite new members to your team and assign different roles to them. You can also make one member the **team admin**, a role that shares the same privileges as the team agent except the right to sign legal documents.

Each of your team members, including yourself, has an **Apple ID**, the **certificates** issued to them by Apple depending on their role and privileges, their **signing identity**, which they use to sign apps, and their iTunes Connect account, if they are given one by the team agent. Certificates allow Apple to know who signed an app that was submitted for review or released, and the best way to get the certificates is to request one directly through Xcode.

Identifiers

With any app that you build, each team member will have an individual ID and certificates that allow them to sign the code for an app and develop, submit, and distribute apps depending on their level of access. Every device connected to Xcode for app testing will also have a separate ID.

Signing identities are unique IDs that are used by developers to **code-sign** apps, which is a security-related step that certifies who created the code for an app and confirms that the code has not been modified since the developer code-signed it.

Apple describes **provisioning** as "the process of preparing and configuring an app to launch on devices and to use app services." This involves choosing the devices on which your app will run and the services it will use. You will download a **development provisioning profile** for the app from your account and embed it in the app bundle.

A **team provisioning profile** in the Apple system "allows all your apps to be signed and run by all team members on all your team's devices." To create a team provisioning profile, you need to connect the devices that you want to use for testing the app and then choose the members of your team. After the team provisioning profile is created, you need to export all your signing identities and provisioning profiles to a single file that can be moved if you want to continue developing on another computer.

Design and Develop Apps

Now you can start building your app by choosing File ➤ New ➤ Project, or by clicking on "Create a new Xcode project" in the Welcome to Xcode window. When you do, you will be asked to choose what type of app you want to create. There are a number of templates available for you to choose from: a Master-Detail Application, a Game Application, a Page-Based Application, a Single View Application, a Tabbed Application, a Utility Application, or an Empty Application.

These templates have pre-designed features to help you set up and structure your app quickly, and you or your developer will choose the appropriate template for your app.

After choosing the template, you will be asked to fill in some basic information, which we looked at earlier. You will also be asked whether you want to use storyboards (you should), whether you want to use automatic reference counting (you should), and whether you want to include unit tests (also recommended).

Apple then creates the needed **signing identities** and **provisioning profiles** for the app. Xcode also creates an **App ID** for your app, which can be **explicit** for a single app or a **wildcard** for multiple apps.

You will also be asked to identify yourself or your organization, the programming language you want to use to build the app, and the devices for which the app is intended. You will then choose where you want to save your project. You can then create a team and develop apps.

The Xcode IDE

When building an app, a developer needs access to three things: the code, the overall layout of the app that shows the screen layout and the connections between screens, and the final result on a set device. The Xcode IDE combines these views into one main interface: the code editor, the interface builder, and the simulator.

The Code Editor

As its name suggests, the Code Editor window in Xcode is where developers write and edit the code for iOS apps. What is present in the coding pane is reflected in the associated screen in the Interface Builder, and any modification of, addition to, or removal from the code is immediately reflected on the associated screen.

The Interface Builder

The Interface Builder allows developers to design the screens for an app using visual resources without writing the code. Xcode automatically translates any layout into its corresponding code in Swift, which can be edited in the coding pane, also known as the Assistant Editor.

The iOS Simulator

At any point in the development process, Xcode allows developers to see how an app will look and work on actual devices using an iOS simulator. The simulator can be activated by pressing the Play button at the top-left corner of the Xcode interface.

Frameworks

Frameworks are shared resources that developers can access through Xcode so that different teams working on different products don't have to reinvent the wheel every time and can save a great deal of time by accessing resources and solutions for basic tasks and functions. Frameworks are used to code apps to perform tasks like displaying user interfaces, playing media, saving passwords, and other standard functions that are common to the vast majority of apps.

Storyboards

A storyboard in Xcode displays all the screens of an app together in different ways. Xcode has storyboard controllers for Table View Controller, Collection View Controller, Navigation Controller, Tab Bar Controller, Page View Controller, and GLKit View Controller. These storyboards organize the screens of an app in different ways, depending on how they want to view the screens and the connections and transitions between them (Figure 7-4). Developers also have the option to build their own storyboards.

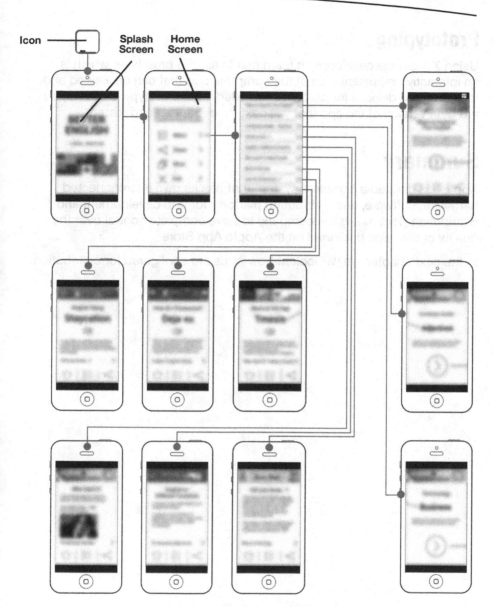

App storyboards and wireframes depict the layouts
of an app's screens and the connections between them
(This one is drawn with graphic design software).

Figure 7-4. A sample app storyboard

Prototyping

Using Xcode, the development team builds an app prototype, which is an interactive representation of the complete app that can be viewed and tested on the devices for which it's intended. This prototype is essentially the beta version of the app that will next be debugged and tested.

Summary

Apple has created a complete system that has its own interconnected hardware, software, and distribution platform for app development and distribution. This allows the company to have complete control over the quality of the apps published on the Apple App Store.

In the next chapter, we will look at how apps are configured for distribution.

Chapter **8**

Configuring Your App

Configuring an app for distribution involves defining important settings related to the frameworks and services your app will use and the capabilities it will have as a result, as well as submitting key identity information about your app to iTunes Connect through Xcode.

In this chapter, we will look in detail at app frameworks, which are shared resources common to most apps; app services, which allow an app to perform specific functions using those resources; and capabilities, which define what an app can do for its users by combining its frameworks and services.

© Hagop Panosian 2017
H. Panosian, *Learn iOS Application Distribution*, DOI 10.1007/978-1-4842-2683-4_8

Configuring a Project

Before choosing the frameworks and services that will support your app, the app's identity and basic information need to be created in iTunes. The following sections lay out the sequence of steps required to create your app's identity.

Create a Bundle ID

In the Identity section of the General category of your app project, you will enter a bundle identifier. A bundle identifier, or bundle ID, is a unique name for an app. It can contain alphanumeric characters (A–Z, a–z, 0–9), hyphens (-), and periods (.), and is written in reverse DNS order (e.g., "com. Company.ProductName"). A bundle ID is used at different times during the development process in Xcode, as well as during distribution by iTunes Connect, iCloud, and Apple services, to identify the app when necessary. You will also be asked to submit the version number of the app and the build.

Identify Your Team

After you identify the team responsible for developing the app, Xcode will create a team provisioning profile to allow all team members to code-sign and run the app. It will also create either an explicit app ID matching the bundle ID or a wildcard app ID for multiple apps, and will then enable app services. Here, you can also enter the version and build numbers of the app.

Input Product Information

You will be asked to input product information, including the product name, the organization name, the organization identifier, the language of the app, and the devices for which it's intended.

Input Deployment Info

In this section, the developer inputs the following information: the deployment target, which is the lowest version of iOS that the app will run on; the target devices for which the app is intended (iPhone, iPad, Universal); the desired device orientations (portrait, upside-down, landscape right, landscape left); and the style of the status bar (light, dark or translucent, and either fixed or hidden).

Submit Visuals

The visuals that must be uploaded as assets into the app bundle include the app icon and a launch-screen file, or splash screen. All visuals that are referenced by iOS are stored in the app build, and visuals that are used by iTunes or the Apple App Store are stored in iTunes Connect. Xcode will store groups of images, such as the app icon in various sizes or resolutions, in an asset catalog.

Set Architecture, Base SDK, and Debug Information

In this section, the developer defines the iOS device architectures for which the app is intended, including armv7 and arm64. The Base SDK setting is the base software level for the app, which is recommended to be the highest possible— namely, the "Latest iOS" setting—so that Xcode can implement debugging on the device on which the app is being debugged. Finally, the appropriate settings that will allow the symbolication (the backtracing of an event to the source code) of crash reporting are chosen.

App Record

The app record contains all the information about an app that must be submitted to Apple before the app can be uploaded onto iTunes Connect for distribution. An app record contains the information that will be published on the app's App Store page and the information that is necessary for managing the app while it is in distribution.

Only a team agent or a team member with Admin, Technical, or App Manager status are authorized to upload apps into iTunes Connect.

App Information

When you create a new app under the My Apps section in iTunes Connect, you will be asked to fill in the relevant fields with identity information that was created in Xcode, like the bundle ID, the app name, and the default language. This information is displayed in the App Information window of the App Store section.

Configurable fields also include restrictions on user access, settings for storing data in iCloud Display Sets, localization information, like additional supported languages, and Pricing and Availability settings, which identify the territories in which the app will be made available and whether the app will be sold with no discount or at a volume discount, or be released privately.

App Frameworks

As we saw in the previous chapter, frameworks are shared resources that developers can access through Xcode to save time and effort when coding. These frameworks implement standard functions that are common to the vast majority of apps. Each framework can be added to an app to allow that app's users to benefit from the framework's capabilities. Adding frameworks to an app is done in the coding phase via code. The following sections discuss the app frameworks relevant to iOS devices.

3D Touch

3D Touch allows an app to react to a user's behavior beyond just recognizing when the user presses the display; it implements different actions depending on how strongly the user is pressing the display. This 3D Touch responsiveness allows users to complete tasks faster, preview content before accessing it, and generally do more with their apps.

App Extensions

As its name suggests, App Extensions allows an app to extend its functions and content throughout the operating system of the device that hosts it instead of simply being an icon-activated separate entity. App extensions, for example, can enable an app to share content on social networks, apply effects to photos from a device's camera, post updates, and provide custom keyboards.

Bonjour

Bonjour is a framework that enables apps to automatically find and connect to devices and services on local networks without any configuration requirements.

CarPlay

CarPlay connects the user's devices to a vehicle's own built-in display, thus making an iPhone's functions, such as playing music, using maps, using messaging, and making calls, available inside the vehicle.

Handoff

Handoff is a framework that enables continuity for a function or activity across different devices, allowing a user to begin an activity on an iOS device, for example, and continue it on a macOS device like a Macbook. It allows users who own multiple devices to use them together to carry out an activity.

Notifications

The Notifications framework enables the delivery of local and push notifications to users on iOS devices. Local notifications alert a user to a change related to an app while that app is in the background, and sometimes they solicit a response. Local notifications include alert dialogs, badges, banner messages, and lock screens. They can also be interactive, presenting the user with a number of options for actions related to the app that can be implemented without fully activating the app. Local notifications are scheduled by the app itself and target the specific user who has downloaded that app. For example, a calendar reminder that pops up on a user's screen is an example of a local notification.

Push notifications or remote notifications, on the other hand, are not scheduled by apps, but are sent by a server to many user devices. Push notifications are created by app publishers to communicate with all or some of the users of their app at the same time. A publisher who wants to use push notifications needs to register for the Apple Push Notifications (APN) service and generate a related certificate.

App Services

Apple provides app developers with a number of services, which are built around frameworks, to enhance their app's capabilities and enable functions that individual apps cannot fully implement on their own, such as payments.

An app's services and capabilities are enabled and configured in the Capabilities window of the project editor in Xcode.

Apple Pay

Apple Pay enables app users to make easy and safe payments and donations from inside the apps they use.

CallKit

CallKit enables apps to make and receive telephone calls using a phone's native user interface.

CareKit, HealthKit, ResearchKit

CareKit is oriented toward health-related apps and enables apps that use it to gather information about a user's health. It then allows that user to access that information and share it with their doctors. Apps that use HealthKit are also able to monitor a user's health and activity metrics and generate health-related information as part of the app's functions. ResearchKit is designed to give data-gathering capabilities to apps designed for medical research; it works with HealthKit to support sophisticated health-related apps.

HomeKit

HomeKit enables apps to connect with and control devices in a user's home, including lights, doors, windows, blinds, cameras, and doorbells.

iBeacon

iBeacon is designed to support apps that use location-based information. These apps connect to devices, or beacons, with iBeacon technology enabled in order to communicate location-related information to the app's users.

iCloud and CloudKit

CloudKit enables apps to access Apple's cloud-based data-storage service, iCloud, and includes authentication, a public database, a private database, and asset storage services.

iMessage

iMessage enables apps to reach users while they are chatting and interact with them without forcing them to end their conversations. iMessage apps allow users to do things like make payments and share content without having to exit Messages.

MapKit

The MapKit framework enables apps to display interactive maps and location information.

SiriKit

SiriKit enables apps to work with Siri, Apple's voice-activated virtual assistant.

StoreKit

StoreKit enables apps to offer in-app purchases of all kinds to app users, including content, products, virtual goods, and subscriptions.

Wallet and PassKit

Wallet and PassKit allow app users to manage and use rewards cards, tickets, boarding passes, and gift cards.

Capabilities

The combination of frameworks and services used by your app defines its capabilities, or what your app can do. As a security measure, Apple allows developers to specify and enable only those services and capabilities that an app needs so as to minimize the likelihood of unauthorized malicious access to and manipulation of apps and their data.

Once developers choose the frameworks and services they want to use, Xcode uses the code-signing and provisioning assets of the development team to grant entitlements to the relevant app based on the app ID. The capabilities associated with each app are switched off by default and can be switched on if they are to be used by your app. The supported capabilities for iOS are App Groups, Apple Pay, Associated Domains, Background Modes, Data Protection, Game Center, HealthKit, HomeKit, CloudKit, iCloud Documents, iCloud: Key-Value Storage, In-App Purchase, Interapp Audio, Keychain Sharing, Personal VPN, Push Notifications, Wallet, and Wireless Accessory Configuration. Let's look at each of these a bit more closely.

App Groups allows apps that are grouped together to share data. Apple Pay was looked at earlier. Associated Domains allows the app to connect to a website (mainly used for deep linking). Enabling Background Modes allows the app to perform very specific tasks in the background if you specify those tasks, including playing media, updating the app's location, handling VoIP calls, downloading content from Newsstand, keeping content up to date with Background Fetch, and communicating with external accessories. Data Protection enables the app to encrypt the data it stores as an extra layer of protection against unauthorized access. Game Center is the social gaming network created by Apple to help players track scores, invite others to join, and play multi-player games.

HealthKit, HomeKit, and CloudKit were looked at earlier. iCloud Documents and iCloud: Key-Value Storage are part of the iCloud entitlements and allow your app to store documents and key values in the cloud. As its name suggests, enabling In-App Purchases allows the publisher to sell features, digital content, and products from inside the app. Interapp Audio allows audio produced by one app to be used by other apps. Keychain Sharing allows an app to share passwords, credit card numbers, and other bits of information with other apps. Personal VPN (Virtual Private Network) allows an app to provide a VPN service on the device on which it's installed. Push Notifications allows apps to send push notifications containing information about updates or new content to the owner of the device. Wallet was looked at earlier. Finally, Wireless Accessory Configuration allows an app to communicate with accessories.

Additional Configurations

If your app is using Apple services, additional configurations may be required, such as for In-App Purchases, which need to be created; defined in terms of type, characteristics, visuals, price, and availability; and submitted to Apple for review before they can be made available to your app's users. This is likely to be an ongoing process throughout your app's lifecycle and is tied to your marketing, growth, and retention strategies.

Game Center is another service that may require additional configuration information. If your app is a game, you will need to connect it to the Game Center so that your players can submit scores, see the leaderboards, and exchange game information.

App Thinning, App Slicing, and On-Demand Resources

Depending on the device they are using, customers who download your app may not be able to use all of your app's features and capabilities. The App Store and iOS download only those features that the device doing the downloading can use, thus reducing the app's footprint and optimizing the user experience. This is known as app thinning.

The App Store will also create variants of your app depending on the device groups your app supports. For example, it will use the target devices you identified in Xcode and the asset catalog you built to create a variant for iPads using images with the appropriate sizes and resolutions for iPads, leaving out resources intended for iPhones. This is known as app slicing.

Finally, to further optimize the user experience through small app sizes and fast downloads, apps can be designed to download resources only when they anticipate the user will access them, such as additional levels for a game or other types of content that do not need to be available until the user requests it. This is known as on-demand resources.

Summary

Configuring your app is about capabilities and efficiency—defining what your app will be able to do, making sure it functions as efficiently as possible, and ensuring access to the services it will need and excluding those it will not. A well-configured app is a sure sign of a professional approach to app development.

Chapter 9

Testing Your App

As part of its complete app development and distribution system, Apple allows publishers to te   before submitting them for review. Although testing is not a requirement for submission, it's always a good idea to test an app thoroughly before submission or release.

Why is it wise to thoroughly test an app? No matter how good the development team is, there's always a possibility that there will be one or more design or programming flaws somewhere in the app. It's essential that finding those flaws and fixing or removing them is done before Apple reviews the app or your users get their hands on it.

© Hagop Panosian 2017
H. Panosian, *Learn iOS Application Distribution*, DOI 10.1007/978-1-4842-2683-4_9

After you submit an app for review, it will be thoroughly checked out by Apple anyway, and if flaws are discovered, the app will be rejected. You will have to go back and fix the flaws before resubmitting the app, with all the disappointment and loss of precious time and resources this would entail.

If your app passes review but flaws remain (which is unlikely, especially for major flaws), they will inevitably be discovered by frustrated and angry users, who will then punish you with bad reviews and bad publicity. After having put so much effort into creating a positive and engaging user experience in your app, why would you risk destroying everything by ignoring the opportunity to perfect your app before you release it?

In short, testing is too important to ignore. Testing an app on TestFlight involves the following stages:

1. Upload a test build onto iTunes Connect.

2. Create iTunes Record for beta testing.

3. Submit the app for beta review.

4. Create a testing team, invite testers.

5. Testers use test app and offer feedback.

6. Gather the feedback to fix and improve your app.

7. Develop final build for release.

8. Submit final build for review before release.

Uploading the Test Build

The first step in the testing phase is to upload a beta version, or test build, of the app onto iTunes Connect. This can be done directly from Xcode or through the Application Loader tool, which can be accessed via the Open Developer Tool button inside Xcode.

Uploading an app build through the Application Loader tool is relevant if your app contains in-app purchases, as it allows the developer to create and configure in detail all the app's available in-app purchases, including their display names, descriptions, prices, and start and end dates between which they will be available.

Once the test build is uploaded, it can be seen in the Activity section of the developer's iTunes Connect account.

Creating an iTunes Record for Beta Testing

Like all apps, this app will require an iTunes Record, but the metadata required for app builds intended for beta testing is much less than that needed for final builds, and the process is therefore simpler and quicker. However, if external testers are involved in the testing process, the iTunes Record will have to include the following: information about what to test, the description of the app, an e-mail address for feedback, URLs for marketing, support, and the app's privacy policy, and the developer's contact information.

Submitting an App for Beta App Review

If an app is to be made available for testing by external testers, the beta version will have to undergo a Beta App Review. To pass that review, it will have to comply with the App Store Review Guidelines, just like a final version. So, even as a beta version, an app must be in very good shape in terms of design and programming before it enters the testing phase.

Creating a Testing Team

The next step is to invite internal and external testers to test the beta version.

To invite an internal tester to your testing team, just insert their e-mail address in TestFlight. For external testers, an e-mail and a full name suffice. These testers then receive an e-mail inviting them to join the testing team and download TestFlight, the iOS app they will use to test your app and submit their responses. Up to 2,000 external testers can be invited to create a testing team, and, unlike internal testers, they don't need to have an Apple ID to participate.

TestFlight Beta Testing

iOS apps are tested using Apple's TestFlight beta-testing utility. TestFlight allows app publishers to test up to 100 iOS, watchOS, and tvOS apps at the same time among up to 25 internal and up to 10,000 testers. Internal and external testers are allowed to test up to 100 apps at any time, for over 90 days per test app.

Internal testers can join a testing team if they have Developer or Admin status, and each can test up to 30 apps at any one time, while external testers who are not part of the development team can be invited to join the testing process through just an e-mail invitation.

Using the TestFlight App to Test a Beta App

Before testing a beta version of an app, each member of the testing team, internal or external, must download the free TestFlight app for iOS from the App Store for each of the devices on which they want to test the beta app. When a tester receives and accepts an invitation to test an app, they can download the beta version onto their devices.

The TestFlight app allows testers to work on a number of apps at the same time. For each app, TestFlight displays the app description and the "What to Test" guidance provided by the publisher.

Testers are expected to provide feedback to the developer about their user experience and any flaws they may have discovered. This is done by pressing the Provide Feedback button on the App Details view, which opens an e-mail window for that purpose. Testers can also use the App Details view in TestFlight to unsubscribe as a tester and opt out from a testing group.

Using Feedback to Develop the Final Build

Feedback from your team of testers will be used to identify the flaws and bugs in your app and to inform the design and coding of the app's final build.

Feedback from testers is sent in e-mail form to the address specified in the Feedback E-mail field of the relevant test information.

Developers use feedback from testers to improve the app, fix bugs and flaws, and upload new builds. They invite testers to test these new versions until the final build is ready to be submitted for review.

Summary

Testing is an important phase in the development process that should be given the attention it deserves. Bugs, errors, and crashes will have a disastrous effect on app adoption and user retention after release, so the testing phase is the time to eliminate them.

The final step, of course, is to submit the final build of the app for review. We'll look at the submission process in the next chapter.

Chapter **10**

Submitting Your App

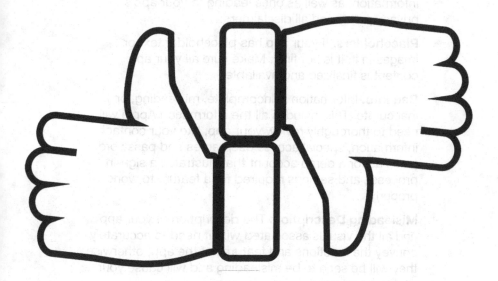

Once your app is ready for release, it needs to be approved by Apple before it can hit the App Store, and to get Apple's approval, it needs to pass an app review. Before you submit, it pays to know that Apple is very strict about approving apps for release; the review process takes at least two weeks. Apple will go through your app thoroughly and can reject an app for a number of reasons. A rejection is a very painful and costly experience in terms of both money and the time wasted trying to find the flaw that sunk your release—not to mention the impact on your team's morale. In short, an app should work perfectly and meet all of Apple's requirements when you submit it, so test it thoroughly and make sure it does before you click the Submit for Review button.

© Hagop Panosian 2017

H. Panosian, *Learn iOS Application Distribution*, DOI 10.1007/978-1-4842-2683-4_10

Avoiding App Rejection

The most common reasons for app rejection, according to Apple, are the following:

- **Crashes.** Your app keeps crashing and has bugs (no surprise there). If your app has a tendency to crash, it will never be made available to users. An app needs to be tested and tested until all bugs are fixed before submission.

- **Dead Links.** You have links that lead nowhere. Ensure continuity for all links inside the app, and make sure there are links to user support with accurate contact information, as well as ones leading to your app's privacy policy and all disclaimers.

- **Placeholders.** If your app has placeholder text or images in it, it is not final. Make sure all your app content is finalized and available.

- **Bad Info.** Information is incomplete, misleading, or inaccurate. This includes all the information Apple will need to thoroughly review your app, like your contact information, special access usernames and passwords (such as for a demo account that illustrates a sign-in process), and settings required for a feature to work properly.

- **Misleading Description.** The description of your app and all the visuals associated with it need to accurately convey the functions and features of the app; otherwise, they will be seen to be misleading and will cause your app to be rejected.

- **Design Issues.** Apple provides design standards and guidelines to developers and designers to make sure all apps on the App Store have consistently good user interface designs. You must follow these guidelines to be approved.

- **Unformatted Web Content.** When an app accesses web content that is not formatted for iOS, this undermines the quality of the user experience.

- **Similar Apps.** Apps that are very similar to each other and could easily be combined into a single app are likely to be rejected.

- **Lack of Ad Functionality.** Your app will need an Advertising Identifier (IDFA) to display ads. If you submit an IDFA, but your app lacks the proper functionality to display ads as it should, it will be rejected.

- **Lack of Lasting Value.** Apple will reject an app that does not offer much use value for its users compared to similar apps in its category.

App Submission Checklist

Before you submit your app for review, go through the following checklist and make sure you answer all the questions in the affirmative.

- **Testing.** Has the app been tested thoroughly enough to eliminate all crashes and bugs?

- **Accuracy.** Is all information in the app up-to-date and accurate, including your contact information?

- **Backend Server.** Are backend services ready and available for access during the review process?

- **Support Information.** Does the submission include all support information for available features?

- **Conformity.** Does the app abide by all of Apple's design and technical guidelines?

- **Configurations.** Have you set up all the configurations the app needs?

- **App Size.** Does the size of the app fall within Apple's set limits?

- **App Record.** Have you verified all app properties for the Game Center (if your app is a game) and iCloud Display sets (which allow multiple apps to access the same data files) and completed the app record, with categories, keywords, the bundle ID, and the App Store version number filled in? These properties cannot be changed after the app is submitted for review.

- **App Sandbox.** Have you configured your app for App Sandbox? App Sandbox provides access control for app security purposes. It restricts an app's access to only the data and system resources and services that it needs in order to function properly. It does not provide foolproof security, but it does limit damage significantly in case of compromise. See Figure 10-1.

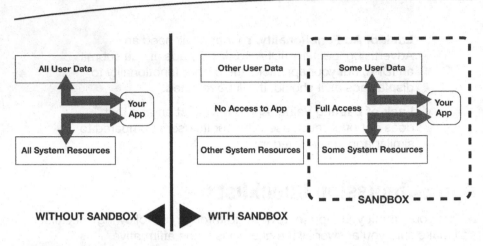

Figure 10-1. The App Sandbox

- ■ **Services.** Have you configured the services your app will use? Make sure all the services your app will use from the list of Apple App Services are configured and are functioning properly: Apple Pay, CallKit, CareKit, CloudKit JS, HealthKit, HomeKit, iBeacon, iCloud and CloudKit, iMessage, In-App Purchase, Maps and Location, ResearchKit, SiriKit, Wallet, and PassKit.

Submit Now!

When you are ready to submit your app, go through the following process:

1. **Specify the App's Build.** An app can have any number of builds uploaded onto the App Store, but only one can be associated with the app at any time, and that will be the build you will submit for review. So, you have to upload the build and choose it from among the available builds for your app. This is known as the current build.

2. **Meet Export Compliance Regulations and Specify Encryption Features.** Your app will be hosted on Apple servers located in the United States, which means it will be subject to U.S. export legislation. iTunes Connect asks app publishers questions regarding the level of encryption your app will require, and where relevant it asks publishers to submit related documents.

If you are not using encryption, you can submit export compliance and encryption-related information while developing your app so that you won't have to go through this process at submission time. You can submit the related documentation through Xcode, have it approved, and receive a key that you can submit with your build.

3. **Confirm Permission to Use Third-Party Content.** If your app will be hosting content from third parties, you will have to confirm that you have the right to use that content wherever the app will available for download.

4. **Confirm Use of Advertising Identifier.** An Advertising Identifier is a unique ID created for each iOS device and is used for two purposes: displaying advertisements inside your app and for the attribution of installation and actions inside the app to that device.

5. **Specify Timing of Release.** If for any reason as a publisher you don't want to release an app automatically as soon as it's approved and prefer to wait for a specific time, you can specify a "no earlier than" date for release after approval. You can also opt to manually release the app whenever it suits you (for example, at a specific moment coordinated with your marketing campaign).

6. **Click Submit for Review** (under App Store on the App Details page of your app, at the top right of the page). The app status will change to "Waiting for Review."

7. **Follow the Status of Your Review.** The status of your app version is grouped into three broad categories, defined by the color of the associated status indicator: red, yellow, or green.

   A red status indicator means either the app has been rejected for a specific reason or the publisher needs to change something before the app can be approved for the App Store. The following statuses are indicated in red: Rejected (app has been rejected for failing to meet acceptance criteria, Metadata Rejected, Removed from Sale, Invalid Binary, Developer Rejected (developer removed build from review), Developer Removed from Sale (developer removed app from review).

A yellow status indicator means the app is in the middle of an ongoing process that is being implemented by Apple or the app publisher. The following statuses are indicated in yellow: Prepare for Submission, Waiting for Review, In Review, Pending Contract, Waiting for Export Compliance, Pending Developer Release, Processing for the App Store, and Pending Apple Release.

A green status indicator means your app has been fully approved and is available for distribution.

8. **Wait.** If your app is rejected, you as the publisher will be notified of the reason for the rejection. Apple has a Resolution Center you can contact for more information and additional guidance.

In the next chapter, we will look at how to monitor your app's progress and gather data about how users are interacting with your app.

Summary

App submission requires diligence and patience. Get everything right before you submit, and passing app reviews will be a breeze. Then, you can focus on post-publishing activities like monitoring your app's progress and gathering data about how users are interacting with your app, which we will look at in the next chapter.

Chapter 11

Distributing Your App

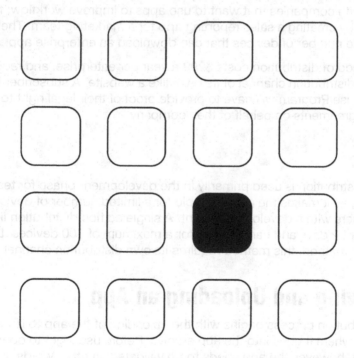

App Distribution Methods

App distribution is the process of making an app available for download.
There are three distribution methods available to publishers of iOS apps:
App Store, Enterprise, and Ad Hoc.

© Hagop Panosian 2017
H. Panosian, *Learn iOS Application Distribution*, DOI 10.1007/978-1-4842-2683-4_11

App Store

This method involves posting your app on the App Store and making it available to anyone for download onto their devices. This is the most popular method among the vast majority of app publishers. It is the appropriate method if you are developing for profit, like most publishers are. The App Store has a marketing and financial transaction system in place to facilitate the process of marketing and selling your apps.

Enterprise

As its name suggests, enterprise app distribution is the process whereby a company distributes apps internally to its employees. This method is popular with companies that want to use apps to improve workflow; for example, by creating a sales reporting app for a marketing team. There is no limit on the number of devices that can download an enterprise app.

This method of distribution costs $299 a year per enterprise, and requires a special distribution channel of its own, like a website. A subscriber to the Enteprise Program will have to provide proof of their legal right to sign binding agreements on behalf of their company.

Ad Hoc

Ad hoc distribution is used primarily in the development phase for testing purposes, as it makes the app available for a limited number of devices and only to users with a developer account. A single ad hoc distribution license is valid for 90 days and can be used for a maximum of 100 devices. Like the enterprise method, this method requires its own distribution channel.

Archiving and Uploading an App

The distribution process begins with the uploading of the app to iTunes Connect, where it goes into the app archive. Before users get to download and use it, however, the app needs to be validated; in other words, it needs to be checked to see whether it's properly configured for distribution on the App Store. Let's look at this process in more detail.

Creating an Archive

Before you upload an app to iTunes Connect, you need to create an archive where it will be stored and validated before being made available in the App Store. This is true irrespective of the distribution method you choose. To do this, the archive scheme settings must first be checked in the Product ➤

Scheme ➤ Edit Scheme pane in the project editor in Xcode. These settings vary depending on the nature of the app. Then, choose Product ➤ Archive to create an archive for your project.

Validating Your App on iTunes Connect

Validating a project on iTunes Connect involves making sure the app is properly configured for the App Store. Validation tests are implemented when an app is uploaded onto iTunes Connect, and afterward as well.

To validate an archive, choose it from the archives listed in the Archives organizer in Xcode and press the Validate button on the right-side pane. A pop-up window appears that displays the app's binary, entitlements, and provisioning profile. Press the Validate button at the bottom right of the pop-up window. Xcode uploads the archive to iTunes Connect to run validation tests.

Uploading Your App to the App Store

When your archive has passed the validation tests, you can upload the archive by pressing the Upload to App Store button on the right-side pane in the Xcode window. In the pop-up window that appears, check the "Include app symbols for your application" option so that your app will be able to send you crash reports. If you want to be able to update your app in the App Store without having to submit new versions for review every time, check the "Include bitcode" option.

When you press the Upload button at the bottom right of the pop-up window, Xcode will upload the archive onto iTunes Connect and run validation tests again.

Your App's Product Page

Your app's product page in the App Store is the first real contact point between the app and its users, and all your marketing channels will probably drive potential users to it. It's therefore very important that the page is well designed so as to maximize your app's discoverability in search, as well as its appeal to visitors.

This is where visitors get all the information they need in order to decide whether to download your app, and they will make that decision in a matter of seconds. It's your job as a publisher to make sure that visitors are not put off by bad design, incorrect spelling, or other errors. You want them to hang on beyond those first few seconds and decide to give your app a try.

Your app's product page in the App Store will display all the key visual and textual information that will interest visitors. It's your first thorough marketing "pitch," one aimed at convincing visitors to download the app. On the App Store page, visitors will see your app's name, icon, price, age rating, review rating, preview video and poster frame (the still from the video that appears in search results), screenshots, description, and information about what's new, as well as the name of the publishing company or individual, the app category, the date of the last update, the app version, and the app size.

When creating your App Store page, you will also be asked to submit keywords, which are words relevant to your app that help make it discoverable and determine its ranking in App Store searches. Apple imposes a 100-character limit on keywords and reviews them to make sure they do not violate regulations.

More information on keywords can be found in Chapter 12, "Marketing Your App."

Managing Your App and Team

As an app publisher, you will be managing your app and all financial activity attached to it through iTunes Connect. As we have already seen, via iTunes Connect you can validate archives, upload apps and distribute them for testing, market and distribute apps on the App Store, create development teams, and assign roles to each member.

After your app has been released, you will be using iTunes Connect to replace your app with new versions, change your app's App Store metadata based on your marketing strategy, create and sell in-app purchases, and conduct business activity, like signing business contracts, conducting financial transactions, and generating financial information. You will also be managing your team, inviting members, assigning roles to them, and signing contracts.

As your app evolves into a business, the developers will be involved mostly with Xcode, and only the people who are involved in the business aspects of the app will need to access iTunes Connect. Therefore, it's very important to control who in your team has access to what on iTunes Connect. For example, if you have a marketing manager, it's logical that he or she is able to modify the app metadata or access analytics or financial reports.

By assigning privileges and roles to different teams and members, the team agent controls different levels of access to iTunes Connect. Some team members have very specific titles and related privileges. For example, a member with the Admin role is given all privileges except the right to sign contracts. An App Manager is given the privileges associated with just that: managing apps, including creating and updating apps and managing the testing process. A team member who has the Developer role assigned is given privileges related to the technical aspects of app development, like handling app builds and testers.

Managing Your Account

Apple requires all apps to be code-signed, which confirms that all code submitted to Apple was created by a registered developer and does not contain anything malicious. Apple requires that all people and devices using its system, as well as any code created on it, have a unique signature in the form of either an ID or an attached certificate or signature. This requirement has two purposes: security and quality.

When creating apps on the Apple system, you will have to create signing identities, certificates, keychains, identifiers, and profiles either during registration or during the development process. You will also have to attach the devices that will be used for testing by adding the Device IDs of test devices to your account.

Signing Identities

A developer who creates code on the Apple system attaches his signing identity to that code, or code-signs the app, certifying that he or she was the last person to edit that code and that the code has not been modified since then.

A signing identity is a combination of a public key and a private key that is stored on a team member's keychain through the Keychain Services API. Authorized team members code-sign an app using both their signing identity, which is created in Xcode, and an intermediate certificate, which is stored in their account.

Certificates

Certificates qualify team members and define their status within the team. A team includes an agent as well as members who have Admin, Developer, or Member status.

A team member who has Developer status is issued a development certificate by a team member with Agent or Admin status, which allows that developer to deploy to devices any apps they have code-signed. A team member with a distribution certificate has the right to submit apps to the App Store. Distribution certificates are also created by team members who have Agent or Admin status.

An intermediate certificate in a team member's keychain confirms that a certificate issued to that member was issued by a certificate authority.

Keychain

A keychain is the collection of keys and identities that belong to a member of an app development team. These keys define the team member's status, their privileges, and the levels of access they have to different aspects of an app project.

Identifiers

Identifiers are unique number–letter–symbol combinations that, besides identifying you and all your team members, also uniquely identify the apps you create and the devices you use for testing on the Apple system. For example, every app you develop has an app ID attached to it. If that app ID is explicit, it will perfectly match the name of the app bundle. If it is a wildcard ID, it will identify one or more apps.

After creating an app ID, the developer is asked to choose which services should be enabled for that app. The available services include App Groups, Associated Domains, Data Protection, Game Center, HealthKit, HomeKit, Wireless Accessory Configuration, Apple Pay, iCloud, In-App Purchases, Inter-App Audio, Wallet, Push Notifications, and VPN Configuration & Control. These services can be viewed in detail in Chapter 8, "Configure Your App."

Provisioning Profiles

Provisioning profiles are normally created by the developer to identify the members of a team and the devices that are attached to a specific app project or phase in an app's lifecycle. They are of two types: development provisioning profiles and distribution provisioning profiles. Distribution includes ad hoc provisioning profiles and store provisioning profiles.

Development provisioning profiles group team members and devices during the development phase. For the distribution phase, ad hoc provisioning profiles are created by Xcode upon request when an app bundle is uploaded for testing, while store provisioning profiles identify the authorized team members when an app is uploaded to the App Store.

Devices

App publishers can attach devices to their account, primarily for testing purposes. Each device that is registered to an account for testing or other purposes has a unique ID attached to it, known as a Unique Device Identifier, or UDID.

App Performance and Analytics

After your app is released on the App Store, you will focus your efforts on managing and optimizing the app's performance, both technically and financially.

Crash Reports

The first concern for an app publisher is making sure the app doesn't crash—and to fix the code if it does. To do that, you will need to know when, how, and why instances of your app are crashing and on what devices. For that, you will need crash reports.

Crash reports for iOS apps are created by Apple's crash service, which generates crash logs that record all the necessary details about app crashes based on data that app users agree to share with Apple.

Crash reports will tell you the location in your app's code where the crash occurred, as well as the number of devices on which it occurred over a specific period of time. Crash reports are very useful in helping you, as the publisher, identify bugs and problems in your app before release so you can fix them in time and release a reliable, bug-free app to the market.

The crash service will begin generating crash reports no earlier than three days after the release of the app in the App Store. To understand a crash, the developer will need to see the source code associated with it, which can be done by opening the crash log in the project. Clicking the Open in Project button will display in the debug navigator the source code and the specific line of code associated with the crash.

Analytics and Financial Reports

Apple will generate highly detailed analytics for your app regarding both usage and monetization once it's in the App Store. App analytics are available on the iTunes Connect home page for team members who have Admin, Finance, or Sales status.

The app analytics interface on iTunes Connect provides detailed app usage and sales data and allows you to apply filters to that data based on your campaign goals.

In the Sales arena, you can view revenue data for app sales, in-app purchases, sales, and paying users. Regarding Usage, you can see how many instances of your app are installed on devices, how many sessions of your app users have launched, how many active devices your app has been installed on over time, including over the past month, and why and how often your app is crashing. This data can give you insight into app engagement.

App analytics will also generate retention reports. These reports will tell you how the usage of your app is changing over time through detailed visuals.

Financial Reports

iTunes Connect also uses analytics data to generate different types of financial reports that you can download. These reports are grouped under two broad categories: *Sales and Trends* and *Payments and Financial Reports*. In each category, select the fiscal month and the regions for which you want the report, then click Create Reports. A download link will allow you to download the report you have requested.

Summary

Publishing an app to the market is a very exciting but also very sensitive moment in an app's lifecycle, as the smallest misstep can derail the whole process. Diligence helps you avoid heartbreak, and, as this chapter shows, there's much more to successfully publishing an app than just pressing a Publish button somewhere. The period immediately after publishing is important from a performance-monitoring point of view because you're anxious to see how your app is being received and what problems, technical or otherwise, may be holding you back.

Chapter **12**

Marketing Your App

"Marketing without data
is like driving
with your eyes closed."

Dan Zarrella

This chapter is a big milestone on your app's path to success. This is because in all the previous chapters of this book, apps were discussed as ideas, as products in development, or as products awaiting review and approval. As of right now, we will generally be treating apps as fully developed products available for download or purchase.

As you will see, however, marketing actually begins before launch and is very much a part of the app design and planning phase. For the experts, an app's concept is somewhat validated by taking into account how effectively it can be marketed to its audience. The pre-launch marketing phase to build interest is also key to an app's successful launch, but, for the most part, marketing will naturally be a post-launch activity as you create momentum and build your audience. You will be constantly searching for new users, managing your existing users, and bringing back users who have abandoned your app by finding out who they are, what they want from your app, how and where to reach them, and what offer will most entice them.

Marketing Refresher

Once your app is published in the app stores, you have to support and promote it, drive its downloads, and generate revenue. As we saw at the beginning of this book, marketing is everything, and everything is about marketing. Let's look at these two principles again.

Marketing Is Everything

In short, this means that marketing is the factor that will decide how successful your app is. Even a well-designed app built around a good idea will not go far without your help. Skillful marketing is key to helping your app shine in the app stores and to driving downloads.

Everything Is About Marketing

This essentially means that everything related to your app—from the design of the app icon, the App Store page, and your own marketing campaign; the speed at which your app loads; the level structure (for games); the content; the color coding; the sharing capabilities for social media; the services it uses; and the functions it performs—literally every single aspect of your app revolves around making sure your users love it and will help you market it, and in this you've got stiff competition indeed, as Figure 12-1 shows.

Among app users, just

8 %

use more than 10 apps a day.
63% use between 4 and 10.

Among app users,

80%

engange with their apps
15 times a day.

Among app users

70%

spend their app time
on just 2 or 3 apps.

Source: https://www.appboy.com/blog/mobile-customer-99-stats/ (April 2016)

Figure 12-1. App use stats

This is the basis of how you should treat marketing: it's everything, and you will do it all the time and in every way you can. Now that you intend to promote your app every way you can, let us look at all the options that are available—all the marketing channels. The success of your app depends on two things: how good the app really is and how well you market it. Again, even a great app won't go very far without marketing, but great marketing can't do much to rescue a badly designed app.

Success in any business depends a lot on good marketing, and nowhere is this truer than in the app business (Figure 12-2). Apps are marketed through online and offline channels, and each channel is used either at a specific moment, like a press release or official launch; at specific intervals, like weekly newsletters mailed to a mailing list; or continuously throughout the lifetime of the app, like AdWords or Facebook ad campaigns.

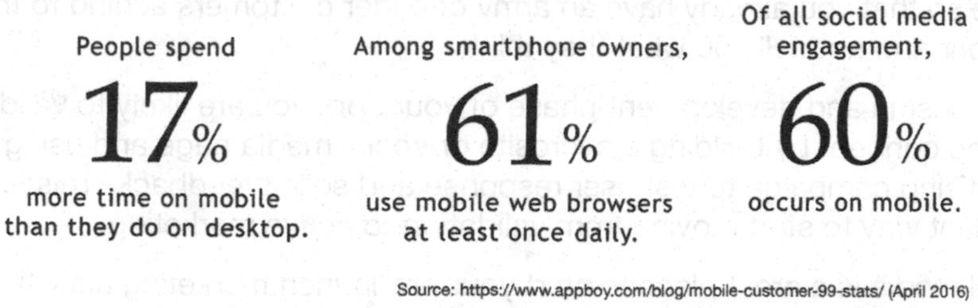

People spend	Among smartphone owners,	Of all social media engagement,
17%	**61**%	**60**%
more time on mobile than they do on desktop.	use mobile web browsers at least once daily.	occurs on mobile.

Source: https://www.appboy.com/blog/mobile-customer-99-stats/ (April 2016)

Figure 12-2. App engagement stats

Effective marketing is a fine art, and the effectiveness of your marketing campaign will be one of the two key factors determining the profitability and commercial success of your app (the other is revenue). App marketing is constantly evolving, with new principles, strategies, and methods appearing all the time, so keeping up is important. Fortunately, there are a number of great app development and marketing companies, like Marketo, Appsee, Buzinga, and Localytics, that constantly produce a wealth of free resources you can use to hone your marketing skills to professional levels. You can find links to these resources at the end of this book.

App Marketing: Key Principles

Now that your app is in the app store, you have to look at how to support it, nurture it, and promote it every way you can. Your app needs more attention now than it ever did.

Marketing Begins Long Before Launch

If you think about marketing as something that begins the moment after you launch your app, think again. If your marketing strategy is not in place and fully operational by launch time, and even before it, you've lost valuable time and opportunity. A marketing campaign takes time to produce its intended results, so if you have to launch an app at zero momentum and wait for that momentum to build up, you've probably lost the game already.

Traction is something an app needs to already have at launch time, not build up after launch. It's your responsibility as the publisher to make sure your app launches with a big bang, lots of media attention, a social media frenzy—everything that is part of your campaign—and gets tons of downloads from day one. How can you do that? By timing the start of your marketing campaign with specific moments in the design and development phase so that you already have an army of eager customers aching to try out your app and tell you what they think.

In the design and development phase of your app, you are likely to validate the app concept by building a microsite or social media page and using an advertising campaign to test user response and solicit feedback. This is an excellent way to start moving from validation to active marketing.

Social media is a great place to start your pre-launch marketing activities. Create a social media identity for your app. Tell people how the app is progressing, and allow people to share their views and offer feedback. Create short surveys asking people what features they would like to see on an app like yours. Ask those who are interested to test the beta version. Create a blog or video log to allow people to follow the app's progress. If your pre-launch marketing has been effective, by the time your app nears launch, you will have an army of Facebook friends or Twitter followers who will give you the precious momentum you need to make your app a success.

Every App Has Self-Marketing Mechanisms

Your app has internal marketing mechanisms that you can exploit to maximize its virality and drive downloads. One is giving users the opportunity to share their experience of your app with their friends on social media. This is an excellent marketing channel that should not be wasted, especially as it's free. Free marketing will go a long way toward reducing your Customer Acquisition Cost (CAC), a very important metric that affects your app's financial sustainability.

Another internal marketing mechanism is cross-promotion, which involves using push notifications and interstitial ads in one app to promote another app. This applies to publishers who have more than one app in the market and is a very useful free marketing mechanism that will also reduce your overall marketing costs.

If you are a smart marketer, you won't do all your marketing on your own, but rather will get your users to market your app for you. The best marketing team is an army of happy users raving about your app to their friends on social media, encouraging their friends and colleagues to download it, and giving you five-star reviews. Best of all, they will do all of this for free! In this sense, creating a strong user support system and feedback loop, updating your app regularly based on user feedback, and generally going out of your way to keep users happy are the most important marketing tactics you will ever employ.

Automate and Personalize Your Marketing Campaign

Approach your marketing campaign as a system that functions on four pillars: information, segmentation, personalization, and automation. First, use your app to gather information about your users. Two, use that information to segment your users based on their characteristics (location, language, gender, etc.) or behavior (frequency and duration of app use, etc.). Three, create personalized messages based on these segments. Four, automate the process (how often you target each segment, which channels you use, what content works best, etc.). All of this can have a major impact on conversions and profit, as the statistics from Appboy in Figure 12-3 suggest.

Marketing automation has raised conversions for	User segmentation in ad campaigns produces up to	A 5 percent increase in user retention results in a
77%	**200**%	**25**%
of companies.	higher conversion rates.	increase in profits

Source: https://www.appboy.com/blog/mobile-customer-99-stats/ (April 2016)

Figure 12-3. App conversion stats

Developing a Marketing Strategy

A marketing strategy is something that you will be looking at early on in your project, as early as the idea-validation phase, because the success of your app will depend on growth and revenue, not just on how good your idea is.

A thorough marketing strategy for an app combines a number of key components that can change over time as your app gets adopted by users and the goals of your marketing campaign adjust to user behavior and feedback.

Your marketing campaign will be based on the goals you have set, the budget you have set for your campaign, the user segment you want to target, the channel or channels you will use to reach that user segment, the content of your marketing message, and your offer, or value proposition. Two vital elements of any marketing strategy are attribution and segmentation.

Attribution

Your marketing strategy can only be effective if you are able to measure what you are doing and how your users are responding. Given that there are so many channels through which you can reach potential customers, one of the most basic measurements that needs to be made is finding out which channel is the most cost-effective and which is the most profitable so you know where to focus your efforts and which marketing content is working best. Are Facebook ads or YouTube videos the most effective for you? Are you making more money through ads or affiliate programs? Which e-mail style is getting the best response?

To measure all this, you need attribution. Attribution involves measuring the instances and frequency of specific events (such as when a user downloads an app, launches the app, re-launches the app, views ads in it, clicks on an ad, etc.). By recording these events and "attributing" to them to users or devices, you can derive a great deal of useful information about customer behavior and draw conclusions about which channels are working the best for you.

Segmentation

Segmentation means dividing your target users into different subgroups so that you can tailor your marketing strategy to their needs and interests. Your users will include different age groups, different professions, and a variety of preferred hangouts. Some of your users may be female teenagers who spend a lot of time on Facebook, while others may be male mid-career professionals who spend less time on social media but use e-mail a great deal. You won't get very far by trying to market the same content to them in the same way. Each will respond positively to different marketing content on different channels. The first group is likely to respond well to content marketing and ads on Facebook, while the second group can be reached through e-mail ads. The way the first group will spend its money, and what they will spend it on, will differ from the spending habits of the second group, and you will have to employ different tactics to get them to part with that money. Segmentation helps you do that.

Marketing Strategy Components

A marketing strategy comprises several components (Figure 12-4): the Goal, the Budget, the Segment, the Channel, the Content, and the Offer. Each of these components will differ for the various campaigns you develop designed to target different user groups on different occasions for differing objectives.

1 GOAL

Do you want to drive downloads, find new users, make your existing users more engaged, stop current users from abandoning your app, bring back inactive users, turn non-paying users into paying users, or generate more revenue from paying users?

2 BUDGET

What is your advertising budget, and how will you allocate it to the channels you plan to use? Will you implement a single, short campaign, or a paced campaign spread over several months or longer?

3 SEGMENT

What user segment are you targeting? What are your target users' demographic characteristics, like location, ethnicity, language, age group, and gender? What are your target users' habits and preferences?

4 CHANNEL

How will you reach your target users? Which channel is the most effective? Are they on social media, or will PPC ads work better? Is a single channel, multi-channel, or omni-channel approach the best?

5 CONTENT

What ad content works best for your target users and your chosen channels? What ad formats, color coding, text, CTAs, keywords, and visuals will produce your intended result? Will you A/B test a variety of ad types and content?

6 OFFER

What value proposition will you offer your users, and how is it monetized? Will you make a single offer to everyone, or segment your target users and create a separate offer for each segment?

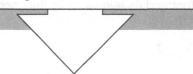

Figure 12-4. The components of an app marketing strategy

Marketing Strategy Component 1: The Goal

What is the driving principle behind your marketing strategy? You are going after both growth and revenue, and in the app world it's tough to get both at the same time, especially early on. So, which will you prioritize?

Experience suggests that the focus at the beginning should be on growth for several reasons.

Adoption

The adoption of your app will increase much faster with a pricing strategy that focuses on growth. In other words, your app is likely to do much better if it is free, because users are used to free apps and have to have a serious reason to pay for one. Users are highly unlikely to pay upfront for a new app, and your adoption rates and downloads will remain very low.

Remember, you will be competing with many other apps, more than 93 percent of which are available for free download, so you are much more likely to maximize download rates with a free version of your app.

Monetization can be part of the app from the beginning—for example, in the form of in-app purchases—but the core functions should be made available for free at the beginning.

Information

When your app is new to the market, no matter how well designed it is, it will be some time before you achieve a strong product-market fit, or, in other words, before you establish a strong relationship between your product and its users. You will need to tweak the app, eliminate its flaws, and release more than one new version or update, possibly with new features you hadn't planned on in the beginning, before you start to build a strong and loyal user base.

To do this, you will need information about your users as well as feedback and reviews from them. For this information and feedback to be useful, you will need a large number of users whose habits and app-use patterns you will track through analytics and whose feedback, opinions, and reviews you will solicit through push notifications. The larger your user base, the more relevant and useful the information you gather will be, and the better the quality of your product and its relevance to the user will be.

Financing

Are you planning to take your app into startup territory with seed funding, venture capital, and so forth? An app with a large user base that has not yet reached positive cash flow is a much better candidate for attracting venture capital than is a monetized app with low revenue and a tiny user base. Market share is more important than revenue in the early stages. When you have market share, revenue is a much easier goal to pursue.

Furthermore, heavy monetization can seriously harm your momentum in the early stages of an app and can keep away your potential user base.

It's true that as an appreneur your goal is likely to be to reach positive cash flow as soon as you can, but focusing on monetization from the outset will not help you do that. Delaying the focus on revenue until you have built a large-enough user base and then targeting users with a well-thought-out monetization strategy at a specific point in time is much more likely to lead to positive cash flow.

At different points in your app's lifecycle, you will be interested in one or more of the following goals: finding more users and driving more downloads, strengthening engagement and retention among your existing users, bringing back users who downloaded your app but have lost interest, turning engaged but non-paying users into paying users, and getting already-paying users to pay more.

You can also see your users as being at different points in the user lifecycle: discovery, engagement, retention, loyalty, and abandonment. You can segment users based on this approach and set marketing goals accordingly. These marketing goals are very different from each other and will therefore require completely different marketing strategies with different marketing content and value propositions.

Marketing Campaign Types

Marketing campaigns differ immensely depending largely on their intended purpose and have names that correspond to that purpose. The most common campaign types are the following:

> **Onboarding** – Onboarding is the process of welcoming a new user or customer who has taken the first step. In the app world, it would be someone who has just launched your app for the first time after downloading it. The purpose of onboarding is to welcome new users and offer guidance on how they can make the most of your app. The effectiveness of onboarding shows in Figure 12-5 below.

Welcome e-mails
to new users have a

60%

open rate, the highest
open rate of all e-mails

Welcome e-mails produce

9

times more transactions
than traditional bulk sends.

Welcome e-mails produce

8

times more revenue
than tranditional bulk sends.

Source: https://www.appboy.com/blog/mobile-customer-99-stats/ (April 2016)

Figure 12-5. E-mail marketing stats

Drip Campaign – A drip campaign is an automated marketing campaign with e-mails sent on a set schedule.

Shopping Cart Abandonment Campaign – Relevant to the online web and e-commerce apps, and targets users or customers who abandon a shopping cart halfway through the purchasing process. The purpose of such a campaign would be to find out why the shopping cart was abandoned and convince shoppers to return. A customer willing to spend money through your app is too precious to lose and should be enticed to return.

Re-subscription Campaign – These campaigns target users or customers who have canceled their subscription to a newsletter or other form of content marketing tool.

Churn Management Campaign – These types of campaigns target users who have abandoned an app and try to bring them back with enticing offers, like an alert about a new version with new features or features that have gone from paid to free.

Product Recommendation Campaign – As its name suggests, this type of campaign promotes products that may appeal to users. You could be promoting products related to your app, including digital products like in-app purchases or paid features, or be promoting someone else's products to your users as part of an affiliate program.

List Growth Campaign – This type of campaign targets new users with the aim of driving downloads and growing an app's user base.

Lead Qualifying Campaign – A lead qualifying campaign is designed to identify those users in your user base who are good prospects for monetization. They are those leads who have a specific need that your app meets and are prepared to pay money to fulfill that need through your app.

Lead Nurturing – Lead nurturing is the process of building a relationship with your user base segments at different stages of the customer journey and helping users move from one stage to the next.

Marketing Strategy Component 2: The Budget

The size of your budget will inevitably determine the reach of your marketing campaign. The secret to marketing budgets is knowing how much to allocate to each of the channels you plan to use and how to make the most of your marketing dollars. It's also important to compare channels to see which is more effective in helping you reach your target segment and goals.

To do that, what you need is a system to measure the ROI of your marketing campaign. You can measure the ROI, or return on investment, of a multi-channel campaign to see how well you did overall, or select a specific channel and measure the ROI to see how productive your marketing campaign is on that particular channel.

Marketing Strategy Component 3: The Segment

Marketing campaigns are much more effective when they target a specific segment than when they are generic in content and try to target everyone with the same message at the same time.

Analytics in your app will generate detailed information about your users and their behavior, which you can use to segment users depending on your goals. There are two fundamental ways to segment users:

Segment by User Characteristics – Separate your users into groups depending on characteristics such as location, age, gender, country of residence, spoken language, and profession.

Segment by Behavior – Divide users into groups based on how they are interacting with your app and where they are on the customer journey: new user, "light" users, deeply engaged users (based on frequency and duration of sessions and session intervals), lapsed users, and users who have abandoned the app. By looking closely at each segment you decide to target, you can determine which channel to use to target that segment and how to approach that segment to get a positive response to your value proposition.

Personalization and Timing

The purpose of segmenting your target market or user group is to create the opportunity to personalize your marketing. Personalization can be based on any aspect of the user's or group's characteristics or behavior. For example, you can use location data to target users based on an event in their town, or target users in a specific country in their language. You can also time marketing messages to maximize the likelihood of a positive response, like targeting busy professionals at off-work hours or weekends, or building up a Christmas-related campaign in late November to early December. See Figure 12-6.

Personalized messaging raises conversion rates by	Customized timing of messages raises conversion rates by	Images in messaging result in a
27%	**38**%	**57**%
compared to generic messaging.	compared to scheduled messaging.	increase in user responses to a CTA (Call-to-Action).

Source: https://www.appboy.com/blog/mobile-customer-99-stats/ (April 2016)

Figure 12-6. Messaging stats

Personalizing your app to your users goes through the following process:

> **Segmentation** – First, segment your users or target market in a relevant way, depending on the purpose of the ad campaign involved and on how much information about users is available.

> **Personalization** – Second, create unique content for each segment. The content of a message—the layout, color coding, call to action—is all designed to appeal to the target segment and to produce useful information about which designs work best. As a further refinement, messages are addressed directly to the user.

> **Timing** – Third, time a messaging campaign to the habits of each specific user to maximize the likelihood of a high open rate and a positive response to your message.

Marketing Strategy Component 4: The Channel

Where are your customers, and what's the best way, the best medium, to reach them with your offer? This is what "channel" means. If you determine that segments consisting of younger users are highly active on social media, then focusing on Facebook, Twitter, Instagram, Pinterest, and other social media sites is the right channel in terms of both content and paid advertising. If your target segment consists of professionals in the 30 to 44 age group, then LinkedIn ads and an e-mail campaign might be the more productive channel combination.

It's important to remember to use every relevant and effective channel to promote and market your app, and to learn the secrets of each channel. There are literally dozens of channels through which you can reach your desired user segment, the most important of which are listed in Figure 12-7. They include digital and non-digital channels, free and paid, traditional and unconventional. All can be highly productive if you match the segment with the right channel or channels.

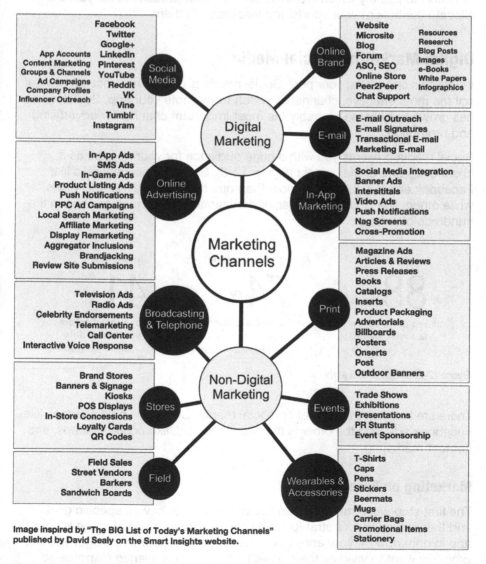

Image inspired by "The BIG List of Today's Marketing Channels" published by David Sealy on the Smart Insights website.

Figure 12-7. App marketing channels

As the following big list of marketing channels shows, it's possible to divide these channels into two broad categories, digital and non-digital, and divide each into further subcategories. For example, digital marketing consists of social media, online branding, online advertising, e-mail, and in-app marketing. Non-digital channels are divided into broadcasting and telephone channels, store-related channels, event-based marketing, print, field marketing, and wearables and accessories. Each channel has its methods, characteristics, and use value in bringing you the customers you want. As you market your app, you will find not all are suitable for you, so make the effort to identify which channels are the most productive for you and allocate the bulk of your efforts and resources to them.

Digital Marketing: Social Media

Ignore this channel at your peril. Social media is one of the most effective, if not *the* most effective, channel by which to promote your app. Social media has grown to become probably the most important channel for advertising and promotion.

Social media presents you with a huge audience for your app, so as a channel it's one of the biggest (Figure 12-8). Social media networks like Facebook and YouTube have more than one billion active monthly users, while others like Google+, Twitter, and Instagram have monthly users in the hundreds of millions.

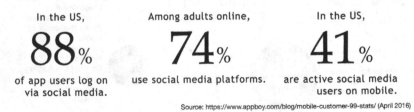

In the US,
88%
of app users log on via social media.

Among adults online,
74%
use social media platforms.

In the US,
41%
are active social media users on mobile.

Source: https://www.appboy.com/blog/mobile-customer-99-stats/ (April 2016)

Figure 12-8. Social media stats

There are two ways to market on social media. One is the paid channel, like Facebook ads, and the other is the "free" channel, like posts, uploads, and content marketing.

Marketing on Facebook

The first step when marketing on social media is to have a specific goal and then organize your strategy and content around it. What stage is your app in right now? If your app is in the concept-development stage, you will probably want to validate the concept and test for audience response to see how people are reacting to your idea and to make projections about downloads. Your goal will be to get people to tell you what they think. If your app is in the development stage, then you will want to build up buzz around the upcoming launch of your app, so your primary goal will be sharing. If you've already published your app, you will be using social media to drive downloads, so your primary goal will be to lead the crowd to your App Store download page.

In each of these pre-launch and post-launch stages, Facebook will provide you with a number of ways to promote your app. One way is via Groups. Create a group for people who are excited about your product, regularly post news about your app as it goes through pre-launch, solicit opinions and feedback from your group members, and encourage the members to share their views with their circle of friends.

Another way to promote your app involves paid options that will help you get more likes and extend your reach, as well as Facebooks Ads, which will advertise the app to a target audience defined by you.

Directives

Once you know what you want from your audience, tell them. Make sure your social media funnel effectively directs visitors to where you want them to go and tells them via the right call to action exactly what you want them to do, such as "Share," "Like this page," or "Download Now."

Marketing on Twitter

The key to effective marketing on Twitter is creating the right kind of short, re-tweetable content and making smart use of relevant hashtags, connecting them to current events to benefit from the public's shifting interest. Following influencers and getting influencers to follow you is another key strategy for raising the exposure of your app across Twitter. Influencers are people whose opinion on their subject of expertise matters; they can give your app a boost simply by tweeting about it to their followers, or by following you and sharing your news with everyone on their list.

Marketing on Instagram

As a photo-sharing social media website and app, Instagram is a great channel for sharing photos related to your app, including screenshots and mockups. Using relevant hashtags—more than one, as opposed to Twitter—will help raise the online exposure of your photos.

Taking Action Early

Marketing on social media is most effective when you have a large following, but this takes time. Ideally, to give your app the maximum amount of momentum, you should have a significantly large audience waiting for you when you publish your app. This means building your audience early on. Trying to build an audience after your app is already published will do very little for your app, so start early. As soon as your app enters the concept-design phase, develop a social media marketing strategy and use it to gauge audience reaction, build a core group of evangelists, and find a broader audience of eager customers.

Your focus when marketing on social media should be on gradually building a loyal and interested audience, which is achieved with a consistent presence, regular posts, and active interaction.

Smart Marketing

When implementing your marketing strategy, it pays to apply the following underlying guiding principles and tactics so as to maximize the positive response from your audience:

> **Appreciation** – Reward your loyal audience with special offers and free stuff related to your app. If you are building buzz around your upcoming release, you might consider giving users an "early-bird" peek at the app. Or, if there are in-app purchases involved, you could offer your social media audience discounts on those purchases.

> **Interaction** – Focus on human interaction, not direct marketing. Your social media audience will grow only if you directly interact with people, and will do so rarely if you approach them with direct marketing content. Share actively, but do not overwhelm your audience will repetitive material.

> **Attitude** – Develop a positive attitude and respond positively to audience feedback. If your users are giving you feedback about your app's weaknesses, the worst thing you can do is be defensive about it and criticize your users. Instead, be positive and thank everyone who gives you feedback, take action to fix those weaknesses, and let your audience know what you are doing about their feedback. Your users will appreciate your efforts, and you will be rewarded with more-loyal users, plus you'll have a strong feedback channel that will help you develop the next version of your app.

Involvement – Let your audience feel they are a part of your project. Ask them for feedback and opinions. Get some of your most loyal followers to test new versions of the app and tell you what they think.

Integration – Make social media a key part of the app itself. Allow and encourage users to share their experience, achievements, and opinions on social media, and they will act like marketers working for you for free. Incentivize sharing through the app with free stuff, and you will raise your marketing momentum significantly.

According to Openxcell (www.openxcell.com), social media marketing is second only to mobile search in the app discovery process and "trumps cross-selling, ad networks, incentivized ads and app discovery platforms in a number of areas, including conversion rate, user quality, and install volume." So, it's easy to see the value the social media marketing channel can have for your app and how useful it is to harness the secrets of this channel.

Is there a complete list of social media platforms that you can use for your social media campaigns? We are all familiar with Facebook, Google+, Pinterest, LinkedIn, Twitter, and the other networks that have become household names, but there are dozens, if not hundreds, of social networks and social and professional spaces of interaction you can join to connect to people who may be interested in your product. The social media networks listed here are some of the biggest and most popular for networking, product promotion, and sharing of information:

Facebook (http://www.facebook.com), with 1.6 billion monthly active users

YouTube (https://www.youtube.com), with 1 billion monthly active users

Google+ (https://plus.google.com), with 440 million monthly active users

Instagram (http://www.instagram.com), with 430 million monthly active users

LinkedIn (http://www.linkedin.com), with 429 million monthly active users

Twitter (http://www.twitter.com), with 325 million monthly active users

Pinterest (http://pinterest.com), with 110 million monthly active users

Profile Visuals Cheat Sheet

For each of these social media networks, you will have to create marketing-related visuals, like cover photos, banners, profile photos, headers, and backgrounds. The sizes of the visuals differ for each network. Use the cheat sheet in Figure 12-9 to speed up your work.

Facebook	Twitter
Profile photo: 180 x 180	Profile image: 400 x 400
Cover photo: 828 x 315	Header image: 1500 x 500
Shared image or link: 1200 x 630	Shared image: 1024 x 512

Google+	LinkedIn
Profile photo: 250 x 250	Profile photo: 400 x 400
Cover photo: 1080 x 608	Background image: 1400 x 425
Shared image: 497 x 373	Shared image: 700 x 400
Shared link: 150 x 150	Company cover photo: 1536 x 768

Instagram	Pinterest
Profile photo: 110 x 110	Profile image: 165 x 165
Shared image: 1080 x 1080	Board covers: 217 x 146
	Shared image: 735 x 1102

Figure 12-9. Social media visuals basic cheat sheet

Digital Marketing: Online Branding and Identity

The majority of the channels you use to market your app will guide target users to a specific location, where they will respond to a CTA, or call to action, like downloading your app or subscribing to a newsletter. The inbound funnel, or people who come across your app on their own without your direct efforts, like by searching on the web or through recommendations from friends, will also arrive at one of these online locations. Such locations include your website or microsite and your App Store page or online store.

These locations will be components of your online brand, or the identity of your app, which means they will have to be consistent in terms of design, layout, color coding, and content in order to present a consistent image to your visitors.

Your customers will likely first discover your app at three key locations: your social media page (especially your Facebook profile), your website (which can be a simple search-enabled microsite), and your App Store page. Your social media profile pages and website should lead to the final destination, which is the App Store page where your app can be downloaded.

Once your app is published, it will make sense to have channels ready to accept feedback and offer user support on your website and within your app. Once you have a significantly large user base, you can also create a forum so that users can help each other and share their experiences. These channels will be an invaluable source of information to help you identify pain points and gaps that should be fixed before you release the next version of your app. Blogs are also very useful tools for building an audience before the release of your app and for improving retention rates after release by offering relevant content.

App Store Optimization

The top way people search for apps to download is through the App Store. App Store Optimization (ASO) is the set of techniques publishers use to draw the maximum amount of attention to their app and "optimize" their app's presence and ability to compete with other apps.

ASO begins with a clear understanding of what your target audience is searching for. The quality of your user research determines how effective your ASO efforts will be, because your research will produce a set of keywords that are likely to generate the highest traffic and downloads for your app. The keywords you have chosen may change from time to time depending on how they rank and how you are performing compared to your competitors.

In ASO, the following are optimized: the app's title, icon, category, description, and screenshots. Other factors that affect ASO include the total number of downloads and app reviews, as they result in higher rankings. App reviews are difficult to optimize, however, because the publisher has little control over them.

Here's how to optimize your app's title, icon, description, and screenshots:

> Title – Based on your user research, choose a title for your app that has the maximum appeal for your target user, using the main keyword from among the keywords you have chosen for your app. According to MobileDevHQ and Apptentive, app titles with keywords in them rank at least 10 percent higher on average than titles without keywords.
>
> It's preferable that your app's title be short, up to 25 characters, so that it won't get cut off on a smartphone screen. It should also be original so that it will be easily remembered and won't get lost among apps with similar generic names.

Icon – Design a visually appealing icon that best communicates what your app does and indicates the main function that it performs for its users. Ideally, the icon should be designed by a professional, as the difference in quality will significantly improve the impression the app makes on users.

Description – An app's description affects ASO beyond just being what visitors to your App Store page read. The natural incorporation of your app's keywords in the description influences how the App Store algorithms classify and rank the apps. Populate the app description with the keywords you have selected to maximize the chances of your app showing up high in search rankings.

Depending on the screen that's displaying your App Store page, the description will be truncated, and visitors will be asked to press the More button to read further. Make sure your app's function and benefits are "above the fold" of the description so that you'll reach all your visitors.

Ratings and Reviews

App ratings and reviews are most useful at a very specific point in the customer journey—when the customer has already arrived at your App Store page and wants to assess how popular the app is and what other users think about it.

When visitors arrive at your App Store page, it means your marketing efforts have been successful and they are interested in your app. You already have a potential customer. Your app's ratings and reviews are probably the last hurdle you need to cross to convince the visitor to download the app, and because of this, ratings and reviews are crucial for your app's success.

The difference between the number of people who visit your App Store page and the number who actually download the app will give you a sense of the impact your page is having on visitors (Figure 12-10).

When choosing which
apps to download,

34%

of people decide
based on peer reviews.

Before downloading apps,

59%

of app users say
they check an app's ratings.

Among app users,

96%

will download a 4-star app
(50% for a 3-star app).

Source: https://www.appboy.com/blog/mobile-customer-99-stats/ (April 2016)

Figure 12-10. App download stats

For the customer, however, there is a risk because reviews are not exactly reliable. Given the importance of reviews on download or purchase decisions, faking app reviews has become a big trend. App publishers pay money to get positive reviews for their app and negative reviews for competing apps.

Digital Marketing: Affiliate Marketing

Affiliate marketing is seen as a potentially lucrative alternative to the most popular monetization models for apps; namely, in-app purchases (payments from users) and freemium (ads-supported).

Affiliate marketing is a form of advertising whereby a merchant selling a product will use advertising space in your app to sell something, and if they close a sale with a customer they got through your app, you receive either a pre-set figure or a percentage of the value of the sale. Affiliate marketing can work for you in two ways—you can use your app to market other apps as a source of revenue, or you can recruit affiliates to market your app as a means of driving downloads.

Affiliate programs also involve rewarding users for referring people they know to your app. Affiliate marketing can be cost-effective because people are more likely to download an app if it's been recommended by someone they know.

Referrals are tracked through software known as affiliate platforms. These platforms follow and report on how affiliate programs are working by measuring specific events for which you can get paid, such as downloading an app, subscribing to an e-mail list, making an in-app purchase, and viewing or tapping on an ad.

It is also possible to develop apps intended primarily for revenue through affiliate marketing. For example, a publisher might develop an app related to food with the intention of referring users to nearby specialty food stores based on their location, building a business model around affiliate marketing revenue from these stores.

While affiliate marketing can be lucrative compared to other advertising methods, there are two key obstacles to consider: difficulties related to thoroughly tracking user behavior, especially knowing which marketing platform a certain ad was displayed on, and those related to using links within the content of the app, which is highly relevant in affiliate marketing. Another obstacle that could undermine your affiliate marketing campaign, especially if you are directing users to products on a merchant's website, is the possibility that the merchant's website is not adapted properly for mobile or does not provide a smooth checkout process, in which case the purchase will be abandoned and your revenues will suffer because of someone else.

Digital Marketing: E-mail Marketing

E-mail is one of the oldest online marketing channels, of course. It's been around more or less since the invention of the Internet, and it remains a major marketing channel with a higher click-through rate than many other channels (Figure 12-11).

In the US, just

20.7%

of e-mails are opened.

Of all e-mails opened in 2015,

57%

were on mobile devices.

In the US, e-mails have a

3%

click-through rate.

Source: https://www.appboy.com/blog/mobile-customer-99-stats/ (April 2016)

Figure 12-11. E-mail marketing stats

There are many companies that can help you automate your e-mail marketing campaigns with mailing lists, e-mail templates designed with best practices, and many other useful features.

Digital Marketing: Push Notifications and In-App Messages

Push notifications and in-app messages are messages from an app that appear on a mobile screen. A push notification is a message from *your* app that appears on a mobile screen while a customer is using *another* app (Figure 12-12), while an in-app message is a message that appears when a customer is using *your* app, or, in other words, a message that is delivered from *inside* your app. Both can contain text, images, and calls to action.

Push Notification

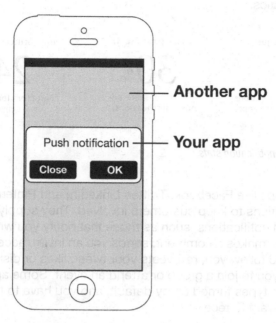

Figure 12-12. Push notifications

Push Notifications

Push notifications are a type of message. They pop up on a mobile screen at specific times or intervals without any intervention by the user. An app that is not being used can still send a push notification even if the user is not actually using his device. The timing of the push notification is chosen by the advertiser, but an app user can decide whether or not they want to receive them at all.

Push notifications on an app screen can be used to advertise the app publisher's other products. They can also be used for remarketing, such as encouraging users who haven't used their app for a while to return; to notify an app user when they receive an e-mail or post; and generally to deliver tailored information requested by the user directly to their lock screen. They can also be used to solicit feedback and information from the user.

Push notifications help you extend your reach to customers who have downloaded your app even when they are not actually using it. Such messages can be used to deliver information to customers, request information for a survey, solicit feedback to improve the user experience, deliver a call to action, or advertise a product or service. Many app publishers with multiple apps in the app stores use push notifications to market each of their apps across all the others. Figure 12-13 reveals some interesting statistics.

Among app users, just

50%

accept push notifications
from their favorite apps.

Among app users,

30%

disable all
push notifications.

Push notifications that are

24

characters long or shorter
convert the best.

Source: https://www.appboy.com/blog/mobile-customer-99-stats/ (April 2016)

Figure 12-13. Push notification stats

Social media apps like Facebook, Twitter, LinkedIn, and Pinterest rely heavily on push notifications to keep customers involved. They supply long lists of options for push notifications, such as those that notify you when someone uploads a photo, makes a comment, sends you an invite, accepts your own invite, decides to follow you, re-tweets your tweet, likes or dislikes your post, or invites you to join a group or attend an event. Some apps have all push notification types turned on by default, and you have to turn off the ones you don't want to receive.

Online push-notification vendors can help you automate the process of sending push notifications and gathering data about your users through them to help you market to your users more effectively. Many allow you to combine location information and behavioral data to personalize your push notifications so as to increase positive response rates.

The effectiveness of push notifications depends on when the user receives the message (timing of notification), what the message says (subject), and how often the user is receiving the same message or different messages (notification schedule). Sending users too many notifications can be irritating and drive them away.

In-App Messages

In-app messages are messages that show up on the mobile screen when a user is actually inside your app (Figure 12-14).

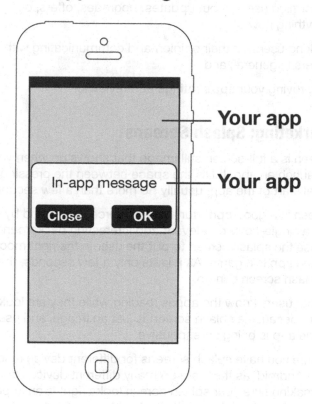

Figure 12-14. In-app messages

These messages vary a great deal depending on where the user is inside the app, what they are doing, and what you want them to do. Many in-app messages are triggered by user actions. According to app design firm Localytics, "in-app messaging should feel like a natural part of the app, not additional marketing, and can be used by marketers to fine-tune app content or promotional strategy." Seamless integration with the user experience through fine-tuned design, timing, and content is the key.

Push notifications and in-app messages are highly effective for

- maintaining user retention rates and keeping your users engaged with your app through new offers and free stuff;

- increasing conversion rates for a specific action, like buying, viewing, or sharing something specific;

- informing users about updates, upgrades, offers, or anything new;

- asking users for their opinion and communicating with users in general; and

- improving your app's ratings and reviews.

Digital Marketing: Splash Screens

A splash screen is a full-screen still image that shows up when you press an app icon to launch an app. It fills the space between the pressing of the icon and the actual start of the app, usually no more than a few seconds.

A splash screen is a good opportunity to reinforce your brand by placing your logo on a single-color or relevant and interesting background. Another option is to use the splash screen to put the user in the right mood, especially if the app is a game. As it lasts only a few seconds, there's little else that a splash screen can do.

Make sure your users know the app is loading while they are looking at the splash screen, because a splash screen is just an image, and users can easily think the app is being unresponsive.

Also, make sure you have splash screens for different device resolutions. In the case of Android, as there are so many different devices and screen resolutions, making sure your splash screen looks right is an important issue. It's impossible to design one splash screen for each screen resolution, so the best tactic is to design three screens, for small, midsize, and large screens.

Paid Advertising

Paid advertising applies to online channels, like ads on websites, blogs, and social media networks, as well as ads in other apps. Paid advertising also includes offline channels, like newspapers, magazines, radio, and television. There are literally hundreds, if not thousands, of options out there depending on your target market and the best ways to reach it. Marketers, however, usually group their marketing campaigns into paid and free, or inbound, to more clearly determine the productivity of their marketing spend. Relevant app monetization statistics can be seen below in Figure 12-15.

Mobile user acquisition cost rose by	Selling to an existing customer is	Among people who spend money in a game app,
84%	**50**%	**13**%
in 2015 to $4.14 per user by September of that year.	easier than selling to a new one.	are willing to spend in a second game as well.

Source: https://www.appboy.com/blog/mobile-customer-99-stats/ (April 2016)

Figure 12-15. App monetization stats

Whether you have a big budget or a small one, it's very easy to overspend on marketing and get little in return, so spending wisely on the right channels is very important in order to produce the results you want. Although it varies greatly across countries and types of apps and fluctuates over time, the average cost of getting a user to install your app, or CAC (Customer Acquisition Cost), is estimated to be between $2.50 and $3.50. This means that if you have set a goal of getting at least 100,000 installs in order to generate the revenue you need to be sustainable, you should expect to spend between $250,000 and $350,000 on marketing.

Digital Marketing: Review Site Submissions

Once your app is online, submit it to as many app review sites as you can. Most are free; some are paid. They're great for free (or paid) exposure for your app.

Visit the following links for lists of the top 200+ app review websites:

http://translatelab.com/android-ios-app-review-sites-list/

http://app-apes.com/2014/09/list-of-the-greatest-app-review-websites/

Non-Digital Marketing: Print and Press—Ads, Articles, and Interviews

Print and press are not channels you will be using constantly; you will not be publishing articles or buying newspaper ads once a week. Advertising in print is something you will be doing at very specific points that are carefully timed to coincide with events like the launch of your app. For example, you can use a full-page newspaper ad to build up interest in your app launch or solicit an article or interview about your startup in a magazine. The most important aspect is timing: you should be prepared to use the interest that ads or articles can generate to promote the app or the event you have planned.

Word of Mouth

Don't underestimate the most traditional of channels: word of mouth. Talk publicly about your app at every opportunity. Create buzz around it before and after release by giving interviews on radio and television and building a highly talkative social media following. Introduce and discuss your app in one or more videos and post them on video-sharing sites.

Don't be the only one talking! After release, get your users to talk about the app by creating a forum where they can share their opinions, offer feedback, and get answers to questions they might have!

Marketing Strategy Component 5: The Content

You will be generating marketing content that will vary depending on the channel and the format, from AdWords ads to articles or social media posts. The content of your marketing campaign needs to be carefully designed to appeal to your target audience, and to do that it should take into account the following:

> **Make content keyword-rich.** Your content not only needs to be read, but also needs to be found easily in search. To do that, it has to contain keywords that match the search terms your audience will use.

> **Use power words.** Power words for marketing, like "discover," "easy," "guaranteed," "free," "instant," and "real," inspire, motivate, and convert. Use them intelligently in marketing copy to get readers to press the Download Now button.

> **Make smart use of calls to action.** CTAs are assertive statements instructing readers to do something, like "Download Now!" or "Join Now!" CTAs that are positioned correctly in a message, with the right color coding and wording, will have a huge impact on the effectiveness of your marketing campaign. The best way to develop a library of effective messages and CTAs is to test a number of variations to see which one works best, a method known as multi-variate testing, or A/B testing.

Marketing Strategy Component 6: The Offer

The final component of your marketing strategy is the offer, or the value proposition. Again, what you offer your target audience depends on the characteristics of that segment, where they are on the customer journey, and your own growth and customer acquisition goals. Are you trying to get a new visitor to download your app, rewarding a loyal user with free stuff to increase user engagement and retention, or urging a lapsed user to return to the app? Each segment will respond positively to a relevant offer, and segmentation, as always, is the key to strong ROI on your campaign.

Extend Your Reach with Smart Tactics

In your effort to make the most of your marketing spend, apply the tactics outlined in the following sections to give your campaign an edge.

Deep Linking

Deep linking in the app world occurs when content inside one app connects to content inside another app. Deep linking is a way for an app to exponentially increase its exposure to users through ways other than direct marketing, and therefore increase user acquisition and (hopefully) retention through organic channels.

For example, say you are browsing through a fashion magazine app A, and you come across an ad for a set of beauty products sold through another app, an e-commerce app B. When you press the link in app A, you will be directed to the product's page inside app B, where your shopping cart will be filled with that particular product, ready for checkout. If you don't have the e-commerce app B installed, you will be directed to the App Store. After you download and launch the app, you will be directed to the product's page inside app B. This is how deep linking works—directing you from deep inside one app to deep inside another app.

However, while it's easy to navigate in this way from one website to another, doing it from one app to another is much more complex because you may be navigating across platforms, apps, and devices. Effective deep linking is valued as a means of decreasing the cost-per-install of mobile apps. Social media ads in particular that contain deep links to content inside your app are a highly effective app marketing tool.

Desktop-to-Mobile Marketing

Desktop-to-mobile app marketing allows you to target users who are using desktops instead of mobile phones to browse. Users submit their phone number on a site, like the Groupon website, and receive a link via SMS that downloads the app to their mobile phone when pressed.

Internal Marketing Channels

Internal marketing channels, for the purposes of this book, are those channels that function from within your app, effectively turning your users into app promoters working for you for free. By sharing their experience or the content they create and giving your app their review or feedback, your users also help you promote your app at no cost to you, and their word as users goes a long way. Thus, from a marketing perspective, your users have very high value.

You can turn your users into promoters by using the following technique.

Ask for Reviews

By asking for reviews, you create an opportunity for users to rave about how great your app is and how much they love it.

The gamble, of course, is that they could provide negative reviews, which will have the opposite effect. A bad review, however, can be very useful for you because it can tell you where you may be making mistakes and turning off users. The value of a good review is for promotion, while the value of a bad review is for feedback to support the design of the next release of your app. However, you want to avoid bad reviews as much as possible.

This means good reviews should be treated differently than bad reviews. Good reviews should be directed to your App Store page, while bad reviews should be directed to you. But how can you tell how your user intends to review your app?

Don't directly ask your users to review your app. First, ask your users in a push notification whether or not they love your app. If they say they do, direct them to your App Store page. If they say they don't, ask them to tell you why and launch an e-mail dialog to help them do so. This way, bad reviews will be directed to you instead of showing up on the App Store page, thus raising your app's average rating.

Good marketing requires that you prompt users to offer their opinion in one way or another. It's up to you to decide how, when, and how often you will prompt users to do so. You can use push notifications to prompt users at regular intervals, like every fourth time they launch the app, or every third time they close it, on exit. It's up to you.

Measuring App Performance

Now that you are marketing your app, you are going to use analytics, KPIs (key performance indicators), and benchmarks to measure how well you are doing and how effective your marketing is. Your decisions will be effective when they are informed and supported by accurate information. There are four main categories of analytics: **User Analytics** provide information about your users and their behavior; **Performance Analytics** measure how your app itself is performing; **Financial Analytics** will tell you how well your app is performing financially; and **Visual Analytics** measure the effectiveness of an app in visually communicating the right information to users.

These different groups of metrics combine to create a picture of how well your app is doing and how effective it is in terms of design, content, and monetization. Most important, analytics will help you identify where the biggest problems are in your app and what to change to fully optimize it.

User Analytics

User analytics provide information about who your users are, how they are interacting with your app, what devices they are using, how often they are using your app, and how much time they spend on it on average. Detailed information about users helps you tailor your app to their tastes and improve their engagement with the app.

Performance Analytics

Performance analytics measure the technical performance of your app, such as how long it takes to load and how often it crashes. The loading time of your app may seem relatively unimportant, but it will affect how much users enjoy using it and how many of them will abandon it in frustration.

Fast, efficient, and reliable performance is a key component of strong user engagement and is the result of skilled programming and extensive testing before release, as well as close monitoring and constant improvement after release. As Figure 12-16 below shows, users value instant responsiveness, and punish apps that don't have it.

Among app users,

96%

value an app's speed
and responsiveness.

After launching an app,

49%

expect it to launch
within 2 seconds.

Among app users,

48%

will uninstall an app
if they feel it is too slow.

Source: https://www.appboy.com/blog/mobile-customer-99-stats/ (April 2016)

Figure 12-16. User behavior stats

Financial Analytics

Financial analytics provide information about your app's commercial performance and consist of two parts: revenue analytics and marketing and advertising analytics.

Revenue analytics will tell you how much money your users are spending on your app, who is spending the most money, and which channels are your best sources of revenue. Marketing and advertising analytics will tell you which marketing channels are bringing in the most users and how effective your spending on marketing really is. Campaign analytics, meanwhile, is a focused part of your overall marketing analytics, and will measure the effectiveness of a specific marketing campaign, or a specific ad type, over a set period of time.

Visual Analytics

Visual analytics involve the use of tools like touch heatmaps, user journey recordings, session playbacks, and real-time reporting to understand how your users are interacting with your app, which buttons or icons they are pressing, and which parts they are ignoring.

By supplying accurate real-time information about whether your users are interacting with the app the way you want them to, visual analytics will help you identify and correct UI problems that are frustrating users, optimize the user experience, and maximize your app's revenue potential.

Metrics

There are literally thousands of metrics and KPIs you can use to measure the performance of an app from different perspectives. Analytics software allows you to customize your analytics reports depending on what questions about your app's performance or your users' behavior and preferences you want to answer.

Metrics and KPIs also differ based on the type of app involved, such as games, enterprise apps, or commercial apps. Each will set its own benchmarks for user engagement, profitability, and virality on social media, use very different metrics to measure success, and monitor user behavior from very different angles.

Key Analytics KPIs

The following analytics KPIs are among the most important ones that markerters use to measure the effectiveness of their campaigns.

Depth of Visit – the number of screens a user views during a single session

Session Interval – the time it takes for a user to launch the app again after closing it

Organic User Growth Rate – the number of new users who do not originate from marketing campaigns but "organically"

Lifetime Value (LTV) – the total revenue a user will generate over their lifetime using an app

Other KPIs like Churn Rate and Retention Rate have been discussed in previous chapters.

Examples of User Engagement and Financial Metrics

User engagement and financial metrics include User Native Language Distribution, Goal Completion Rate, Number of Sessions in First Week, Peak Usage Times of Day, Abandonment Rate, Session Interval, Number of Active Users, Brand Awareness, Behavior Flow, Retention Rate, Number of Screens Visited, Number of Content Uploads, Number of Shares, Depth of Visit, Churn Rate, Conversion Rate, Session Frequency, OS Version Distribution, Device Type Distribution, Geographic User Distribution, Session Duration, Organic User Growth Rate, Download Count, Permissions Granted, User Lifecycle Duration, Number of Product Likes, Average Revenue per Transaction, Pay per Click (PPC), Total Revenue from Acquired Users, Cost per Click (CPC), Number of New Customers per Month, Cost per Install (CPI), Cost per Thousand Impressions (CPM), Paid Conversion Rate, Shopping Cart Abandonment Rate, Peak Transaction Times, Customer Acquisition Cost (CAC), Percent of New Leads, Average Revenue per User (ARPU), Number of User Likes, Transactions per Second, Hour, or Day, Application Latency, Number of Items in Shopping Cart, Network Error Rate, Number of Subscriptions/Registrations, API Latency, Customer Lifetime Value (LTV), App Load per Period, Percent of Mobile Influenced Customers, App Crash Rate, App User Review Frequency, Throughput, and App Load Time.

How Do I Use Analytics in My App?

Apple will automatically produce analytics reports for you after launch, but you may also want to use other analytics providers as well. Using external analytics suppliers in your app is easy. First, register with an analytics provider (see our list in Chapter 15). Second, create a unique tracking ID that will be part of your app's code. The analytics supplier will create that ID for you once you fill in the necessary information about your app. Third, insert a snippet of code with this ID in your app's code before release.

That's it! Your app will start creating reports.

Summary

Marketing is a science and an art whose efficiency increases with user data. The more information you have about your users, the better you will get at marketing to them. Therefore, the very first step toward successful marketing is to get as much information about your audience as you can, and then to get your app users to share as much as possible about what they like or don't like about your product.

Chapter **13**

App Marketing Concepts

The evolution of digital marketing has spawned and keeps spawning new concepts, strategies, techniques, and methods that marketers employ to target, reach and convert potential customers. The following are some fundamental assumptions and observations that underlie the majority of these concepts:

- App users behave in different ways and use the app they have downloaded differently than other users do.

© Hagop Panosian 2017

H. Panosian, *Learn iOS Application Distribution*, DOI 10.1007/978-1-4842-2683-4_13

■ Users at different stages in their engagement with an app, a brand, or a product respond differently to marketing content, and therefore marketing campaigns need to segment users based on different factors and tailor marketing content to the habits and preferences of these segments.

■ New technologies allow a great deal of marketing-related activities, like buying ad content (programmatic marketing), to be automated. Companies that automate their marketing processes can create higher levels of efficiency and increase marketing ROI.

Let's look at the most popular marketing concepts that are employed in app marketing.

Predictive Marketing

Predictive marketing involves using data science that is based on customer behavior and habits to make smarter marketing decisions (Figure 13-1). By gathering and analyzing data about user behavior and identifying patterns, marketers are able to make forecasts about user behavior and make informed decisions about the likelihood of the success of their marketing content and offerings.

Analyze customer's habits, preferences ⟹ Present customer with the right offer at the right moment ⟹ Maximize success of marketing campaign

Figure 13-1. Predictive marketing

Marketers can get better returns on their marketing spend by targeting the right user at the right time with the right offer. Predictive marketing is usually optimized in combination with personalization.

A/B Testing

A/B testing (also known as split testing or multi-variate testing) involves the use of several versions of the same ad, distributed to different groups, with different designs, color coding, calls to action, and message content, to determine which version produces the highest conversion rate. Normally, predicting which ad design will work best is impossible, so A/B testing fills in the gap as users themselves tell the marketer which is most convincing.

Remarketing/Retargeting

A very small percentage of people who come across an app will respond positively to a call to action and download the app. Among customers who engage with the app, another significant number will quickly abandon it, or will keep it but use it very rarely. In general, over 90 percent of visitors to a website leave without converting, and 70 percent abandon shopping carts.

Remarketing targets everyone who has come into contact with your product but hasn't converted, or who converted but later abandoned the app. It allows marketers to reconnect with these categories of users and "bring them back," or increase the time they spend engaging with the app.

Customers who are on your remarketing list are more valuable than an average customer because they have already expressed some form of interest simply by downloading your app or visiting your website or app page. This means that a campaign designed to convert them is likely to be more effective than one targeting new customers.

Personalization

Personalization, also known as customer-centered marketing or one-to-one marketing, involves customizing the timing and content of marketing messages to the target user based on their preferences, habits, and behavior patterns. Personalized messages refer to every user by name and entice the user to become more engaged with an app with the right kind of incentive based on their characteristics, like age, gender, location, profession, and financial segment. The aim of personalization is to raise the effectiveness of marketing campaigns by approaching users with the offer that is most likely to appeal to them.

Personalization is a very powerful tool for converting customers. Over 40 percent of consumers say they value companies that remember past shopping behavior, and just under 70 percent say they prefer personalized shopping.

Marketing Funnel

A marketing funnel is a visual representation of the different phases in a customer's journey toward conversion and their relationship with a product (Figure 13-2).

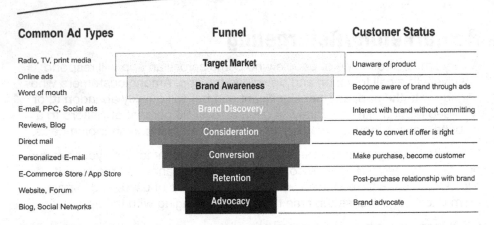

Common Ad Types	Funnel	Customer Status
Radio, TV, print media	**Target Market**	Unaware of product
Online ads	**Brand Awareness**	Become aware of brand through ads
Word of mouth		
E-mail, PPC, Social ads	Brand Discovery	Interact with brand without committing
Reviews, Blog	Consideration	Ready to convert if offer is right
Direct mail		
Personalized E-mail	Conversion	Make purchase, become customer
E-Commerce Store / App Store	Retention	Post-purchase relationship with brand
Website, Forum		
Blog, Social Networks	Advocacy	Brand advocate

Figure 13-2. Marketing funnel

One way of segmenting users is by their location on the marketing funnel, or their location on the customer journey. Are they new users, or are they users who downloaded the app some time ago and are now not as engaged with it as they used to be? By segmenting customers based on where they are located in the funnel, marketers target these groups much more effectively, sending the offer that is most likely to move them to the next level. For example, turning unaware visitors into brand-aware potential customers requires a different approach through a different channel than what would be used when trying to turn leads interacting with your brand into converted customers.

Funnels are usually divided into three broad sections—TOFU (Top of Funnel), MOFU (Middle of Funnel), and BOFU (Bottom of Funnel)—and separate marketing strategies are assigned to each.

Incentivization

The incentivized model (also known as the sponsored, reward-based, or value-exchange ad model) is the strategy of making a product, program, or other offering more attractive to customers by offering an incentive in exchange for buying or participating.

In the app business, incentivization is normally used to quickly amass app installs. For example, a retail company may offer its customers discounts and/or loyalty rewards if they make purchases through its app. A content publisher could offer exclusive content available only on its app, or a game may offer first-time downloaders a certain amount of virtual currency they can use in the game. Publishers and marketers use incentivized installs to generate installs more quickly and cheaply than if they used non-incentivized methods, as the incentive offered makes it much more likely that a potential customer will install the app on their device. However, since customers who download an app because of the attached incentive are less likely to keep the app, they should be targeted with a focused retention strategy to prevent churn.

Thought- Leadership Marketing

Thought-leadership marketing is the process of positioning a company as a leader in a specific domain by supplying customers with top-quality information. This is usually done by creating a special section on a company website that offers free e-books, infographics, and other downloads; launching a blog and populating it with content from top-notch authors; organizing webinars; and launching a video content channel on YouTube or Vimeo that offers customers quality content, like how-to's, guides, and other information that the company's existing customers and new visitors are likely to find very useful.

The idea behind thought-leadership marketing is to build a company's reputation to the point where that company is the first thing that comes to a customer's mind whenever they want to fix a problem or answer a question.

Programmatic Marketing

Programmatic marketing is the automated, algorithm-based, real-time buying and selling of advertising space through a bidding system, with the aim of reaching the right customers at the right time.

According to iab.com, programmatic marketing involves "four main types of transactions—open auctions, invitation-only/private auctions, unreserved fixed rate/preferred deals, and automated guaranteed/programmatic guaranteed deals."

Programmatic marketing greatly increases the level of personalization of the ad content and its timing, and greatly increases the efficiency of marketing campaigns and spending.

Programmatic ad buying grew from around $10 billion in 2014 to just under $15 billion in 2015, out of the total $58.6 billion spent on digital advertising.

Identity Resolution

Identity resolution is a process through which large amounts of data in separate databases are analyzed to find identity matches and "resolve" identities. In the app business, identity resolution is used primarily to prevent a customer from engaging with a brand or an app through multiple devices or through several identities being counted as different people. It is also used to avoid having different people with the same name get counted as the same person. Another important use for identity resolution is the prevention of fraud and identity theft.

Single-Channel, Multi-Channel, Omni-Channel Marketing

Single-channel, multi-channel, and omni-channel marketing refers to the number of channels that are used to reach customers in a marketing campaign. A single-channel marketing campaign involves reaching users through a single channel, like Facebook ads, for example. A multi-channel campaign uses more than one channel, while an omni-channel marketing campaign attempts to reach users through all available channels.

The main purpose of an omni-channel campaign is to ensure that customers are offered a consistent, seamless experience across all the channels or devices through which they are interacting with a brand. An omni-channel strategy employs search, social media, SEO, a corporate website, print, apps, forums, online ads, and all other available channels to acquire customers.

Mobile App Attribution

Mobile app attribution is the process of recording and measuring the actions of app users, such as installs, level completions, in-app purchases, and other milestones.

Mobile app attribution differs from traditional online attribution, which uses cookies and pixel tags. These methods do not work in mobile app attribution, and mobile marketers and platform developers like Apple and Google have come up with new methods of attribution. The most universal methods are the following:

- **Device Fingerprinting** – An ad that is displayed on a device gathers information about that device to create a unique identity and submit that information to the marketer.

- **Unique Identifier Matching** – A mobile attribution tool automatically compares unique identifiers in real-time, matching these identifiers to each other, from ad clicks to installs and other actions.

Mobile app attribution is essential to app marketing because it helps produce the data that is gathered and analyzed to measure how well marketing campaigns are working. It supports higher-level performance tracking, as well as marketing strategies like personalization and predictive marketing.

Content Marketing

Content marketing is a marketing strategy that involves producing content that potential customers find useful, valuable, and relevant. Content marketing has grown in popularity and relevance alongside the evolution of social media, which is now the primary medium for the dissemination of content to users.

One big advantage of content marketing is that ads or links embedded in that content survive ad-blockers and are more reliably delivered to customers. For example, an ad embedded in an article as a link to the advertiser will not be removed by ad blockers.

Content marketing is highly effective at building a loyal user base and converting leads into customers. It's also useful for helping a company build up its reputation as a leader in its field, and in that respect it's part of thought-leadership marketing. Game developers who post walkthrough videos of levels in their game on YouTube are employing content marketing. One example of great content marketing is used for the Clash of Clans game, as fans of the game are allowed to post their own game art on the Clash of Clans Facebook page.

Loyalty Marketing

Loyalty marketing is a marketing strategy that focuses on nurturing existing customers rather than acquiring new ones. Loyalty marketing sets goals like raising the average revenue from existing customers, turning loyal customers into evangelists by asking them to share content about your product or brand, and increasing an existing customer's level of engagement with a brand by offering them incentives.

Behavioral Marketing

Behavioral marketing involves segmenting your app's user base based on user behavior with the aim of refining your marketing strategy and more effectively targeting users. For example, a user who downloads a clothing manufacturer's app and searches for offers on leather jackets is sent notifications about discounts on leather jackets or a new collection that has just arrived. Another example is a "Well done!" message sent to a language app user who has just completed a basic level; the message also contains discounts or special offers for the paid higher levels for that language.

Behavioral marketing helps marketers understand the different subgroups that make up their customer base, and therefore helps them create targeted content and ads customized for those groups based on their choices.

Summary

Marketing is a field that is evolving very fast as new technologies create new ways to amplify the effectiveness and efficiency of marketing campaigns. Keeping up with marketing methods as they become available is key to maintaining your edge over other competing apps and maximizing the return on your marketing budget.

Chapter **14**

Prepare for Success

**"At first they'll ask why you're doing it.
Later they'll ask how you did it."**

Anonymous

© Hagop Panosian 2017

H. Panosian, *Learn iOS Application Distribution*, DOI 10.1007/978-1-4842-2683-4_14

What any appreneur fears most is, of course, failure. But, as we'll see in this chapter, there's something worse than failure—success for which you are unprepared. It's worse because the aftertaste is more bitter when you know you almost succeeded than when you never had a chance. It's therefore imperative to be prepared to adapt very fast and grow with your app when it becomes a hit.

Sudden Success

It's every app publisher's dream: you design and release an app to the world, and all of a sudden it's an overnight super-hit, with fast-growing downloads, special attention from investors and the media, and maybe even talk about an award or two. You, in the meantime, are ecstatically trying to absorb your success.

Not so fast. This dream could very easily turn into a nightmare if you are unprepared for sudden success and rapid growth. If you fail to adapt very fast, the popularity of your app will deflate just as fast as it grew, and your app will be dead in the water.

This does not mean you have to invest large amounts of money beforehand, when there is no indication that your app is a surefire super-hit. This would be unrealistic and foolish. However, the whole team involved in your app project needs to know and understand the components of rapid growth should it be necessary and be prepared as much as is possible to adapt to the new situation. If you think about these components only after you have achieved sudden success, it will probably be too late, and that would be a real shame, wouldn't it? An app that "could have been and almost was" is even worse than one that "never had a chance," so don't let it happen to you.

Let's start by taking a closer look at what can happen in a worst-case scenario, when your app unexpectedly becomes an overnight success but you are completely unprepared and unable to adapt.

First, you start to see a snowball effect in the number of app downloads and active users. People are using your app heavily, sharing their experience with others, and giving it rave reviews, while you and your team are celebrating your success, convinced you've hit a home run and that your success is permanent (Figure 14-1).

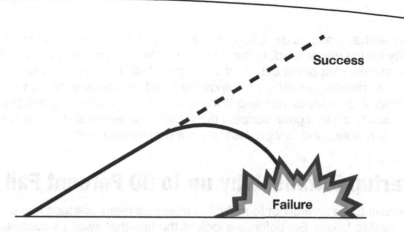

Figure 14-1. The worst-case scenario for an app startup

After a number of positive reviews by top app industry blogs, the media are banging on your door. This draws the attention of investors and venture capitalists, who are interested in your app's potential. Meanwhile, you and your friends are still busy celebrating.

Then, things start to go wrong. Your servers and backend cannot handle the traffic from so many users. You need bandwidth to maintain your app's response time for content delivery and space to store all the data you are gathering and processing.

Your users are starting to get unhappy. Many have come across bugs in your design and pointed them out to you, but there seems to be no response, or your response is not quick enough. You simply can't respond to user complaints with your small team, and you probably don't have a Customer Relationship Management unit yet. The crash rate is rising along with the number of users. No one is working on a new version. As the bugs remain unfixed, people are starting to complain, and five-star and four-star reviews are turning into one-star and two-star reviews. Eventually, your users start to abandon the app because there's a better-designed alternative by another publisher available.

In the meantime, the app industry media have already moved on to the next superstar, and investors who were originally interested have also moved on to other projects because you simply did not have a detailed vision for the future of your project or a detailed business plan to prove you know how to get there.

Finally, your team members are jumping ship to start other projects on their own or are getting hired by the competition. You are left alone in your empty office, wondering how and why this happened.

A somewhat dramatic depiction, yes, but one that could easily become a reality for the unprepared. In this situation, failure has nothing to do with your original idea or the design of the app. In fact, the early success of your app proves you did many things right and found the success you were seeking. The failure of your app is the result of your failure to manage that success. You had a great concept but terrible implementation. A concept, no matter how good, is worthless without great implementation.

Startup Pitfalls: Why up to 90 Percent Fail

You have to be careful not to make the mistakes many startups make that lead to failure. So, before we look at the fate that awaits a successful startup, let's look at the most common reasons why startups fail.

Estimates of the percentage of tech startups that fail vary between 75 percent and over 90 percent. It is also an open secret that venture capitalists expect four out of ten of the tech startups they invest in to fail, and only one out of ten to be a big success. With the odds stacked so highly against you even before you start, it pays to know the traps that await you.

The causes of failure for tech startups fall into four main categories: technical, financial, strategic, and behavioral. All can undermine a startup to the point that it falls apart before reaching the milestone of financial sustainability. Some startups still fail after they reach that milestone, having consumed millions of dollars in investor money.

- Technical
  - Choosing the wrong platform, or trying to develop for all platforms at the same time
  - Launching the app too early
  - Launching the app too late, after it's been overtaken by competition
  - Failing to test for bugs before release
  - Launching a badly designed app
  - Failing to include promotion methods (social media sharing, push notifications) in the design of the app
  - Failing to include analytics
- Financial
  - Not raising enough money
  - Raising too much money

- ■ Spending too much (especially by paying hourly rates and spending highly on paid promotion channels)

- ■ Spending too little

- ■ Using the wrong monetization strategy for your app (like charging users upfront without offering a free version and failing to include attractive in-app purchases)

■ Strategic

- ■ Failing to combine the necessary skills in the startup's founding team

- ■ Targeting a niche that is too narrow

- ■ Choosing an unfavorable location with no access to the support environment suitable for fast-growing startups.

- ■ Investing in an idea for which there is little demand

- ■ Failing to target a clearly defined user category

■ Behavioral

- ■ Insisting on pursuing a bad idea

- ■ Not wanting to get involved in the day-to-day management of the startup

- ■ Conflicts in the founding team

- ■ Conflicts with investors

- ■ Hiring the wrong people

Changing Your Mindset

As part of an app development team, the very first and most important step you have to take to prepare for success is to change your frame of mind and your understanding of what your project needs. You have to shift from the inventor mindset to the investor mindset.

If you haven't noticed by now, you already are an investor. You've invested a great deal of time, money, and effort to create "sweat equity," and you probably already own a large part, if not all, of an app that's hopefully on its way to becoming a full-fledged business. So, start treating your app like an investor treats a prized asset and give it the attention and planning it deserves so it can become a success.

If you are committed to steering your app to success, you don't need to wait until your app is actually a success to change your frame of mind. Do it as soon as you can. The benefits will be tremendous for you, your team, and your app.

At this point, your energy is probably focused on preventing failure rather than chasing success. You're most likely trying to keep your app afloat, especially in the crucial few weeks after release, and to build up momentum. However, success can hit you unexpectedly, and the bottom line is that you and your team need to know exactly what needs to be done to best exploit the opportunities created by that success.

What a Successful Startup Needs

What does an app startup need in order to have a good chance of success? It needs a great idea, a team to turn that idea into a product and a business, a market to consume that product, and money to make it all happen. Each of these components functions well when it has the right characteristics or features, as Figure 14-2 shows.

Figure 14-2. The four components of a successful startup

The Idea

The idea is where everything begins, right? However, not all ideas are created equal, and even a great idea in your head is of little tangible value if others don't get a chance to qualify it. To do that, an appreneur needs to go two steps further: one, to validate the idea, and two, to create what is known as a Minimum Viable Product (MVP).

- **Validated Idea** – There is a big difference between an idea and a validated idea, and that difference can be worth millions. For venture capitalists and other people who can influence the fate of your app, an idea that has not been validated is nothing more than a curiosity, because the burden of validation falls on you, and presenting an unvalidated idea is unwise.

- **Minimum Viable Product (MVP)** – According to Eric Ries, entrepreneur and author of *The Lean Startup*, a Minimum Viable Product is "the version of a new product which allows a team to collect the maximum amount of validated learning about customers with the least effort." Another way of describing a Minimum Viable Product is "the bundle of features that helps you avoid building a product that customers do not want."

  An MVP allows you to save time and money by leaving out the features of a product that are unrelated to its main function while also gauging customer response to its core function. If the response is positive, then the additional features that were initially left out are gradually added with each iteration of the product.

- **Protection** – Protecting your ideas is expensive but necessary. Without it, no investor or venture capitalist will take you seriously, because no one wants to put money into a product only to see it being copied left and right by competitors and be unable to do anything about it.

  Getting full protection of your idea at the beginning is a heavy financial burden if you want to register trademarks and copyrights internationally. There are other means of protecting your idea that are just as important.

  One method involves asking anyone to whom you formally present your project to sign a non-disclosure agreement. This is a simple way to stop people from sharing your idea with others. One way to prove you were the first to think of an idea is to put everything about your app concept in a document, like a PDF or Word document, and e-mail it to yourself without opening it. Do this before sharing your idea with anyone else. That way, no one can claim they thought of your app before you did.

One counterintuitive way to protect your idea is to go in the opposite direction and share your idea formally with the world, especially in tech meets or competitions. When everyone has seen your idea and associates it with you, it's difficult for anyone to copy it and present it as their own. An important advantage of this is that it helps build up buzz around the coming release of your app, which you are going to do in the development phase anyway.

The Team

The purpose of an app startup's founding team is to perform the core tasks that drive growth and to steer the app to success and an eventual exit. For this to happen, the members of the team need to have (or create) synergy between themselves and bring the complete set of skills needed to implement the core tasks of the business. These are tasks that cannot be outsourced at the early stage because of cost or privacy concerns.

When the startup has to scale very rapidly, the relationship between the founders will need to evolve to meet the demands of that growth. Let us say, for example, that an app startup founding team has three members, one of whom is responsible for programming, the second for financial issues, and the third for marketing. This is a pretty good combination of skills, by the way. Ideally, a founding team should be large enough to combine all the skills needed to get a startup going, but small enough to keep the likelihood of conflict low and to avoid diluting ownership.

When the startup has to scale rapidly, each of these members will take their tasks to the next level, creating a department and hiring new employees. To do this, the members will have to make an assessment of the human resources they are likely to need in the coming 18 to 24 months to grow effectively. Each will have to learn new skills fast so that jobs get done, especially managing teams and creating the right accountability hierarchies.

Care must also be taken to gradually establish the right corporate culture, one that is consistent with the app's image and encourages maximum employee productivity. The right company culture is also important because it's a key component of a company's image as a workplace and will help draw the new talent the company needs to grow.

The Market

To sustain your app, you will be looking for a market for it. For the app to be worth the investment, that market will need to be large enough and still be growing. To keep up with your market, you will need a way to know who your users are and what they want from you, or, in other words, a feedback cycle.

- **Market Size** – Needless to say, if your app is to have any chance of success, it needs a market large enough to support it. This does not mean targeting as many people as you can without caring who they are. It means targeting enough intended users who are willing to pay to use your app to make your business sustainable. This will help you quickly achieve one of the most important milestones in your business—positive cash flow. Having 1,000 users who pay you $10 each month to use the premium version of your app is better than having 100,000 users who pay you a total of $1,000 a month on the ad-supported version. Each of these groups is in a different category. You will probably start by advertising to a million potential users, out of whom 100,000 will download the freemium version and 1,000 will get the premium version. The important point here is to get to the core group of paying users who can sustain your app business.

- **Positive Growth** – Are you headed in the right direction? Are there more paying users downloading your app every month than users who are abandoning your app? There are a number of metrics that tell you whether your app is building up momentum and moving in the right direction, like your churn rate, but the most important measurement you need to make in terms of your market is whether the profitability of your app is improving.

- **Feedback Cycle** – Establishing a feedback cycle with your users is fundamental to your relationship with both your market and your users. If you give your users the right tools, they will tell you almost everything you need to know to improve your app and make sure it meets their needs. They will tell you what you're doing right, what you're doing wrong, and what your app is missing. They may use your app in unexpected ways (depending on what type of app it is) and open up new opportunities for you.

The Money

Money is the most important factor that will decide the future of your app startup. How much of it you can get, when you can get it, and how you spend it will determine whether your app succeeds or fails. Scaling successfully requires that you have access to funding when you need it, which means you have to take steps to make sure it's available before you anticipate you will need it. If you start looking for money after the problem appears, you are too late, because by the time you get the money to do what you want, the opportunity to grow with your user base will be lost.

The best strategy to ensure you have money when you need it is to gather pledges. Build your business plan, make forecasts about key milestones for your app, and talk to investors who are likely to be interested. Ask them for information about how much they would be prepared to invest should your app hit a specific growth milestone or benchmark. Have a large-enough group of investors ready to make sure your app will have the money it needs when it needs it.

Investors will put their money in your app if they see you have a well-thought-out business plan that shows you understand the key elements that drive growth, are committed to steering your project to success, and can produce the returns they expect.

Managing Rapid Growth

To successfully scale a startup, you have to be ready for success when it happens. As Figure 14-3 shows, you have to scale your company in several directions at the same time to accommodate the changes success will bring, and you have to be ready for it when it happens.

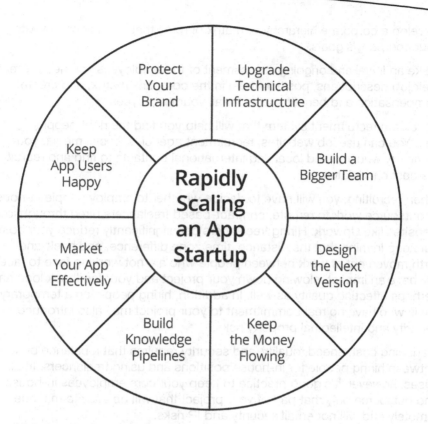

Figure 14-3. Aspects of app startup scaling

Scale Effectively: Hardware and Software

If your app is a sudden success, you will need to grow quickly to keep up. There are several aspects to this, and one of the most fundamental is infrastructure and hardware. You will need bigger servers to handle the increased traffic, and you will need a sophisticated backend to manage your users and regularly update the content of your app.

Scale Effectively: People & Space

To scale your app effectively, build and manage a new backend, serve your users, market your app, and implement all the activities related to scaling, you will also need to launch a big recruitment round. You will need programmers, UI/UX designers, marketers, accountants, lawyers, and managers to manage different departments.

Develop a corporate hierarchy or matrix of roles that is in alignment with your company's goals.

Make an initial and ongoing assessment of the employees you need. Create their job descriptions, position them in the company matrix, and create compensation and benefit scales for all your employees.

Develop a recruitment system that will help you find the right people fast. You can use job websites, recruitment agencies, social media, your company website, and local and international contacts to find and recruit the best candidates.

When recruiting, you will have to decide whether to employ people in-house or outsource work to remote, contract-based freelancers hired through job websites like Upwork. Hiring freelancers can significantly reduce your costs, but keep in mind that the distance, time zone difference, and back-and-forth movement of work between people who are not working face to face will have an impact, slowing down your project and your feedback loop and perhaps affecting quality as well. In addition, hiring people on a temporary basis who have no real commitment to your project may also introduce security and intellectual property risks.

Managing cost, speed, quality, and security requires that a balance be found between hiring people for in-house positions and using freelancers. In all cases, however, it's good practice to keep your core employees in-house and outsource only that part of your project that will be easy to manage remotely and will not entail security and IP risks.

Your new team, of course, will also need office space. An office that is perfect for your needs should be strategically located but affordable, and should be larger than your current needs require so that you will not have to relocate again as you expand. It's wise to plan at least a year ahead in terms of your human resources and office space needs and find an office accordingly.

Protect Your Brand

A successful app will need a rethink of its image. The app or MVP that you originally built is unlikely to have a logo and image that are of the needed quality. Thus, you will need to rethink the app's marketing visuals, including the logo, advertising and App Store images and screenshots, website design, and video content for promotions. To do this, you can contract a professional marketing agency if your budget allows, or, if not, you can hold an online competition on a jobs website like Upwork or eLance.

Intellectual Property Protection

Take action to protect your brand. If your concept is worth the investment, it needs to be protected in every possible way. That protection will come in three forms—copyrights, trademarks, and patents—that apply to different types of assets you feel are worth protecting.

- **Copyright** – Copyright is the way to protect any original authored or artistic work. In the case of your app, it would protect your app's content in the form of text, images, sounds, icons, and so on.

- **Trademark** – A trademark protects a company's logo, name, and anything directly related to its identity. It prevents competitors from using your company's identity and from using very similar but not identical logos and names to benefit from your success.

- **Patent** – A patent normally applies to devices and inventions. If your app involves a new device or combination of devices to perform a function, it's wise to patent it to prevent others from copying the technology.

Incorporation: When, Where, and Why

Incorporating an app startup is not absolutely necessary for publishing apps, because you can do it under an individual's identity. However, the value of incorporating is in formalizing your identity, which is very helpful, if not essential, if you plan to raise funds for your startup.

The process of registering a company differs depending on your location and country. You may want to register in your own country as a natural choice if you plan to expand your business there, but there are numerous other alternatives as well. One is to register a company in the U.S .State of Delaware.

Registering a company in Delaware through a quick online process is a popular option for many tech companies because of the speed and low cost of registration and the favorable tax laws. If you are outside the United States, the downside of registering in a foreign location consists mainly of legal issues and unexpected fees and charges related to operating as a foreign company in your own country.

If you are interested in the MENA (Middle East and North Africa) region, one option is to register a company in one of the Dubai Free Zones in the United Arab Emirates, like the Dubai Silicon Oasis or Dubai Internet City.

In this case as well, there are advantages, like no taxes, 100 percent ownership (which does not apply outside the free zones in the UAE), and direct access to markets and human resources.

Incorporate Early: The Advantages

Incorporating your startup early has a number of advantages, one of which is that it clarifies ownership—who owns how much of the company, and who is just an employee.

Ownership

If your company suddenly becomes a success and you have to look at incorporating it, there is a risk that everyone who has ever worked there for a short time or even delivered fast food once or twice will feel they are entitled to a percentage of the company, and there will be little you can do to avoid the legal nightmare.

Stock Value and Profit

A second advantage is that as a founder or co-founder you will own stock in your company. Early on, it is very easy to set a very low nominal price to buy the stock as opposed to much later, when the product has registered its intellectual property and has a large number of users. The value of the company's stock at a later point will be much higher and not nominal. This also means the profit potential of incorporating a startup is highest for the founders the earlier it is done.

Financing

Incorporating early is also advantageous if you plan to finance growth through venture capital, loans, or other forms of external financing later on. A startup that has corporate status will attract funds much more easily than would a motley group of developers who plan to incorporate after they secure financing.

An important point here is to know which types of companies are allowed in your country and which are most attractive to investors. Limited Liability Companies (LLCs), for example, are known to be unattractive for investors in the United States for a number of reasons related to laws that regulate their financing and operation. For example, they are known as pass-through entities, which means they do not pay income tax. Instead, the owners of an LLC pay income tax depending on their share of the company's profits.

Intellectual Property

Incorporating early allows startups to maintain a maximum degree of control over all the intellectual property related to their app, as all assets will have been developed after incorporation by employees or outside contractors who cannot claim ownership over any of these assets.

Protection for the Founders

Incorporating allows the founders of a startup to protect themselves from any personal liability with regard to their project, as all legal and financial liability toward creditors will belong to the company.

Scaling Well: Tips on What to Do

The following sections provide some insight into how to build a successful app project.

Keep Users Happy

Probably the worst thing that can happen to an app startup that meets with unexpected success is to have thousands upon thousands of people download the app, but then see users abandon the app in growing numbers because of dissatisfaction with the product or user support. Users might complain about crashes or glitches in the design of the app but realize they are being ignored and abandon the app.

This kind of situation is even worse than not attracting any users at all, and to avoid it you need to build a system to cater to your users, use them for valuable feedback about how to improve the app, and get them to leave positive reviews of your app on the app stores, your website, or on social media and forums.

In short, without users you have nothing, so make them happy and keep them happy. Build a strong relationship with your users, responding to their complaints and encouraging them to share their reaction to your app. They are your free marketers, and their word goes a long way.

Monitor negative reviews. They will tell you a lot about where your weak points are. Respond fast and fix what needs fixing quickly. Make it easy for your users to reach you with their complaints, and make them feel you are listening. Be prepared to listen to them, incorporate their feedback into your iteration process, and release the new version of your app quickly.

Market Effectively

Building on the success of your app requires a whole new level of thinking about positioning your app as a product and marketing it. The early success of your app will attract a lot of attention your way, and your task in this situation is not to stand out (you've already done that), but rather to establish your product in the market and in the minds of your users, building the critical mass to become stratospheric.

To do this, your marketing strategy will pursue three goals: getting more users, keeping your existing users, and getting your existing users to bring in more users. Each of these goals requires a different strategy with different approaches, message content, and CTAs (calls to action).

Build Knowledge Pipelines

Your startup's marketing and product-design efforts will only be as good as the information that supports them. To get the information you need, you will have to build knowledge pipelines that supply you with data to help you monitor and understand your users' behavior and design products that match their expectations. Otherwise, everything you do will miss its target and will be a waste of time and money.

Use analytics everywhere you can to monitor your users and gather information about them—their patterns, preferences, and habits. Use this knowledge to segment your user base in different ways, then design marketing campaigns tailored to them.

As your startup scales into a larger company, your knowledge pipelines will become more and more elaborate. The more automation you introduce into this process of gathering and analysis, the more efficient and affordable it will be. You will need to develop internal knowledge pipelines as well, like performance dashboards, to keep the company running efficiently as it grows.

Having information about your company and your users is also crucial when you have to attract investment. Much will depend on performance metrics, including the valuation of your company by investors or venture capitalists interested in betting their money on you. Therefore, the more accurate and rich the data is, the better the accuracy and quality of the conclusions drawn from it will be.

Keep the Money Flowing

Creating and maintaining a stable flow of financing will allow you to scale your startup at the necessary pace to achieve your goals. As we saw earlier in this chapter, building that flow needs to begin before you scale, not after, or scaling will deflate and collapse at the worst possible time. As you scale your startup, update your business plan regularly using the data you have, and have that business plan ready for presentation at any moment.

Upgrade Your Technical Infrastructure

A fast-growing app will need more and more computing power and storage space to handle its fast-growing customer base, and you have to make sure the infrastructure you are using can be expanded to keep up. Stay ahead of the curve in terms of what you expect to need so that you will have time to switch service providers or relocate if you need to do so.

Build a Bigger Team

Another fast-growing aspect of a successful app project is the size of your team. Rapidly growing a company to keep up with success is no easy task, as finding and attracting a talented team will not only take time, but will also be costly. It also requires that you accurately forecast your human resources needs. How many designers will you need to create graphics, digital products, and game levels? How many programmers will you need to add to your team, and when will you need them? Too few will keep you lagging behind your audience, and too many will eat up your finances, so accurate forecasting is key here.

Design the Next Version of Your App

Research suggests that apps that are updated frequently do better in the apps stores than apps that are not. The first version of the app you publish is unlikely to be perfect, nor is it likely to be the last version you publish. Why is this so?

First, despite all the pre-release testing, your app is bound to run into a glitch or two after release.

Second, your users could use the app in unexpected ways, or like or dislike a very specific part of the app or something specific that it does. This will suggest to you that there are aspects of your app that are worth keeping and parts that you need to remove to make your app leaner and more attractive.

How will you know which parts of your app should stay and which should go? The design of the update will be affected by information from a number of sources:

- Your own analysis

- User feedback in the form of reviews, ratings, and e-mail

- Crash reports, which tell you at which point in the app there may be a coding problem that is causing the app to crash

- Analytics about user behavior, which will tell you if there are "pages" in your app, or parts of it, that users like and spend a lot of time on, or parts that they do not like and are largely ignoring.

All this information, when combined, will tell you a great deal about how to design the next version of your app. In general, the more information you gather, especially about what your users like or dislike, the more informed and effective your next design iteration will be.

What Next?

Your app is doing well. What do you do next?

Capitalize on a Skill

By the time you've released an app and monitored its progress for a few months, you've likely picked up some new skills you did not have a few months ago. In fact, if you've applied the advice in this book, you've become quite an expert on one or two aspects of app publishing. One way to grow in the app industry is to capitalize on one of the skills in which you excel and build a business around it. Maybe you have become adept at app marketing or have discovered you're an app design genius!

Coding, app design, UI/UX design, ASO (App Store Optimization), app marketing, and analytics are all fast-growing industries in their own right, and experts in these fields are always in demand.

Sell Your App

This is probably the quickest possible exit from an app project if you decide your app is not as successful as you'd hoped and you want to move on to other things. Should you opt to sell your app, there are online exchanges where you can buy or sell apps and games, like chupamobile.com and flippa.com.

Launch a Startup

This is the way to go if your app is a surprise hit and you choose to capitalize on its success. You will need to grow fast to keep up with your growing number of users—hiring new employees, investing in new technology, and planning the next version of your app. To do all this, you will need infusions of cash. To get that cash, you will need to build a strong team, write a well-thought-out business plan, and create a legal entity that will grow into a business that revolves around your app.

Exit Strategies

An exit does not necessarily mean the original team of founders has to leave. Many stay on after the exit to manage what has become a full-fledged company. It simply means the way a startup's investor will get the return on their original investment.

A well-thought-out exit strategy is something that you have to present to investors and venture capitalists before they even invest in your startup, rather than something you figure out after your app startup succeeds.

The exit is a major milestone in your app's journey. It is the defining event for your app, the culmination of all the effort you have put in from the moment the idea was born.

The four most likely types of successful exits are a merger, an IPO (Initial Public Offering), a buyout, and a cash cow.

Let's look at each of them in detail.

Merger

A merger is a combination of two companies whereby one company is fully absorbed by another. The two companies in the merger may see each other as equals, in which case the merger is friendly, or one side in the merger may be aggressively trying to merge with the other, in which case the event is known as an acquisition, or in some cases a hostile takeover.

The main reasons why two companies might merge are to increase market share, eliminate competition, and achieve economies of scale.

IPO

An IPO, or Initial Public Offering, is the sale of a percentage of a company's shares on a securities exchange, whereby the company is known to go from private to public.

Buyout

A buyout is the process by which the majority of shares or ownership equity in a company is acquired by another company or an individual. In effect, the acquirer "buys out" the company's current owners. A buyout also involves the purchase of the target company's outstanding debt.

The main reasons for a buyout are 1) profit through the sale of the target company's assets; 2) entry into new markets; 3) acquiring a new customer base; and 4) eliminating competition.

Cash Cow

A cash cow is a company that has simply become highly profitable, producing significant revenue from its activities. The owners decide to keep the company as it is, protect it from aggressive takeovers, and refuse to surrender ownership in a merger, buyout, or IPO.

App Industry Trends

Things change quickly and all the time in the app world. App design, marketing, and distribution are all affected by trends that are set off by user behavior and preferences, new regulations set by app stores, and the capabilities of new devices built by smartphone and tablet manufacturers.

Breaking Down the Man–Machine Barrier Further

AI (Artificial Intelligence), machine learning, big data, and growing interconnectivity are helping devices respond better to user requests and giving users a higher-quality experience. Apple's Siri and Microsoft's Cortana are early examples of this, and the coming advent of bots will push this trend further.

Greater Device Capability

The ever-increasing capabilities of devices are placing more and more power in the hands of designers, who are investing in subtle and sophisticated interactions. Such increased capability also allows advertisers to use ad types like video ads in the hope of improving user engagement.

New Tricks to Keep Users Engaged

App designers are constantly coming up with new ways to keep users engaged with an app and prevent them from abandoning it. One of the most talked about trends for 2017 is called **hapnotic feedback**, which combines the words "haptic" and "hypnotic." Haptic technology simulates the sense of touch in user interaction. Hapnotic feedback involves using subtle haptic cues to point users to the desired action, like a pulsing button to direct a user to a desired activity, or a pleasant texture or image to prevent a user from abandoning an app.

Improving the User Experience

Sometimes, users do not engage with a product the way they are expected to. **Failure mapping** is an aspect of UX design that involves mapping non-ideal scenarios that show the unanticipated ways in which users have interacted or could interact with apps, allowing these designers to better manage unpredictable usage patterns and improve user experience. Another user experience trend is known as **user offboarding**—improving the user experience after the desired actions have been completed, when the user has completed their interaction with the app, or wants to abandon or delete the app. Good user offboarding practices include letting users know whether or not their personal data will be kept after they delete your app, and asking them to tell you why they are deleting it.

More Personalization

A new trend in personalization is **age-responsive design**, which involves segmenting users by age and providing different user experiences for each segment for the same product.

Availability of New Technologies

The advent of Augmented Reality (AR) and **Virtual Reality (VR)** is creating a new market for AR and VR apps and video advertising. Video is a fast-growing advertising medium supported by growing device capabilities and increased available bandwidth. According to the Digital Marketing Association, **wearables** is also a medium that is growing fast, with at least one in four Americans expected to carry a wearable by the end of 2016, thus creating a new channel for advertisers to target.

Big Data

Extensive knowledge about user habits and preferences is supporting the greater **personalization** of ads and content based on location and age, as well as leading to more **predictive advertising** based on what a user is likely to do in a given situation or at a given location.

Power to the User

Ad blocking allows users to disable advertising on their mobile device, and as a result it is forcing advertisers to find less-intrusive ways to reach app users.

Buy Now

The **integration of e-commerce and social media**, like the Buy Now Facebook button, allows users to buy directly through social media without visiting an e-commerce website.

New Types of Apps

As the advent of the **Internet of Things, or IoT**, continues, millions of new apps designed to help users interact with various devices will flood the app stores. Partly encouraged by IoT and the integration of sensors and other devices into the Internet, the use of apps is also spreading to industries that have so far been slow to adopt them, like the construction and agriculture sectors.

The Future of Apps

Apps are about empowerment. Each of us now has the power of a supercomputer in our palm, combined with access to colossal amounts of data, to entertain us, keep us informed, and support our decisions.

Apps allow us to do things no one would have thought possible just a few years ago. Every day, app creators are coming up with new things we can do and new and better ways we can do what we've always done.

What about future trends? Apps today are currently evolving from entities running in the foreground to services running in the background, analyzing the user's history and making predictions about where they will be and what they will do. This is made possible by the evolutionary leap created by apps.

The Evolutionary Leap Created by Apps: Big Data

The very first games that were made available on smartphones were Snake, Pong, Tetris, and Tic-Tac-Toe. Each was in monochrome and was a few kilobytes in size. Snake first appeared on the Nokia 6110 in 1997. Today's apps are a world away from these now archaic apps, but the differences are not just about size, color, resolution, or engagement capability; the biggest technological leap that apps and games have made is the way they generate colossal amounts of information about their users. Apps and games have gone from programs that perform a function to programs that watch everything you do and generate big data, which is used by developers and marketers to create better products and market them more effectively by personalizing them for their users, making these products an integral part of their user's lives.

Where is the app revolution headed? Is the app bonanza dead?

App industry trends suggest the app revolution is indeed slowing down and that it's time to think about the next big thing. Why is this so? It's because smartphone shipments and smartphone use growth are slowing down, and because app users are simply not downloading that many apps anymore.

It is true that the opportunities to make a big hit in the app stores have shrunk. All this, however, is not a sign that the app boom is dead, but rather is a sign that the industry is maturing and the capabilities of apps and what you can do with them, which were once a magical curiosity, have now become familiar. It's much more difficult these days to impress people with something that hasn't already been done.

The app industry, however, is not going to disappear, just like the Internet, which was a wonder in its infancy, has also not disappeared. All these waves of new technologies that spring up once every few years are simply layers of the technological revolution we are currently going through, the foundation of the society of the future. The new layers of that revolution, like robotics, the Internet of Things, drones, and 3D printing, will open up new frontiers for tech-savvy designers and inventors, who will come up with new ideas for how these technologies can be applied to making our lives better.

Apps are just software, and nothing can be done without software. Software used to come in the form of a program you would download or buy. Now, it's in your hand. Tomorrow, it may be accessible in a different form through hardware other than a smartphone. It's only the form of the hardware and the form of the software that are changing to serve users' needs better, but the opportunities never dwindle.

The revolution is only just beginning, and there will be no lack of opportunity to change the world and become obscenely successful and rich in the process.

So, what are the key directions in which apps are evolving now? In which direction are we headed?

More Empowerment

As much as apps have helped us do what we could not do before, they will help us do much more in the future. This wave of empowerment will be further supported as more and more devices, like household appliances, cars, and homes, become accessible via the web and through apps.

Who would have thought a few years ago that technology would put very powerful software programs and machines (like robots and 3D printers) at our disposal, allowing us to control them through apps?

Personalization

Supported by the constant supply of information provided by analytics about your location, preferences, habits, and responses to different kinds of content and ads, apps will increasingly tailor their content, notifications, and even design and color to you.

The Nature of the App

According to some, the very nature of apps is changing, from an app as a program sitting behind an icon on your screen to a system that is constantly operating in the background, bringing you the information you need in the form of notifications, to which you can respond by issuing commands.

This means that apps no longer offer a browsing experience, but rather talk to the user only when necessary, using sensors and user-generated data like history of use to make forecasts and communicate accordingly. A user would not launch an app every time they need it, instead downloading and running it just once. The app would then combine a set of automated functions to run in the background and deliver the desired content to the user at regular intervals. In this context, the purpose of apps will change from performing tasks on request to providing services in the background.

Single All-Platform Apps

Apps are headed toward a single design for all platforms for desktop, mobile web, iOS, Android, and any other online platform or device at the same time.

The Influence of AI

AI is a fast-evolving sector that is improving every aspect of computing and user–computer interaction. More than wowing users with human-like robot behavior, AI is being used to improve the quality of services and content supplied to consumers through apps.

According to an article in TechCrunch, "rather than introducing a layer of AI to help users make use of a given app, these AI programs are operating in the background, making the apps better."

Bots

Bots are intelligent bits of software that function from inside bigger programs, helping you solve problems and get what you want. Bots are a new trend that some say could potentially spell the end of many types of apps, replacing them with text-based services, booking airline tickets, making restaurant reservations, or reserving hotel rooms for you through chat. Will bots replace apps, or, as some say, will apps "be replaced only by better apps"? Time will tell.

Deep Linking

Deep linking involves building closer and closer links between apps and blurring the gap between mobile apps and web apps.

Deep linking is designed to merge the lightweight and browsable nature of the web with the high user engagement and personalization of mobile apps, while eliminating problems like very low app discoverability for the vast majority of apps on app stores.

Ubiquity and the Internet of Things

The Internet of Things (IOT) is a vision of the Internet in which everything in the environment is connected to and communicating with everything else, including devices (like cars, home appliances, smartphones, and computers), materials (like "smart" or "self-healing" concrete), and spaces (like our homes and offices). Some 26 billion devices are expected to be connected to each other through the IoT by 2020.

The Internet of Things requires an exponential growth in the amount of accessible information, and that information is generated by equipping devices, materials, and the environment with sensors that constantly measure numerous parameters and supply the information to analytics programs that derive useful conclusions from the data.

Our own interaction with these programs will be through apps, and these apps will give us access to and control over a vast new array of parameters in our environment. Armed with new knowledge and awareness capabilities, apps will also allow us to automate many aspects of our environment and our daily rituals, such as automating our grocery shopping or monitoring our health.

We can easily conclude from the factors mentioned earlier that the industry is looking at very strong growth and multiple directions of evolution. Developers who are capable of imagining new things that can be done by merging new technologies with the capabilities of apps will be the most successful.

Closing Thoughts

The advent of new technologies is continuing at an ever-increasing pace, and it's now clear for even the completely uninitiated that the world is riding a wave of innovation that will transform every aspect of our lives, for better or for worse. The robot revolution that's just round the corner will wipe out many jobs, but will also open up possibilities we cannot even imagine today. The power technology gives us to monitor, understand, and transform our environment is tremendous and is inspiring the boldest among us to dream up things that were inconceivable just a short while ago.

Apps are nothing more than programs, just like the programs we were used to before apps came along. What makes them magical is their ability to put so much computing power, communication capability, and access to information in the palm of our hand through another technological "marvel," the smartphone, which more than two billion people currently carry around with them everywhere they go.

Summary

The app industry is a young and fast-evolving piece of a much bigger revolution in information technology and computing. Its future is closely tied to all the other pieces of that revolution, like robotics and AI, which are creating new potential and possibilities on a literally daily basis. Developers searching for the next phase in the evolution of the app industry need to keep up with the momentum of this revolution in order to predict what these new technologies will help us achieve next and be among the first to explore new frontiers as they emerge.

What's next? As we discussed earlier, current trends point to the next wave that will be built on this one, but it is safe to say that much of what is to come hasn't even been imagined yet.

Apps and smartphones have not just put tremendous capabilities into your hands; they have made it possible for you to be a part of the revolution they are bringing about, and that was the main reason why I wrote this book. Technology is more accessible to the uninitiated today than it has ever been, and it's inviting you to be a part of it every time to look at your smartphone screen. The purpose behind this book was to give you, the reader, every reason to dive into the world of technology and app publishing and to eliminate any reason that could hold you back. I trust I have succeeded.

Appendix

Online Resources

With so many contributors and an industry that is evolving as fast as the app industry, it is impossible for us to include everyone in our Resources section. However, no exclusion is intentional, and to make this book as useful as possible we intend to include everyone who is a leader or innovator in any part of this industry.

If you consider yourself a part of the industry too important to be left out of this book, drop the author a line at contact@hagoppanosian.am, and you will definitely be included in the next edition!

App Development

Andromo	http://www.andromo.com/
Ambrowse	http://www.ambrowse.com/
Appery	https://appery.io/
Appmachine	http://www.appmachine.com/
Appmakr	https://www.appmakr.com/
Appsbar	http://www.appsbar.com/
Appsme	http://www.appsme.com/
Appypie	http://www.appypie.com/
Biznessapps	https://www.biznessapps.com/index.php
Buzztouch	http://www.buzztouch.com/
Codiqa	https://codiqa.com/

(continued)

© Hagop Panosian 2017
H. Panosian, *Learn iOS Application Distribution*, DOI 10.1007/978-1-4842-2683-4

Como	http://www.como.com/
Eachscape	https://eachscape.com/
Fabric.io	https://get.fabric.io/
Good Barber	http://www.goodbarber.com/
Infinite Monkeys	https://www.infinitemonkeys.mobi/
Kinvey	http://www.kinvey.com/
Knackhq	https://www.knackhq.com/
Learn App Making	https://learnappmaking.com/
Mippin	http://www.mippin.com/appfactory/
Mobile Roadie	http://mobileroadie.com/
Pubnub	https://www.pubnub.com/
Shoutem	http://www.shoutem.com/
The App Builder	http://www.theappbuilder.com/

Game Development

Cocos 2d	http://cocos2d.org/
Corona Labs	https://coronalabs.com/
Game Salad	http://www.gamesalad.com/
Getmoai	http://getmoai.com/
Scirra	https://www.scirra.com/
Stencyl	http://www.stencyl.com/
Unity 3d	http://unity3d.com/
Yoyogames	http://www.yoyogames.com/

Market Information

Comscore	http://comscore.com/
Consumer Barometer	http://www.consumerbarometer.com/
Device Atlas	https://deviceatlas.com
Flurry Blog	https://blog.flurry.com/
Forrester	https://go.forrester.com/

(continued)

Gartner	http://www.gartner.com/
IDC	http://idc.com/
Net Market Share	https://netmarketshare.com/
Smart Insights	http://www.smartinsights.com/
Statista	https://www.statista.com/

Developer Websites

Android	https://developers.google.com
Apple	https://developer.apple.com/
Microsoft	https://developer.microsoft.com/
Blackberry	https://developer.blackberry.com/

App Marketplaces

Chupamobile	http://www.chupamobile.com/
Code Canyon	https://codecanyon.net/

Cloud Based Back-End Services

Amazon AWS	http://aws.amazon.com/mobile/
Apiomat	http://www.apiomat.com/
Appacitive	http://appacitive.com/
Appery	http://appery.io/
Applicasa	http://www.applicasa.com/
Backbeam	https://backbeam.io/
Backendless	https://backendless.com
Google	https://developers.google.com/cloud/
Kii	http://en.kii.com/
Kinvey	http://www.kinvey.com/
Kumulos	http://www.kumulos.com/
Microsoft Azure	http://azure.microsoft.com/

(continued)

Netmera	http://www.netmera.com/
Openkit	http://openkit.io/
Parse	https://parse.com/
Quickblox	http://quickblox.com/
Shephertz	http://api.shephertz.com/
Telerik	http://www.telerik.com/

Free eBooks

Appsee	https://www.appsee.com/ebooks
Apptamin	http://www.apptamin.com/blog/
Apptentive	https://www.apptentive.com/resources/
Buzinga	http://www.buzinga.com.au/
Localytics	https://www.localytics.com/resources/
Marketo	http://blog.marketo.com/
Openxcell	http://portfolio.openxcell.com/resources/ebook.html
UXPin	https://www.uxpin.com/knowledge.html

App Development Companies

Affle AppStudioz	http://www.appstudioz.com/
Algoworks	http://www.algoworks.com/
Apadmi	http://www.apadmi.com/
Appster	http://appsterhq.com/
Apptology	http://apptology.com/
Apptraction	http://www.apptraction.com/
ArcTouch	http://arctouch.com/
Belatrix	http://www.belatrixsf.com/
Blue Label Labs	https://www.bluelabellabs.com/
Blue Whale Apps	http://www.bluewhaleapps.com/
Borne	http://borneagency.com/
Brightec	http://www.brightec.co.uk/

(continued)

Buzinga	http://www.buzinga.com.au/
Cheesecake Labs	https://www.ckl.io/
Chelsea Apps Factory	http://chelsea-apps.com/
ChromeInfo	http://www.chromeinfotech.com/
Clavax	http://www.clavax.com/
Cleveroad	https://www.cleveroad.com/
CodigoDelSur	http://www.codigodelsur.com/
Creative 27	http://creative27.com/
Creative 360	http://creative360.co/
Credencys Solutions	http://www.credencys.com/
Customer Lifetime Value	http://customerlifetimevalue.co
Debut Infotech	http://www.debutinfotech.com/
Digital Brand Group	http://digitalbrandgroup.com/
DMI	http://dminc.com/
Dogtown Media	http://dogtownmedia.com/
Dom And Tom	http://domandtom.com/
Dot Com Infoway	http://www.dotcominfoway.com/
e-Legion	http://www.e-legion.com/
Eleks	http://eleks.com/
Elinext Group	http://www.elinext.com/
Ethervision	http://ethervision.net/
Fan Studio	http://www.fanstudio.co.uk/
Five	http://five.agency/
Fueled	http://www.fueled.com/
Future Platforms	http://www.futureplatforms.com/
Guarana Technologies	http://guarana-technologies.com/
Halcyon Mobile	http://halcyonmobile.com/
Hedgehog Lab	http://hedgehoglab.com/
Hidden Brains	http://www.hiddenbrains.com/
Iflexion	https://www.iflexion.com/
Impiger Technologies	http://www.impigertech.com/
Infinum	https://infinum.co/

(continued)

IntellectSoft	http://www.intellectsoft.net/
Intersog	http://intersog.com/
July Rapid	http://julyrapid.com/
Kogi Mobile	http://www.kogimobile.com/
Konstant Infosolutions	http://www.konstantinfo.com/
Lemberg	http://lemberg.co.uk/
Live Typing	http://livetyping.com/en/
Locassa	http://locassa.com/
Macadamian	http://www.macadamian.com/
MentorMate	http://mentormate.com/
MindInventory	http://www.mindinventory.com/
Miquido	http://www.miquido.com/
MLSDev	http://mlsdev.com/
MOBIKASA	http://www.mobikasa.com/
Mobits	http://mobits.com.br/
Mubaloo	http://mubaloo.com/
Nomtek	https://www.nomtek.com/
Octal Info Solutions	http://www.octalsoftware.com/
OpenXcell	https://www.openxcell.com/
Peerbits	http://www.peerbits.com/
PointClear Solutions	http://www.pointclearsolutions.com/
Polidea	https://www.polidea.com/
Prismetric	https://www.prismetric.com/
QBurst	http://www.qburst.com/
QSoft Vietnam	http://www.qsoftvietnam.com/
QuyTech	http://www.quytech.com/
RaizLabs	http://www.raizlabs.com/
RapidOps	http://www.rapidops.com/
Ratio	http://www.weareratio.com/
Ready4S	http://www.ready4s.com/
Red C	http://www.red-c.co.uk/
Redmadrobot	http://www.redmadrobot.com/

(continued)

Reinvently	http://reinvently.com/
Reliant Tekk	https://www.relianttekk.com/
Robosoft Technologies	https://www.robosoftin.com/
Savvycom Software	http://savvycomsoftware.com/
SIMPalm	http://www.simpalm.com/
Skylark Infotech	http://www.skylarkinfotech.com/
Small Planet Digital	http://smallplanet.com/
SnapMobile	http://www.snapmobile.io/
Snowman Labs	http://snowmanlabs.com/
Softeq	http://www.softeq.com/
Somo Global	http://www.somoglobal.com/
Sourcebits	http://sourcebits.com/
Stanfy	https://stanfy.com/
Stuzo	http://www.stuzo.com/
TechAhead	http://www.techaheadcorp.com/
The Software House	http://tsh.io/
The Sound Pipe Media	http://thesoundpipemedia.com/
Touch Instinct	http://touchinstinct.com/
UruIT	http://www.uruit.com/
Ustwo	https://ustwo.com/
Viteb	http://www.viteb.com/
White Widget	http://whitewidget.com/
Willowtree	http://willowtreeapps.com/
Worry Free Labs	http://worryfreelabs.com/
Y Media Labs	http://www.ymedialabs.com/
Zco	http://www.zco.com/

Cross-Platform App Development

5 App	http://5app.com/
Alpha Anywhere	http://www.alphasoftware.com/
Apache Cordova	https://cordova.apache.org/
Appcelerator	http://www.appcelerator.com/
Corona Labs	https://coronalabs.com/
Famo.us	http://famous.co/
Feed Henry	http://www.feedhenry.com/
Ionic	http://ionicframework.com/
JQuery Mobile	http://jquerymobile.com/
Kony	http://www.kony.com/
Lungo	http://lungo.tapquo.com/
PhoneGap	http://phonegap.com/
Qt	http://www.qt.io/
Ratchet	http://goratchet.com/
Sencha	https://www.sencha.com/
Visual Studio	https://www.visualstudio.com/
Xamarin	https://xamarin.com/

App Design

2ttf	http://2ttf.com/
365psd	http://365psd.com/
99 Designs	https://99designs.com/
Adam Whitcroft	http://adamwhitcroft.com/wirekit/
Adobe	http://sketch.adobe.com/
Android App Patterns	http://www.android-app-patterns.com/
App Cooker	http://www.appcooker.com/
App Icon Template	http://appicontemplate.com/
Arttolstykh	http://arttolstykh.com/lookamore/
Awesome Kit	http://awesomekit.me/
Axure	http://www.axure.com/

(continued)

Balsamiq	https://balsamiq.com/
Bitique	http://blog.bitique.co.uk/
Bootstrap UI Kit	http://bootstrapuikit.com/
Brusheezy	http://www.brusheezy.com/
Cabana App	http://www.cabanaapp.com/
Creative Market	https://creativemarket.com/
Creattica	http://creattica.com/
Deal Jumbo	http://dealjumbo.com/
Design Crowd	http://www.designcrowd.com/
Design Related	http://www.designrelated.com/
Design Shack	http://designshack.net/
Design Shock	http://www.designshock.com/
Design TNT	http://www.designtnt.com/
Designious	http://www.designious.com/
Deviant Art	http://www.deviantart.com/browse/all/
Dexigner	http://www.dexigner.com/
Dezinerfolio	http://www.dezinerfolio.com/
Dmonzon	http://www.dmonzon.com/
Dribbble	https://dribbble.com/
Endloop	http://www.endloop.ca/imockups/
Fiftythree	http://www.fiftythree.com/
Fluid UI	http://www.fluidui.com/
Free UI Kits	http://www.freeuikits.com/
Freebbble	http://freebbble.com/
Freebies Bug	http://freebiesbug.com/
Freebies Gallery	http://www.freebiesgallery.com/
Freepik	http://www.freepik.com/
Graffletopia	https://www.graffletopia.com/
Graphic River	http://graphicriver.net/
Graphics Fuel	http://www.graphicsfuel.com/
Gusto	http://horseandtherook.com/gusto/
Heat Maps	https://heatma.ps/

(continued)

Inspired UI	http://inspired-ui.com/
Interface Sketch	http://interfacesketch.tumblr.com/
Invision App	http://www.invisionapp.com/
iOS Fonts	http://iosfonts.com/
Lookback	https://lookback.io/
Lovely UI	http://www.lovelyui.com
Make App Icon	http://makeappicon.com/
Media Loot	http://medialoot.com/
Mobify	http://www.mobify.com/
Mobile Mosaic	http://www.mobilemozaic.com/
Mobile Patterns	http://www.mobile-patterns.com/
Mockuuups	https://www.mockuuups.com/
My Color Screen	http://mycolorscreen.com/
New Old Stock	http://nos.twnsnd.co/
Omnigraffle	https://www.omnigroup.com/omnigraffle/
Oxygenna	http://www.oxygenna.com/
Patterntap	http://patterntap.com/
Pixeden	http://www.pixeden.com/
Pixel Push	http://www.pixel-push.com/
Pixels Daily	http://pixelsdaily.com/
Placeit	https://placeit.net/
Premium Pixels	http://www.premiumpixels.com/
Pttrns	http://pttrns.com/
Public Domain Archive	http://publicdomainarchive.com/
Sketch App Resources	http://www.sketchappsources.com/
Sketch Gems	http://www.sketchgems.com/
Spark Tech Soft	http://www.sparktechsoft.com/
Streamline Icons	http://www.streamlineicons.com/
Symbol Set	https://symbolset.com/
Symbolset	https://www.symbolset.com/
Teehanlax	http://www.teehanlax.com/
The Noun Project	http://thenounproject.com/

(continued)

The Ultralinx	http://ui.theultralinx.com/
The Web Blend	http://thewebblend.com/
Theme Designer	http://themedesigner.in/
UI Cloud	http://ui-cloud.com/
UI Fest	http://uifest.com/
UI Parade	http://www.uiparade.com/
UI8	https://ui8.net/
Ultrashock	http://www.ultrashock.com/
Unsplash	http://unsplash.com/
User Centered	http://usercentred.net/
Vector Finder	http://www.vectorfinder.com/
Vector Portal	http://www.vectorportal.com/
Visually	http://visual.ly/
W3 Markup	http://w3-markup.com/
Web Design Shock	http://www.webdesignshock.com/
Wikichen	https://github.com/wikichen/sketch-android-kit
Yosemite UI	http://yosemiteui.com/

App Advertising, Marketing, Monetization & Analytics

Accengage	http://www.accengage.com/
Ad Buddiz	https://www.adbuddiz.com/developers
Ad Colony	http://www.adcolony.com
Adjust	https://www.adjust.com/
Aerserv	https://www.**aerserv**.com/
Airpush	http://www.airpush.com/
Amplitude	https://amplitude.com/
App Analytics	https://appanalytics.io/
App Annie	http://www.appannie.com/
App Codes	http://www.appcodes.com/
App Figures	https://appfigures.com/

(continued)

App Statics	`http://www.appstatics.com/`
Appboy	`https://www.appboy.com/`
Appdriver	`https://appdriver.asia/`
Appflood	`http://appflood.com/`
Appia	`http://www.appia.com/`
Apple	`http://advertising.apple.com/`
Applicasa	`http://www.applicasa.com/`
Applift	`http://www.applift.com/`
Applovin	`http://www.applovin.com/`
AppsFlyer	`https://www.appsflyer.com/`
Appsee	`http://www.appsee.com/`
Apptamin	`http://www.apptamin.com/`
Apptentive	`http://www.apptentive.com/`
Apptimize	`https://apptimize.com/`
Apptopia	`https://www.apptopia.com/`
Apsalar	`https://apsalar.com/`
Asking Point	`https://www.askingpoint.com/`
Avazu	`http://avazuinc.com/`
BlisMedia	`http://www.blis.com/`
Branch	`https://branch.io/`
Brokerbabe	`https://brokerbabe.com/`
Byyd	`https://byyd-tech.com/`
Chartboost	`https://www.chartboost.com/`
Cheetah Media Link	`http://www.cheetahmedialink.com/`
Clickdealer	`https://www.clickdealer.com/`
Clicksmob	`http://clicksmob.com/`
Clicktale	`http://www.clicktale.com/`
Clicky	`http://clicky.com/`
Conversant Media	`http://www.conversantmedia.com/`
Converser	`http://converser.io/`
Countly	`http://count.ly/`
Crashlytics	`http://try.crashlytics.com/`

(continued)

Criteo	http://www.criteo.com/
Devtodev	https://www.devtodev.com/
Digital Turbine	https://www.digitalturbine.com/
Distimo	http://www.distimo.com/
Everyplay	https://everyplay.com/
Fabric	https://get.fabric.io
Flight Recorder	http://flightrecorder.io/
Flurry	http://www.flurry.com/
Fyber	http://www.fyber.com/
Geckoboard	https://www.geckoboard.com/
Good UI	http://www.goodui.org/
Google Admob	http://www.google.com/admob/
Google Analytics	http://www.google.com/analytics/
GoWide	https://gowide.com/
Heat Maps	https://heatmaps.io/
Heyzap	https://www.heyzap.com/
Hockeyapp	https://hockeyapp.net/
Imobitrax	https://www.imobitrax.com/
Indicative	http://www.indicative.com/
Inmobi	http://www.inmobi.com/
Jammp	http://www.jampp.com/
Kimia	https://kimia.mobi/
Kissmetrics	https://www.kissmetrics.com/
Kissmyads	http://www.kissmyads.com
Kochava	https://www.kochava.com/
Lead Bolt	https://www.leadbolt.com/
Leadbolt	http://www.leadbolt.com/
Leanplum	https://www.leanplum.com/
Life Street	http://www.lifestreet.com/
Localytics	http://www.localytics.com/
Madvertise	http://madvertise.com/
Marchex	http://www.marchex.com/

(continued)

Marin Software	http://www.marinsoftware.com/
Matomy	http://www.matomy.com/
Mdotm	http://www.mdotm.com/
Medialets	http://www.medialets.com/
Millenial Media	http://www.millennialmedia.com/
Mixpanel	https://mixpanel.com/
Mobfox	http://www.mobfox.com/
Mobidea	https://www.mobidea.com/
Mobile Action	https://www.mobileaction.co/
Mobilecore	https://www.mobilecore.com/
Mobvista	http://www.mobvista.com/
Mobyd	http://www.mobyd.com/
Mojiva	http://welcome.mojiva.com/
Monetate	http://www.monetate.com/
Mopapp	http://www.mopapp.com/
Mopub	http://www.mopub.com/
Mpire Network	https://www.mpirenetwork.com/
Mundo Media	https://www.mundomedia.com/
Nativex	http://nativex.com/
Nend	http://nend.net/en
New Relic	http://newrelic.com/
OneSkyApp	https://www.oneskyapp.com/
Optimizely	https://www.optimizely.com/
Performance Revenues	http://www.performancerevenues.com/
Phunware	http://www.phunware.com/
Playhaven	http://www.playhaven.com/
Revmob	https://www.revmobmobileadnetwork.com/
Sensor Tower	https://sensortower.com/
Slice Intelligence	https://intelligence.slice.com/
Smart App Marketer	http://www.smartappmarketer.com/
Soomla	https://soom.la/
Sparkpage	https://www.sparkpage.com/
Startapp	http://www.startapp.com/

(continued)

Straply	https://www.straply.com/
Supersonic	https://www.supersonic.com/
Swrve	https://www.swrve.com/
Tapjoy	http://home.tapjoy.com/
Tapstream	https://tapstream.com/
Taptica	http://www.taptica.com/
Tune	https://www.tune.com/
Unilead	http://www.unileadnetwork.com/
Upsight	http://www.upsight.com/
Urban Airship	https://www.urbanairship.com/
User Onboard	https://www.useronboard.com/
Wap Empire	http://wapempire.com/
Wire Stone	http://www.wirestone.com/
YeahMobi	http://en.yeahmobi.com/
Youappi	http://www.youappi.com/

App Review Sites

Android Apps	http://www.androidapps.com/
Android Central	http://www.androidcentral.com/
Android Tapp	http://www.androidtapp.com/
Androlib	http://www.androlib.com/
App Apes	http://app-apes.com/
App Brain	http://www.appbrain.com/
App Chatter	http://www.appchatter.com/
App Chronicles	http://appchronicles.com/
App Craver	http://www.appcraver.com/
App Scout	http://appscout.pcmag.com/
App Shout	http://www.appshout.com/
Apps Zoom	http://www.appszoom.com/
Appsized	http://www.appsized.com/
Appsmile	http://www.appsmile.com/

(continued)

Fresh Apps	http://www.freshapps.com/
Gamespot	http://www.gamespot.com/
Gizmodo	http://gizmodo.com/
iPhone Gamer Blog	http://www.iphonegamerblog.com/
iPhone Games	http://www.iphonegames.com/
iPhone Life	http://www.iphonelife.com/
I Use This App	http://www.iusethisapp.com/
Mashable	http://mashable.com/apps-software/
Pocket Gamer	http://www.pocketgamer.co.uk/
Preapps	http://www.preapps.com/
Slide to Play	http://www.slidetoplay.com/
Tech Chrunch	http://techcrunch.com/mobile/
The iPhone App Review	http://www.theiphoneappreview.com/
Wind8apps	http://wind8apps.com/
Wired	http://www.wired.com/reviews/
WP Central	http://www.wpcentral.com/

Apps Without Code

Andromo	http://www.andromo.com/
Ambrowse	http://www.ambrowse.com/
App Factory	http://www.mippin.com/appfactory/
App Machine	http://www.appmachine.com/
Appery	https://appery.io/
Appmaker	https://www.appmakr.com/
Appsbar	http://www.appsbar.com/
Appsme	http://www.appsme.com/
Appy Pie	http://www.appypie.com/
Biznessapps	https://www.biznessapps.com/index.php
Buzztouch	http://www.buzztouch.com/
Codiqa	https://codiqa.com/
Como	http://www.como.com/

(continued)

Eachscape	https://eachscape.com/
Good Barber	http://www.goodbarber.com/
Infinite Monkeys	https://www.infinitemonkeys.mobi/
Kinvey	http://www.kinvey.com/
Knack HQ	https://www.knackhq.com/
Microsoft Power Apps	https://powerapps.microsoft.com/en-us/
Mobile Roadie	http://mobileroadie.com/
Shoutem	http://www.shoutem.com/
The App Builder	http://www.theappbuilder.com/

Social Media Platforms and Other Sites For App Promotion

Bing	https://www.bing.com/
Blab	https://blab.im
Blogger	https://www.blogger.com
Buffer	https://buffer.com/
Delicious	https://del.icio.us/
Digg	http://digg.com/
Facebook	http://www.facebook.com
Flickr	https://www.flickr.com/
Ghost	https://ghost.org
Google+	https://plus.google.com
Hi5	http://www.hi5.com
HootSuite	https://hootsuite.com/
Howcast	http://www.howcast.com/
Instagram	https://www.instagram.com/
LinkedIn	http://www.linkedin.com
Medium	https://medium.com
Meerkat	https://meerkatapp.co
Movable Type	https://movabletype.com
Mylife	http://www.mylife.com

(continued)

MySpace	https://myspace.com/
Ning	http://www.ning.com
Path	https://www.path.com/
Periscope	https://www.periscope.tv
Pinterest	https://www.pinterest.com/
Plaxo	http://www.plaxo.com
Quora	https://www.quora.com/
Reddit	https://www.reddit.com/
Scribd	https://www.scribd.com/
SlideShare	http://www.slideshare.net/
StumbleUpon	https://www.stumbleupon.com/
Tumblr	https://www.tumblr.com/
TweetDeck	https://tweetdeck.twitter.com/
Twitter	http://www.twitter.com
TypePad	http://www.typepad.com
Vimeo	https://vimeo.com/
Vox	http://www.vox.com/
Wix	http://www.wix.com
Wordpress	https://wordpress.com
Wikipedia	https://www.wikipedia.org/
Xanga	http://xanga.com/
Xing	http://www.xing.com
Yahoo	https://www.yahoo.com/
Yelp	https://www.yelp.com/
Youtube	https://www.youtube.com/

Index

© Hagop Panosian 2017
H. Panosian, *Learn iOS Application Distribution*, DOI 10.1007/978-1-4842-2683-4

Get the eBook for only $5!

Why limit yourself?

With most of our titles available in both PDF and ePUB format, you can access your content wherever and however you wish—on your PC, phone, tablet, or reader.

Since you've purchased this print book, we are happy to offer you the eBook for just $5.

To learn more, go to http://www.apress.com/companion or contact support@apress.com.

Apress®

Printed in the United States
By Bookmasters